WAKING UP

Learning What Your Life
Is Trying to Teach You

John Earle

The material in this book is not intended as psychological or religious advice. If you have a psychological issue or illness, consult a qualified psychologist or psychiatric medical doctor. It you have a religious issue; please consult your religious adviser, priest, or minister.

Published by Allawalla Books, Miami. Florida

http://www.wakinguponline.com

ISBN 978-0-615-54620-9

For My Wonderful Kids

Contents

"One thing we do know: Life will give you whatever experience is most helpful for the evolution of your consciousness. How do you know this is the experience you need? Because this is the experience you are having at this moment."

Eckhart Tolle

Introduction

For the past 23 years I have worked with individuals, couples, and organizations as a counselor and interpersonal communication consultant. There are many components to this work but, at its core, it always boils down to helping people to speak their truth, to ask for what they want, and to overcome the obstacles that prevent this. Learning to speak in this powerful manner requires psychological and spiritual changes that are lasting and liberating. Before I could help anyone else, I had to do much of this work myself. This continues to be a fascinating journey.

I became interested in interpersonal communication through exploring intimacy. My wife, Babbie, and I experienced the work of Don and Martha Rosenthal who taught us how to reframe our intimate relationship as a spiritual path. Our work with them evolved into a partnership, and for several years we co-produced a weekend long couple's retreat called *Relationship, the Noble Adventure*. The retreats focused on recognizing and acknowledging the power of the ego to create emotional pain and separation, and learning how to open the heart when the ego is demanding that it stay closed. This is deep work, and the retreats were often intense and life altering. Don was trained in psychology, and he and Martha had been spiritual seekers for many years. They taught new ways of understanding and transforming relationship difficulties, using these difficulties, as Don used to say, "as compost for personal and spiritual growth." With the Rosenthals we produced over fifty retreats in which we practiced concrete exercises for effecting relationship change with hundreds of couples.

After our collaboration with the Rosenthals ended, Babbie and I worked with parent groups and couples who were interested in developing better interpersonal skills. Over time, my view of this work expanded. I realized how important the ability to communicate the truth is, not only in intimate and personal relationships, but also within larger groups and organizations. I began working with the business and institutional world and became a consultant in interpersonal communication. I used the same basic principles to help organizations achieve better interpersonal communication in order to solve problems. This work is especially useful in challenges associated with low morale, feelings of disempowerment, anger, cynicism and despair; all issues that hinder teamwork and synergy. Many problems in business and institutions have their roots in people feeling invisible, unappreciated and not heard. I have found that the full creative power of an organization or group cannot be manifested without creating a safe atmosphere in which the truth can be spoken, as well as developing the wisdom to know how and when to do so. When those in power become skillful listeners and sensitive speakers, an entire organization benefits. When employees are allowed to speak up for what they believe, while offering concrete suggestions for change, rather than simply complaining or acting out, they create new and helpful awareness. None of this threatens the organization or detracts from the power or responsibilities of its members. Everyone benefits from the harmony created and the creativity released.

All of this work centers on authentic communication, the ability to speak the truth without judgment or blame. This is a challenge that has been around for a long time. Authentic communication is described by cultural anthropologist Angeles Arrien as "the seventh initiation of indigenous people." Listening with an open mind and heart is the necessary corollary. This is very difficult work. To speak the truth sometimes means taking risks: the risk of isolation, the risk of ridicule, the risk of job loss, the risk of change, and the risk of embarrassment. These risks can be attenuated by creating a safe environment for speaking up, and by making agreements that honor one another's truth. Most important, personal changes seem to be accompanied by risk. It is through the action of speaking our truth that we discover our personal power, and simultaneously diminish the influence risk has to dissuade us from seeking change. Arrien teaches that authentic communication is the realm of the visionary. If we want change in our lives, or to influence the lives of others positively, we need to be able to envision what that change will look and feel like. The visionary is not hemmed in by blaming circumstance for their current condition or by using judgment as a false foundation for change. Of course, it is not necessary to be a visionary, in the cultural sense, in order to communicate authentically, but, without authenticity, our vision can be hapless and misleading and we may suffer from disillusion.

Authentic communication is a doorway into a more profound journey. It doesn't take long to realize that authentic communication is the tip of an iceberg because it is a practice that requires much self-discovery. We can't speak our truth if we do not know what it is. Also, we can't speak our truth if we don't feel safe doing so, and the safety required has much less to do with the world around us than with ourselves, and the personal obstacles that arise when we make the choice to speak out or ask for what we want. Thus speaking our truth brings us directly into contact with our hidden and repressed fears. We can respond to these fears consciously or react to them unconsciously. There are strategies for both paths. Here we take the view that the conscious path is preferable.

Embracing a conscious approach to our difficulties, especially in our relationship to others, lies at the heart of my counseling and consulting practice. This book concerns itself with four important strategies for manifesting conscious responses to life's challenges. It is about living a more aware and more conscious life. The conscious approach, well known by now, takes the view that the difficulties or discomforts we experience in life are our teachers, that there is always some lesson to be learned when difficulties arise, and that there is something we have either forgotten or never learned that is brought forward by the challenging areas of our lives. These challenging areas turn out to be exactly the places in which we have not completed our growth or are not completely whole. One of the beauties of life is that all of these difficult places invariably contain the seeds of what we need to do to create the life we really want. As a counselor, I help individuals and couples first to express their emotionally painful stories clearly and then take responsibility for them. This can be hard work. Then we work to understand the core challenges that these stories demonstrate and, using specific views and tools, do the inner work for which these challenges call. Using the four strategies contained in this book my clients do the discovery work. They learn the power of awareness in identifying clearly what is really occurring in their lives. They learn the absolute necessity of taking personal responsibility. They seek out teachers, teachings and practices that enhance the inner work necessary to create the change of heart or to create a new view necessary for changing their outer world. They take new action to discover the power of their own change. They experience the benefits of embracing a conscious approach and experience their own power to create change in their lives. I believe this approach is very helpful because it teaches and encourages all of us to take personal responsibility for our lives. Eventually, we realize it is not helpful to dwell on old stories or keep looping back through previous experiences. What we need is usually right in front of us right now, although, of course, we sometimes have to go back and deal with some old demons that have resurfaced in new guises in the present.

Once new and more powerful ways of viewing situations are understood, and specific tools are learned, these tools can be applied to any similar situations that arise. For my clients there is no need to keep coming back to see me. Nothing gives me greater pleasure than a client who empowers themselves with the little wisdom and knowledge I can share. I measure my success on how quickly a person self empowers rather than how many clients of long standing I have. Many people have asked me to record my approach to creating a more conscious life and to share the strategies my clients and I use. This book is the result of these requests.

My understanding of living more consciously has come from many sources: my work, my own experiences, diverse teachers, religious and spiritual studies and interacting with hundreds of fellow travelers including, of course, my workshop participants and my clients who have been very wonderful teachers. In addition to these more obvious sources, I have lived in many places and cultural environments and have experienced many people. Since my late teens I have taken a keen interest in the metaphysical. For thirty years I lived in Vermont, where I built a house with my own hands and where Babbie and I raised five children out in the country.

Relationship has always been one of my biggest teachers. I have been a hospice volunteer for 30 years and taught the hospice communication component to new hospice volunteers many times. Hospice has been an extraordinary teacher. I became an emergency medical technician and drove and rode with a busy volunteer ambulance group for five years. My wife Babbie and I spent a season on the volunteer staff of the Omega Institute in Rhinebeck, NY where, like many others, we taught in addition to our assigned jobs. At Omega we presented workshops in interpersonal communication to staff and did relationship counseling. We were honored to be asked back as full time staff in this capacity.

My greatest teacher is Babbie who has been my best friend and working companion for 43 years. We share a conscious and very active (umm... what does that mean?) relationship that is always teaching us more and taking us to greater depths. Once a teacher of mine said, "Have you ever noticed that most gurus are single?" The meaning of this is that there is nothing that can challenge the open heart and bring forth the ego like intimacy. We believe that relationship is an intense and deep spiritual path.

The need or desire to speak our truth skillfully is not the only reason we make the decision to take up the conscious life. It is simply one of the ways we arrive at the beginning of the path. Its distinction perhaps lies in the fact that we can choose it; we are not necessarily forced into it. There are other classic reasons, not of our choosing, for which we find ourselves at the head of the path: someone close to us dies, our world is turned upside down by an unexpected event, a divorce or painful relationship, a job loss, bankruptcy, personal or social issues, or perhaps we are inspired by a powerful teacher who wakes us up. Something happens, and we find ourselves on the threshold of a new realm, and we realize that a new and more powerful way of being in the world exists. Regardless of how we arrive there, I have discovered that the four strategies presented here are essential components of the conscious life and by using them we can finally discover what our sometimes complicated lives are trying to teach us. We can finally wake up from the long dream in which many of us dwell.

The Four Strategies

Awareness
Personal Responsibility
Inner Work
Action

Awareness

"We sleep in God's unconscious.
We wake in God's open hand."

Rumi - Emptiness

Awareness Overview

The first of the four strategies for learning what our lives are trying to teach us is awareness. Before we can create beneficial change in our lives, we need to be aware of what is happening. This seems obvious but, in reality, most of us prefer to experience our lives selectively, embracing that which is pleasant, and avoiding that which is unpleasant or causes fear. Over time we develop a personality that is an elaborate network of strategies for dealing with what makes us uncomfortable and what we fear. Avoiding our emotional discomfort keeps us forever separated from the full depth and power of our experience and its usefulness as a teacher. Unfortunately, these strategies can become so much a part of our personality that we become unconscious of what is actually happening in our inner world. Our system runs on autopilot. In a sense, over time, we actually develop and expand our unconsciousness.

This unconsciousness spills over into the outer world. It affects our relationship with the world because, when we disconnect with our own inner world, when we don't have the map for this world, we disconnect with the inner world of others, which is so like our own. Why does this matter? Why is it important to be aware and compassionate? Why not just build a psychological fortress? Many try. The most successful become sociopathic. But, without the true understanding of the like experience of others, without empathy and compassion, we feel isolated, lonely, disconnected and even more fearful.

As long as we remain unconscious or unaware, we will fail to learn what life is trying to teach us, and we will find it difficult to harmonize with others in a relaxed and fearless manner. We will be

19

unable to transcend our self-imposed limitations to personal or spiritual growth, simply because we will not be able to discover them. We will keep experiencing the same kinds of stories over and over. We will have trouble moving on.

We need not blame ourselves for taking up the unconscious model or for any other current unskillful behavior we may have. We are not bad or stupid for acting this way. Most of us simply lack the skills and wisdom to respond in any other way. In fact, most of us have never been taught any other way. By default we all seem to work toward unconsciousness. It is, after all, the ocean we swim in. This is the condition of the majority of people in the world.

By developing and honing our awareness, we move beyond the coping and separating mechanisms and into the lessons of our life. Like the mythical hero, we move into the unknown. We stop running away from unpleasant feelings and emotions, we allow them to exist and we observe them. Our most important lessons are usually securely attached to the very emotions or feelings we are avoiding. As we shall discover, awareness allows us to be detached and engaged simultaneously, to be objective while simultaneously experiencing subjective states. Like many spiritual conditions this seeming paradox (the coexistence of objective and subjective) is, in fact, a very real state. We have to practice this state and not return to our old ways of denial and indulgence if we want to make progress. But, of course there are tricks for doing this effectively, as well as traps and distractions that pull us out of awareness.

The four strategies for learning what our life is trying to teach us are linked together in interesting ways, and they act both symbiotically and independently. For instance, in order to become fully *aware* we have to take *personal responsibility* seriously. If we are spending our time creating a life story in which our discomfort and discontent is usually someone or something else's fault, that story is as far as we will ever go. We will keep looping at this level. How can we become aware that there is much more to life? As soon as we take personal responsibility seriously, we embrace the belief that we play the central creative role in our story, and an entirely new perspective is gained; a new world of understanding opens. Returning to awareness while taking personal responsibility, we make deeper discoveries about what at first seemed like a simple matter of judgment and blame. In a like manner, we are often required to embrace inner work before we can move to new action. Yet we can take action at any time, independent of the other three strategies, and learn from the results. This is a very flexible system that we can enter from any of the four strategies. But no matter where we start, awareness is always a necessary component. It is the indispensible, non-judging eye that sees all.

I, A Bumper Car

The Necessity of Awareness

Every summer when we were young, my sister Elinor and I were allowed one or two trips to the small amusement park in York Beach, Maine. We liked to see what new rides had been added or removed over the winter, and then we rushed to drive the bumper cars. We would drive the bumper cars for as long as our money lasted. The snap of electricity, the humming motors, the smell of ozone in the air, the rumble of the cars racing around on the iron floor all blended themselves into an intense adrenaline rush. We loved the suspense, the uncertainty, the constant danger of being hit, the thrill of the predator and the terror of the victim. There were the ecstatic moments, ramming an unsuspecting sitting duck (especially Elinor) at full speed and the moments of despair, when I was the duck (especially Elinor's duck). And oh, the camaraderie when the two of us would gang up on other drivers! If you have ever ridden the bumper cars you know both the joy and the misery these colorful, iron wheeled demons can generate.

Many of us live lives that have a great deal in common with a bumper car ride. You could say we live a bumper car lifestyle. In the bumper car lifestyle everything seems to be going along fine when suddenly we are hit by an event (large or small) and we are thrown off balance. Or maybe we get locked in the corner, paralyzed for a while. We work hard to get back on track and, poof, almost magically, we are in the groove again; everything is going great, right on plan, we're doing the driving, we're doing the scoring, and we think, "Now I am so happy." We might even become bored or complacent. Then, from an unexpected quarter, we take another hit

23

and down we go, and on it goes. Life seems like a perpetual series of highs and lows, unexpected attacks and surprise events. If we stop long enough to check, we find that our lives contain a constant and subtle undercurrent of fear because living the bumper car life style is so unpredictable. We never really know what is going to happen next.

Our response to the unpredictable is to try to make it predictable. We try to control our environment, or the people in it, in ways both subtle and gross. We develop personal strategies for threats real and imagined. We spend much time and energy trying to make our world safe and solid. We engage in ongoing, and often futile, planning. We plan for old age, for sickness, for disaster, weaving our bumper car through the never-ending obstacles. But just when we think everything is under control, we get hit; we lose our job, we break a bone, our child gets sick, we discover our boyfriend has been secretly seeing someone else, or someone close to us dies. The list of possible hits is vast. As long as we are alive there is the possibility of a surprise hit. In the bumper car lifestyle, instead of accepting change (the inevitable) we fear it. We deny its constancy.

The bumper car ride is the perfect metaphor for the unconscious life, the unaware life; the life lived in constant reaction to the world. While many of us remain in the bumper car existence for our entire lives, a few of us find ourselves desiring something different. This desire for change seems to be motivated in a few predicable ways: our bumper car crashes and burns, or it is harried by a seemingly endless series of hits, what Rumi called "all the irritation with the ants."[1] We might become overwhelmed by our discontent or, maybe, if we are fortunate, someone or something inspires us. Whatever ignites it, the desire for change is the sign that awareness is ready to birth, that it is time to wake up to a deeper more complete reality. In fact, this is the first moment of our awakening. Taking notice of our discontent, admitting that we are not really as "in control" of things as we assumed, becoming aware

---

[1] Barks, Coleman, with Moyne, John. *The Essential Rumi*. Castle Books, 1997. Page 138

that, more often than not, we have been "at effect" rather than "at cause" in the story of our life, our head pops out of the sand. The understanding dawns that there is more to life than the bumper car ride, and, with this understanding, the desire for change intensifies. What this "more to life" might be is unknown, but the desire for change is a certainty. This moment of awareness and desire occurs throughout our lives, but unfortunately, it often defines both the beginning and the end of our experience of change. We often stop moving forward right at this point and return to our habitual ways of dealing with the world. Why? In part, it is because we have programmed ourselves to avoid the discomfort that change often requires. It is more natural to seek comfort and pleasure. But another important reason we don't move on from here is that we simply do not have the skills or the knowledge that allow us to do so. These skills are not taught in our schools; neither did our parents pass them down to us. As Buddhists say, we are simply "ignorant." This is not a pejorative term. It is not a judgment. In this case, it means that many of us have little or no understanding of awareness; the primary tool for significant change. Yet, awareness is the pathway into the "more" that so many of us seek in life.

As I said, many of us will spend our entire lives in the bumper car. And, even if we escape, we will return to the ride from time to time. As Jack Kornfield says in his book, *After the Ecstasy, the Laundry,* and as the title implies, there is no such thing as "enlightened retirement."[2] According to Kornfield, even if we experience enlightenment at some point, we return to the everyday world to integrate this experience, and so we still may have to drive our bumper car a few more laps. In any case, for those of us who are not yet enlightened, we can use the four strategies in this book to grow and change, to find peace and equanimity by learning from our experiences. These strategies do not need to be used in a linear fashion, but awareness is as vital as a cornerstone. We begin with awareness, learning how to get out of the bumper car and into a different, more profound, reality.

---

[2] Kornfield, Jack. *After the Ecstasy, the Laundry.* Bantam Books, 2001, page 123

Awareness here is defined as being with whatever is happening at the moment without engaging the natural compulsion to change it, worry about it, or fix it. It is about not taking action every time we feel our habitual reactions to uncomfortable circumstances arise. It is not about certainty, about labeling, blaming, judging or putting things in a convenient box. It is simply noticing what is happening, like watching a river go by, but with the important difference that we are simultaneously in the river while watching from the bank. Through the practice of awareness, as we observe the world around us and our reactions to it, we eventually become more comfortable with change, with uncertainty, with paradox, and with difference. Awareness is the first step in understanding what our life is trying to teach us; in seeing what is offered rather than refusing the gift when we feel uncomfortable and afraid and want to run away. As we have structured our lives around avoiding risk and change, we have simultaneously created an inflexibility toward the new, the different. Avoiding risk, trying to stay emotionally safe all the time, is a way of being that is often passed on from generation to generation. Sometimes our unquestioned and often unconscious inherited beliefs act like an invisible curse that prevents us from understanding and embracing the personal changes that can lead us into a more peaceful and joyful existence.

As stated above, we often arrive at a pivotal moment in our lives, at the opportunity for change and turn back, shutting the gate on a different future. We grab an old strategy for temporary relief of our emotional aches and pains and return to our faithful distractions; more goods, more work, another drink, a new car, sports, more volunteerism, another workshop, another relationship, or a new psychodrama. It seems perfectly logical that we want to avoid all the discomfort and emotional pain that so often accompany a budding awareness. Thus it is that so many of us do not choose awareness but are propelled into it by a dramatic, life-changing event or personal, emotional crisis.

However, it is not necessary to wait until we find ourselves in crisis or in a situation in which we feel helpless or deeply frustrated. We can begin this practice at any time, regardless of our current condition. We may simply be tired of the status quo. We may be wondering what life is really about. We may want to find more meaning in our life; more aliveness. The rewards or awareness are supreme and life altering, regardless of why we embrace it or when we do.

What is extraordinary about awareness is that, in a sense, there is really nothing to do, no skill to learn. Consciousness, or awareness, is actually a state that is accessible for all of us at any time. It is always there. As we access it we sense its familiarity. Rumi opens his wonderful poem about love and consciousness, *No Room for Form*, with these lines:

> *"On the night that you leave your house and your shop*
> *and cross the road to the cemetery*
> *You'll hear me hailing you from inside the open grave*
> *And you will know how we have always been together.*
> *I am the clear consciousness core of your being*
> *The same in ecstasy as in self-hating fatigue"*[3]

The gift is ours all along. In our busy home and work life, the house and the shop, we seldom realize its presence, and yet we and our consciousness "have always been together."

While the terms *being aware, being the witness, noticing* and *being conscious* are interchangeable; the concept of *being the witness* is very helpful for understanding the mechanics of awareness. The part of us called "the witness" is that part that watches and observes everything as it happens in our lives. It is Rumi's "clear consciousness core," and it is "clear" because it is not distracted by judgment of unfolding events or by comparison or blame, or need for change. It is at the core, the center; it is the truth of things. The great clue about consciousness that is offered in this verse is that it is "the same in ecstasy as in self-hating fatigue." In other words, it is not defined by emotion; it is beyond emotion and our reactions to the world. Awareness is benign; it does not deepen our feeling of fear or emotional upset. It does not make us feel worse. It simply

---

[3] Barks, Coleman with Moyne, John. *The Essential Rumi.*Castle Books, 1997. Page 138

reveals fully what is true, what exists, whether it has been hidden or present, whether it is joy or pain or fear.

Often when we witness our interactions with others we focus on how they are "making us feel" and "what they are doing to us" and on how "they" behave. When people first come to see me for relationship counseling, their attention is invariably focused on "other" and "outer." It seems so obvious that another person's behavior is "making" us feel upset. Sometimes a client will talk for quite a long time about what is being done to them, and focus keenly on how their friend or partner or employer is treating them. They will carefully analyze the other person's behavior and tell me how, if someone else would only change their behavior, all would be well. Usually, there is a good portion of judgment and blame in these stories. Sometimes we take pride in knowing exactly how other people behave and more, how they should behave, especially to make us happier. We all do this. This is the bumper car ride. Chances are that the other folks in our stories are surmising about our behavior, and judging how we are acting. Undoubtedly, they have suggestions for us as well.

Being an expert on someone else's behavior usually doesn't change that behavior, and demonstrating our expertise about the way they behave can annoy them. In addition, the negative and positive expectations we often have for behavior changes in others can create a series of disappointments and further frustration. If we want change in our lives, it is vital to take the view that the lessons life is trying to teach us are found in our own behavior and reactions, not in the behavior of others. By focusing our awareness on our selves we facilitate the evolution of self, the discovery of who we really are. As we become more aware of our own reactions, and our own sometimes-unskillful behavior we quickly realize we have enough work of our own to keep us quite busy! We don't need to judge and worry about others. We begin to see that others are simply pushing our buttons, and that we are reacting, sometimes unskillfully, from our own reservoir of fear or sorrow or anger. The source of these emotions is our self; our reaction to their behavior belongs to us. We are the agent of our own action and the choices we make. As Eckhart Tolle states in his book *The Power of Now,* when we practice awareness we no longer define ourselves by our emotions or thoughts. "You no longer *are* the emotion; you are the watcher, the observing presence. If you practice this, all that is unconscious in you will be brought into the light of consciousness."[4]

The witness might see us judging and blaming, but it does not get caught on these hooks. Thus, as life unfolds, the witness might say of our behavior, "Look, there is judgment" or, "Look, there is blame" or, "Look, there is anger" (or lust or greed or fear). Again, awareness is not about making things either bad or good, including our own behavior. So, we don't feed the hungry demons of judgment and blame by judging ourselves when we witness our own unskillful moments. We don't say to ourselves, "There I go judging them again." We simply notice this is happening. Self-judgment can distract us from our noticing. Whatever arises in the moment is simply noticed. Awareness happens in present time. Although we can witness our reactions, it is very important to remember that awareness is not about reacting or creating a response.

At this point it is helpful to remember the bumper car metaphor. Awareness is like standing outside of the bumper car arena and watching the drama inside. But the big trick about developing awareness is that we must simultaneously stay in our bumper car and avoid the temptation to escape the ride through objectivity (just standing outside the arena). This is a very important understanding. We experience subjectively while our witness observes our feelings and reactions simultaneously.

Awareness is often confused with objectivity. Objectivity is often used to separate ourselves from what we perceive to be unpleasant and emotionally trying by disassociating an event from the feelings it engenders. Because we find this easier and less stressful than experiencing our feelings, we end up denying that our reactions and emotions exist at all. Denial is not awareness; it is a way of coping with emotional pain and discomfort. Over time it ends up numbing us to life. The confusion between objectivity and full awareness, which includes awareness of what we are feeling, is the big trap on the awareness trail, the pitfall. Objectivity is the abode of many of us who appear to be above life's trials, but in

---

[4] Tolle, Eckhart, *The Power of Now*. Namaste Publishing, 1997, page 22

reality it is a dry and a lifeless condition, a go-nowhere plan. As we come to realize that we can access our witness at any time; we are often tempted to withdraw from emotional content and just watch from the sidelines. This kind of objectivity and denial can seem like a good painkiller, but it is not helpful if our intention is to learn and to grow. In fact, it brings personal growth to a standstill. Remember the humorous reminder that, "Denial is not a river in Egypt." We are all tempted by denial from time to time. But, when we choose this route we eventually end up shutting down all feelings, including passion and joy.

The fact that developing awareness is not about taking action, that it is simply about noticing with no restrictions, and with no denial of feeling, is one of the reasons it is a wonderful strategy for beginning to learn more about ourselves and our relationship with others and the world. It does not require the participation of others or our ego. It is not about change. It is not about becoming a different or a "better" person. In fact, when we first begin our awareness practice, it is important to avoid taking any action based on our observations. Rather, we just let situations flow. We try to stay aware at all times until this state becomes more familiar and accessible. We will often be forgetful. We will slide out of awareness, away from consciousness, and back into the story, our personal soap opera, our bumper car ride. Yet, when we remember to be aware, we can experience being with anger as it rises and ebbs away; we can go deep into sorrow; we can witness and hang out with our fear. Awareness brings us deeper into the experience of life and the experience of others. We use awareness to feel what others are feeling, again without judgment or blame. Our awareness of others and their emotional reality is the first step toward compassion, empathy and kindness. It is a source of civility.

When we first practice awareness, it is good to leave repair, and change for later. By practicing awareness we will be less likely to fall into our old stories, will not be so easily swept away by our fear, our sorrow or our anger. Acknowledging our emotions is not the same as abandoning ourselves to them. Although we may be tempted to do so, this is not the function of this practice. If we do fall into an old pattern and join an old story we simply notice that.

With our budding awareness, we sometimes see how we act unskillfully, and we may not be pleased with this discovery. Our tendency is to want to immediately change our behavior. Though understandable, this is counterproductive because it takes us out of awareness and into a "fix it" loop. It is important not to get distracted by this often-compulsive reaction to events. Fixing things removes us from the flow, from the practice. It is yet another way the ego removes us from true experience. The ego likes to be in charge. Fortunately, with awareness we can even see this happening and come back to what we are experiencing now. Letting go of the need to fix things is an important step in the discovery component of learning what our lives are trying to teach us.

Over time, as we implement the four strategies in this book, we will discover that the answers to our fears and dilemmas present themselves to us exactly when we are ready; that the answers are within and do not need to be forced. In order for this to be revealed we must be present with what is happening moment by moment. Over time we develop the patience that knows that the answers we seek will come when it is time and no sooner. We cannot force them with the intellect.

In his poem, *The Music*, Rumi writes, "For sixty years I have been forgetful, every minute."[5] Like Rumi, we can remember that the many, many moments in which we are unconscious are simply moments of forgetfulness. We have forgotten to use our awareness; we have forgotten that we can choose to be conscious beings, that awareness is always available. Often we find ourselves back in the bumper car arena. When we become aware that this has happened, it is helpful to have mercy on ourselves, to remember that we all slip back into the arena frequently. We are not in a contest. When we become aware that we have forgotten consciousness, in that moment we can choose to reenter awareness without self-judgment. We begin our journey again right there. We are all forgetful, but now we find little reason to live entirely in forgetfulness. There are too many riches to mine in the conscious dimension.

---

[5] Barks, Coleman with Moyne, John. *The Essential Rumi* , Castle Books, 1995, page 98

Back at the amusement park the bumper car ride was over before we knew it. As we grow older it seems that life has flown by. In the end, the difference between a life well lived and one which we review with regret has nothing to do with what we have acquired, where we have lived, how wonderful our family life has been or how many friends we have made. These are all fine things, but in the end, the depth and beauty of our life will be a result how present we were for all that transpired. How deeply did we immerse ourselves in the passing river? How present were we for the glorious gift? Did we feel the grace, the aliveness?

The practice of awareness changes our lives forever. There is no dousing the fire once it has been lit, try as we may. Understanding that we are not really defined by others, or even by what is happening in our lives, we experience a kind of freedom for which we have often longed.

An Unexpected Ally
Your Personal, Trustworthy Guide

When we decide to make awareness a daily practice, we will begin to see many events in new ways, sometimes disturbing; often revealing. We discover that things are not what they have always seemed. We begin to see and feel our own reactions as they happen and watch as specific interactions trigger our emotions. We discover where our emotions take us when we do not unconsciously and instinctively react to old provocations. We suddenly notice how often situations evolve in predictable patterns.

As we become more aware, each of us is challenged differently, depending on the well-established strategies we have created or chosen to deal with emotional discomfort. Those of us who have repressed our emotions begin to experience them more fully, especially when we do not instantly react to incoming stimulus in habitual ways. If we have been denying our emotions for some time, and unconsciously reacting to discomfort in well-established patterns, moments of awareness in which we allow our emotions to arise in their full glory can be very confusing at first. Often we have trouble identifying what we are actually feeling. This experience is very common for those of us who have been taught, or have decided, that acknowledging or expressing our emotions is a sign of weakness, that we need to "grin and bear it," to pretend we don't have feelings, and be tough.

At the other extreme, some of us have been indulging our emotions with little restraint. With awareness, we will notice how easily we let emotions rule us. We will begin to see that this strategy leads toward inner chaos and feelings of helplessness. It disturbs others, often profoundly. With our new awareness we are now watching this happen as we experience our emotions. We soon discover that we are at choice. As we learned earlier, noticing our emotions and indulging them is not the same. Our work is to simply be aware of our feelings rather than abandoning ourselves to them.

Often we avoid what we are feeling by describing our *thoughts* as emotions. We might say things like, "I feel you should be more....," or, "I feel like I am always the one to...," or, "I feel like she is not being...." Fill in the blanks, but these are not feelings. They are thoughts and ideas. If we have this habit, we need to recognize the difference between what we think and what we are actually feeling and start paying attention to what we are feeling, to our emotions, without denying or over indulging them.

I have a very simple system I use in counseling for getting to the real emotion underlying a situation. When someone is confused and using "I feel" as the prelude to a thought, (rather than relating an actual feeling) I simply ask, "And how does that make you feel?" So, if someone says, "It makes me feel like he doesn't care about me," I say, "And how does that make you feel?" They might answer, "It makes me feel like he lives in his own world." "And how does that make you feel?" Eventually, we will "drill down", as they say in computer lingo, to the core emotion. "It makes me feel angry," for instance. For some reason, most of us think there might be quite a few emotions, but in reality there are very few, and most, it seems, are variations of anger and sadness. We can use this technique on ourselves, and keep asking the question, "And how does that make me feel?" to get to the core of what we are really feeling as well as refocusing on ourselves.

The reason that it is important for us to know the exact feeling(s) we are experiencing is because our feelings are where our truth resides. When we want to connect with others we need to speak our truth. To do this we will need to know exactly the emotion(s) we are feeling or have felt, because emotion is the place where our truth joins that of others. We have all felt sorrow and anger for instance. We all know what "hurt" means. Truth resides in the heart and is communicated from the heart.

Awareness gives us the ability to see the connection between our emotions and our habitual reactions. When we choose to stop instinctively reacting to uncomfortable situations, we realize that we have control over our connection with the world; we are not victims of circumstance. Awareness brings with it the understanding that, although we experience emotion, we are not defined by our emotions. Our core consciousness is free of emotion and intellect, as Rumi says, "The same in ecstasy as in self hating fatigue."[6] This can be a very liberating revelation. This is why practicing awareness, even for a short time, allows many of us to experience hope for change for the very first time. As Eckhart Tolle says, "Ego implies unawareness. Awareness and the ego cannot co-exist."[7] For the first time, we feel what it is like to be free of the ego.

Awareness is especially useful for revealing the way fear works in the world, and how it shapes our perceptions and behavior. Most of us have little understanding about fear, which seems amazing when we eventually discover what a huge role fear plays in our lives and the world. Long ago, when Don Rosenthal first explained the role of fear in my life, I didn't understand what he was talking about. I had been living in fear my whole life, and was not even aware of its presence. As the saying goes, "The fish is usually the last to know about the ocean in which it swims." This was certainly true of my lack of awareness about the fear in which I swam. Often, when I tell my clients that, as they practice awareness, they will come into contact with their fears, they cannot grasp what I am talking about.

The Tibetan Buddhists believe that current incarnations of former great teachers become suddenly aware of complete teachings (which they call "treasures") created long ago. Sometimes hundreds of years pass between the time a wisdom teaching was first constructed and its appearance in the world. These treasures appear fully formed, usually through the current incarnation of the ancient teacher or Rinpoche who first created them. It is said that a teaching remains hidden until the moment the ancient master had envisioned, as he looked into the future, that mankind would need it. Discovering the incredible influence of fear in our lives is like this kind of revelation, a treasure of great value. Awareness often allows

---

[6] Barks, Coleman with Moyne, John. *The Essential Rumi.*Castle Books, 1997. Page 138

[7] Tolle, Eckhart, *A New Earth,.* Plume, 2005 , page 64

us to get our first glimpses of fear and its work in the world. It is not long before we see how ubiquitous it is.

One unexpected place that we find fear is in perfectly logical ideas: of course one plans for the future, of course one tries to make as much money as possible to gain the good life for themselves or their family, of course one tries to be a good citizen, of course one wants to please others, of course one wants to excel. These are all very logical and accepted ideas, but they are all based in fear. Each has an answer to the question, "What am I afraid of?" This is a good question to ask, especially about many of our most strongly held beliefs. If we have difficulty holding something lightly, if we are rigid about certain ideas, if we have to be right about everything, it is good to ask, "What am I afraid of?"

With awareness it becomes very obvious that fear is the source of so much of life's action; so much of our reaction to others and events; so much of our politics and even religion. However, I still remember simply "not getting it" years ago, even after Don patiently laid it out. This often happens when we encounter areas of unconsciousness. They are so close to us, so familiar, that we can't see them objectively. This is one reason why it is often important to seek help from others wiser and more experienced than we are. A good teacher can help us discover these blind spots. Without outside help, without exposure to new and different ideas, it is possible to stay blind to these areas for many years or even an entire lifetime.

Staying aware of what we are feeling, staying with our emotions instead of denying them or indulging them, is made even more powerful when we see the fear that is often the foundation for our beliefs and feelings. It is amazing how many of the ideas and beliefs we blindly accept are rooted in fear.

Seeing how omnipresent fear is can be quite a revelation, a door opening out onto a vast kingdom. We suddenly see the fearful workings of the world for the first time; understand the huge quantity of ignorance that supports it. We see how it is used to market things, start wars, and deny compassion.

But becoming aware of fear and seeing how much it dominates our lives and the actions of our world is only an understanding. What then? How can we use this awareness? When the nature and action of fear is fully revealed, and the myriad unskillful reactions it spawns are seen clearly, how do we alter our relationship to fear? How do we discover a more powerful genesis for our actions? How do we stop using typical, often unskillful reactions every time fear arises?

A powerful device for dealing with and transforming fear is contained in the teachings of Don Juan, the Yaqui sorcerer from the books of Carlos Castaneda. We can treat fear as an ally. Don Juan taught that a man of knowledge (a warrior) always had an ally, that an ally was formless and that an ally was perceived as a quality. Fear makes a good ally.

Because we have trained our whole being to avoid fear, we do not understand its nature or realize its potential for helping us change. Instead, we have developed as many ways as possible to avoid it and smother it. Much of our action in the world is derived from our particular fears. For instance, we might create a career that pleases our peers and parents because we are afraid of their bad opinion. Rather than following our heart, we may work for years at an enterprise that is not satisfying to us. Yet, until we do what we love, live the way we desire, we will not be truly content or happy. We will not feel inner peace. When we fear other's opinion and try to satisfy their vision of what our success or what our life should look like, the results can be disastrous.

We can start working with fear by becoming aware of the thousands of tiny fears we live with each day. We fear peer opinion. We fear the voices in our heads, which say, "You should do this" and, "You must do that." We fear financial troubles; we fear encounters with certain people; we fear authority; we fear the future and the past. We fear for our lives and we fear death. We fear pain. We even fear quiet. We fear that we will never have enough. We fear the judgment of strangers; friends and spouses. We fear loneliness and anger. And the list goes on. For each of our fears we have developed one or more strategies, of avoidance, indulgence, smothering or denial. In addition, many of our most unskillful behaviors come from fear. Many of our goals are fear-based. Fear can even masquerade as worthy action, such as compassion, when we are afraid for ourselves and project our own fear into helping others. (Helping others is noble but helping is much more effective when done out of love rather than fear). We might take up martial arts because we don't feel safe or because we fear attack or feel helpless. Fear is at work when we don't feel safe to be who we are in our relationships. Sometimes, when we encounter a disaster or a big negative event in our lives, the very things that we have feared the most become our reality and create even more fear.

One way to become acquainted with our fear is through awareness of what is going on in our bodies. If we are out of touch with our emotions this is a good way to notice that they are occurring. For instance, when we feel tight sensations in the throat, chest or stomach area, fear may be present. When we become aware this is happening we need to breathe. The mind has a habit of traveling out of the present, following fearful stories, tales of the past and fantasies of a bleak future. When we become aware this is happening we need to come back into the present moment. One method of bringing ourselves into the present, in addition to using the breath, is to access gratitude, to focus on all the positive things in our lives, and on beauty rather than fearful imagery.

Reading all of the above, one might think that fear makes the world go around, and, unfortunately, it does. Our entire culture is based on fear, the fear of not enough, the fear of peer opinion and the fear of change. One could logically say that, because fear motivates so much of our lives, it must be OK, but this is not really so. Most of us would prefer lives based on love and understanding, but fear can become a surprise gift when we understand its real function, and to do this we have to start paying attention to it. Fear cannot serve its function when we ignore it; pretend it doesn't exist, or numb it out in a thousand ways; when as an individual or a nation we continue to act out of fear rather than acknowledging the part it plays in our judgment, opinions and actions. We need to understand the real function of fear. And it is here that the notion of fear as an ally comes in.

Fear and pain have something in common. They are both messengers. Their job is to let us know that something is not functioning properly, is hurt or broken. Physical pain tells us that there is a problem in the physical body. If we ignore the pain it may increase to get our attention more fully. It has been found that when we stop resisting pain it often diminishes in intensity. I have experimented with this. Sitting in meditation sometimes my hip will send pain messages. When I focus on my hip and breathe into the pain, it diminishes or even disappears completely. Like pain, fear is also a messenger, but from our psycho-emotional body. It too is warning us that something is wrong, or not quite right. If we ignore it, the fear can also grow bigger and, most importantly, there will be no healing for the unacknowledged part of us that is sending the message. Avoiding fear and pain can cause them to grow stronger. The trick with fear is to go with it, to let it do its work. Once fear has put us in touch with our inner issue it can diminish. In fact, simply acknowledging fear seems to lessen it.

An example: A client of mine was having financial difficulties. She had a great deal of fear about not having enough money. Before she acknowledged this fear, she reacted to it by indulging herself in terrible fantasies about what was going to happen in the future, about fiscal disasters, about not being able to feed her family and other dreadful imaginings. This was paralyzing. We decided this would be good opportunity for some awareness practice. As her awareness grew, when fear about money arose, she began to acknowledge it, witnessing it, she told herself, "Look, there is fear about money." She learned to avoid the stories of a grim and hopeless future and to stay with her fear. Letting it be present. At first this was uncomfortable. This fear was used to hanging out just under the surface for days without abating. As she began to practice awareness, to acknowledge a specific fear, she noticed that its duration diminished. Over time, her fear and terror about money reduced its presence from days to less than an hour and finally to a time span not much greater than the acknowledgment. She saw that she had been feeding her fear. However, there is no way we can *force* fear to diminish. It is another paradox that, although acknowledging fear reduces its length and strength, if we consciously seek to reduce fear through some technique or strategy, we will become diverted by the attempt and the fear will maintain its force. It is more beneficial to trust the process of pure awareness and "go with the flow." Awareness is not a technique as much as it is a state.

Verbal acknowledgement of fear is very powerful (we will discuss the power of vocalizing our truth in a later chapter). When a client of mine had a business failure and was in fear about money, his wife was also in fear, but rather than express this, both of them acted out, blaming each other for spending too much, complaining about errors in the check book and criticizing each other about not being more organized around money. This failed to address their fear, the "elephant in the room." Finally, one night my client said this simple and truthful phrase to his wife, "I'm really afraid about our financial situation." And she replied, "So am I." It seemed such a simple exchange, and yet, suddenly they noticed a real energetic shift that allowed them to become allies in working with their fear about money. It was a powerful moment in their relationship. Later in this book we will explore the power of vulnerability, but, for now, this example demonstrates how much release can be gained from acknowledging fear instead of trying to pretend it does not exist.

When we become aware of fear and stay present with it, rather than trying to avoid it, it begins to reveal its sources. Fear shows us the beliefs from which we operate that no longer serve us. Since our life is forged out of our beliefs, this is why fear is a very powerful ally. Once we are able to see the beliefs that are not serving us, we can begin to question them fully (see *Who Says So?* for more on this idea). Our fear shines a light on the areas where we are not whole, the places where we are incomplete, the places where we have stopped growing and the places where we don't trust God, the plan, the universe, what Rumi calls "the elegant patterning."[8]

A note on this type of revelation: It is helpful to remember that the mind desires instantaneous revelation and solutions. The mind says, if revelation is not instantaneous the process is not working; try something else. The revelations we receive from being with our fear, by witnessing and acknowledging it, do not always happen instantly. Accepting fear, therefore, is not a formula for instant understanding. This is because sometimes we are not ready for revelation. By trusting that there is plenty of time, and that we will be given what we need at the appropriate moment, we reduce the tension of expectation, we practice trust and we develop mercy for ourselves by accepting ourselves as we are right now. Again, even without solutions, once our fear is acknowledged ("Look,

---

[8] Barks, Coleman, with Moyne, John. *The Essential Rumi.* Castle Books, 1997.

there's fear") and accepted ("This is what fear feels like"), it begins to diminish, sometimes long before the deep inner message or story is revealed. The diminishing longevity and force of an acknowledged fear is an amazing thing to experience. It usually happens slowly, over time, but it happens. However, you actually might want to forget this fact. Remember, we do not help or expedite the diminishment of fear by expecting or wishing for it. It is better to stay in pure awareness.

Sometimes, when we acknowledge fear and recognize an old fear, an image arises in our mind. This is often something forgotten from the past, sometimes our childhood. This image is often the clue to, or the actual point of origin of, our fear. When we do our inner work we can go to that place and, using mercy, alter our relationship to the event and thus do the healing work that will diminish or dissolve our fear. This is what is called "reframing" in Neuro Linguistic Programming (NLP). NLP can be a useful tool in doing inner work.

Fear is a very powerful and necessary ally. Practicing awareness with this understanding keeps us alert to the places where our fears are lurking. These fears tell us where our personal work lies and alert us to the areas where our beliefs need attention, and where we don't trust. Where there was once a rejected knot, a terror inside, now resides a powerful ally. Now, by acknowledging our fear, we can work with our inner demons and, rather than deny them, enlist their help as we work to discover what our life is trying to teach us. It is right at this point that we access and apply another ally, mercy, the wonderful balm that makes inner change possible and softens our worldview.

Have Mercy!

Often Overlooked, Always Important

A budding awareness is an exciting and amazing process. I have experienced the wonder of this process myself, as well as bearing witness to the unfolding of awareness in others. It takes courage and perseverance to choose awareness, but the rewards are rich. Those who embrace this practice will come to live in the world with less fear and with a greater understanding of life. Many will experience wisdom, a great grace.

Developing awareness is not the usual way we work on our problems and issues however. As stated earlier, awareness often requires patience and trust in an organic process in which solutions present themselves only when we are ready. The usual western approach for creating change, the approach most of us have learned, is to carefully identify and outline a problem and then attempt to create a solution based on our understanding of the problem, even though this is like looking at the wake to steer a ship. This well worn system often lacks vision and forgoes intuition.

It does not take a very sharp eye to see that our culture is obsessed with problems. Our news media is very responsive to this obsession. We enjoy identifying problems precisely and then going over them time after time. We believe that our minds can solve all our problems. Thus, when we practice awareness, our first response is to attempt to create solutions to what we are experiencing as disturbance and problems. As stated earlier, we immediately want to fix things. It's an old habit.

By now we see that practicing awareness is about hanging out with our discomfort and letting it reveal whatever lesson we need. Rather than giving in to our immediate compulsion to fix things, we accept them in the moment just as they are. This also includes fixing other people's and the world's problems. Just being with unpleasant emotions or fear, rather than leaping to fix things, is definitely a new way of being! I can't count the number of hours I have spent "thinking about things" trying to solve my problems with my mind. When my grandmother used to tell me, "Worry never helps anything," she meant thinking about things, letting the mind go around and around in circles. It has taken me years to understand this. I thought worry was a special class of distressed thinking reserved for important challenges. Now, I see it is actually any continuous, "try to fix it" loop. It is no wonder she was so relaxed and easy with life. She didn't obsessively ponder over problems, with the hope that a solution would suddenly appear.

When Babbie and I worked as seasonal staff at the Omega Institute, we received, as part of our stipend, free attendance at a workshop. Out of the hundreds offered, we chose a workshop with Stephen & Ondrea Levine. The workshop was named after his book, entitled *A Year to Live*. We had always admired the words and wisdom of Stephen and Ondrea. Like the Levines, we had been hospice volunteers for many years. Stephen had also written a seminal book about conscious life and conscious death entitled *Who Dies?* In our own relationship and working with couples, we had often accessed the Levine's book *Embracing the Beloved*.

The Levine's work comes directly from their personal experiences, and their teachings ring with the truth of real trials. Stephen and Ondrea are compassionate and filled with deep insight. At the workshop, there was humor and sorrow, joy and anger, but the one thing that has stayed in my mind and heart above all others was Stephen's constant encouragement to "have mercy." Participants would stand up and tell about their difficult experiences and, in the telling, many of us judged ourselves. "Have mercy people," he would say over and over, and each time he said it, it was like a bell ringing, reminding us of how little mercy we have for others and, especially, for ourselves. Mercy is an important ingredient in developing deeper awareness, while self mercy is often necessary for creating significant personal change.

With mercy we are able to view the parts of ourselves that we dislike without judgment, and to see our unskillful acts and those of others as the manifestation of ignorance and fear. We come to see how very alike we all are, and, often for the first time, we feel what it is to be accepting of ourselves, just as we are, in the moment. And with mercy, we can go to the deep places in our being where the real source of our fear and misunderstandings lie.

Once Babbie helped young woman practice awareness and gave her the opportunity to experience some mercy in a dramatic way. The young woman had a terrible relationship with her mother, who was unkind and jealous of her daughter. The daughter felt frightened and completely unsafe around her mother. She wanted the relationship to change somehow. Babbie encouraged her to introduce us to the parents in an informal setting so that we could be there with her as she interacted with them. We got together to celebrate Saint Patrick's Day and the party atmosphere allowed everyone to relax and feel comfortable. At one point during the party, Babbie stood behind the young woman, encouraged her to simply observe her mother from across the room, practice awareness of her own feelings, and work to let go of her judgments. I remember watching the young woman's eyes as, safe with Babbie, she saw her mother for the first time in a new light. She looked astounded. For the first time she was able to see her mother with some mercy and compassion instead of instant anger and fear. It was a very healing moment. We often have to do for ourselves what Babbie did for this young woman, hold ourselves in kindness and mercy and then look out at the world with awareness. As we release self-judgment, it becomes so much easier to drop the judgment of others and empathize with their suffering and difficulties. This is the beginning of true healing and more profound insight. Mercy is a complete loop.

Judging ourselves is another way that we avoid or miss the inner voyage. By repeating the stories of how bad we are, or how unskillfully we have acted, we stay in the seeming safety of our familiar world rather than seeking to experience the challenge of real change. This is usually unintentional, simply a product of ignorance. Sometimes self-judgment is so recurring that it becomes natural, and arises simply as a feeling of discomfort. We need to use our awareness to discover when this happens.

There is no need to judge our self for self-judging. It is simply what we know. When we choose mercy rather than self judgment, no part of us is separate, no part bad. We act out. We have fear. We are unskillful. Have mercy.

At a talk I gave recently, a person asked a very provocative question. "If we have mercy for ourselves, if we forgive ourselves, isn't that the same as not taking responsibility for our actions? Isn't that like going to confession and having been forgiven, we then have permission to do the same sin all over again?" The ego likes to confuse mercy with indulgence and irresponsibility. This is a trick it uses to talk us out of compassion for ourselves and, as a result, others. But mercy is not the same as permission to act irresponsibly. Irresponsible behavior represents a separate choice. In fact, mercy for ourselves, because it engenders mercy for others, means that we will be kinder to others and more skillful in our relationships. Put simply, the belief that mercy for ourselves fosters irresponsible and harmful behavior is false. Mercy does not deny our unskillful behavior. In addition it is difficult, if not impossible, to manifest true compassion if we are self-judging and unkind to ourselves. If we can't have mercy for ourselves how can we manifest it truly for others?

As we are more merciful to ourselves and others, we find that we are much more relaxed in the world, much less preoccupied with gossip, tale-telling and judgment. There is a tangible physical and emotional release of angry energy. We feel lighter and happier. We act more kindly. We often become more generous. There is a great, grace filled reward in mercy.

As we focus mercy on ourselves, we begin to release the negative and uncomfortable energy that is stored in our body. There is a wonderful technique for helping this aspect along, perfected by Lester Levinson in his work on abundance, called the "release technique[tm]."[9] As mentioned earlier, when we encounter self-judgment, or fear, or sorrow, or anger, they create a palpable tightness in the body. We can focus our mercy on this tightness and envision it unwinding and releasing, reentering its normal unwound state. Drop the head to chest (to stop thinking) and simply envision this energy leaving the body. Breathe. Envision more and more of

---

[9] Levinson, Lester. *The Abundance Course*, Lawrence Crane Enterprises, Inc. 1998

this energy returning to the outer world where it is easily assimilated. We can do this over and over until one day the energy is no longer stored in the body. Self-judgment and fear have been locked into the physical body, but in a state of mercy we can release them and actually feel the difference physically. This simple technique is very powerful.

When we first practice awareness we can't help but want to make changes as new understandings occur. We might say to ourselves, "But what about becoming more skillful? What about changing things? What do I do when I notice that I am feeling attacked, angry or sad? I want to do something! Just being with what is happening doesn't make sense." The mind wants to know how things can change if all we do is practice awareness. We have to tell the mind to be patient. Before we can change things we have to learn how to simply be with them and understand their message. Most of us have never approached situations in this way. This is a new way of being with our emotions, observations and thoughts; with what is, and the only way we can understand it is by practicing.

There are practices for personal change that we can and will learn, but the linear journey begins with awareness. We have to make sure that awareness has strong roots before the wind starts blowing. We develop these roots by simply being with what is and we need mercy to do this. As the Zen Master Susuki Roshi once said, "Nowhere to go, nothing to do, just being."[10] It is a nice relief knowing that we are not required to fix or change things all the time. By being with what is happening, by staying in the present, we are also beginning to practice trust, a key element of any spiritual progress. In this case, we are trusting that things will be OK without our immediate intervention. Many new practitioners of awareness are surprised by the freedom given through this discovery. For most of us this approach is new but, we can be encouraged by the knowledge that others have gone before us. The path is worn. Our job is to stay with the practice.

In the beginning, at least two weeks of awareness without action is recommended. We might feel some urgency to move on, so it helps to take the view that there is plenty of time (see chapter

---

[10] Roshi, Suzuki, *Zen Mind, Beginners Mind*. Weatherhill, 1970

What's Time to a Pig?). You will know when you are ready to move on by the difference in your response to challenges. Keep the watch. The rewards are great. As the Taoists say, "Don't try to push the river, learn to flow with it." We are entering the world of trust.

Letting Go Of the Branch
The Necessity of Risk

Once there was an atheist who fell off of a cliff. On his way down he was able to catch hold of a branch of a small tree. He clung, terrified, to his small branch high over the valley. Suddenly the tree started to come free of the cliff wall, jerking away slightly every few seconds. There was no way to climb back up and jagged boulders loomed far below. He thought, "Only God can save me now. But I have never believed in God. But I might be wrong. Anyway, I don't have anything to lose." So he cried out, "God, you know I have never believed in you, but, if you exist, please help me now, and I will believe in you." Nothing happened and he pleaded again. "God, if you help me now, I will do anything that you tell me for the rest of my life." Suddenly a great voice came from the heavens. "I have heard this talk before from people in desperate situations. Why should I believe you? I know your kind. As soon as I save you, you will go back to your old ways." The branch gave way a little more. "Oh God, please, I will do anything you say, just save me now!" the man pleaded, and God responded saying, "Anything?" "Yes, God, anything!" "OK, let go of the branch." "Let go of the branch?" the man cried out. "Do you think I'm crazy?"

Staying in awareness requires some trust that we will be safe when we choose to do so. Like the man hanging over the valley, often as we practice awareness, we have to let go of the branch and trust that we will be safe. There is a religious expression, "Let go and let God." There is wisdom in this expression. Whether we believe in an ultimate deity, a perfect universe, or Rumi's "elegant patterning" at some point we have to let go of our usual reactions, defenses and escapes. The moment of choice happens when, with awareness, we suddenly notice ourselves feeling angry, vulnerable, frightened, hurt or attacked. Instinctively, our ego kicks in and we feel the strong desire to immediately return to our old reactions, to simply let go into our emotions. Because our usual reactions are so instinctive, it almost seems natural to follow them, but if we want to learn what our lives are trying to teach us we need to quickly choose to stay present and aware of everything that is happening, especially our own feelings. We need to trust that this choice is safe for us.

The good news is that awareness allows us to let go of the branch one event at a time. Trust in our ultimate safety is not something that happens right away, nor does just saying we are safe bring it about. Rather, it results from cumulative experiences. Thus choosing awareness in difficult situations gives us glimpses of personal safety that eventually expand into an entire view. Each time we maintain awareness, let go of our instinctual fear-filled reactions and stay aware of what is happening in the present, we become more certain of our own safety. Over time, we begin to see that letting go of the branch is perfectly safe. Awareness is both the exercise of trust and simultaneously the foundation for deeper trust. Over time it diminishes the constant underlying fearful state in which many of us live.

I had a client whose husband was verbally mean to her and financially abused her by not letting her control her own money. He knew exactly what to say to get her agitated and angry. She was successful in business but, being a very successful business person himself, he demeaned her accomplishments. He seemed to enjoy getting her upset. Meanwhile, as she became upset, he remained frustratingly calm. He was unwilling to take any responsibility for his behavior or to do any personal work. She and I began working with awareness. Rather than instantly reacting to his prodding and getting trapped on the same old merry-go-round, her work was to watch and be aware of her reactions. It was necessary to stop being provoked into blaming and judging him and look at what was happening within herself. What was really going on? At first she found this very difficult. She had never considered the idea of not responding to his obvious taunts and provocations. They argued often, and usually he overpowered her. The act of focusing awareness on her reactions, rather than going with her instinctive responses, was very difficult. It required her to make one of the most difficult gestures known to man, putting her ego aside. The ego tells us we are not safe, that our dignity is being attacked, and that we must take some kind of action. This is the voice of fear.

She had a very hard time at first. She frequently called me, very upset, to tell me that he had said this, and he had said that, and that she had become very angry and lost control. She would list all the reasons why her upset was his fault. I coached her out of the story and into her reactions, her feelings. I encouraged her to stop blaming him for her feelings. When she did react she needed to become aware of what she was feeling in those moments. Removing herself from the stories of judgment and blame and focusing solely on her part of the encounter, on her arising emotions, she was able to discover the parts of her that were trying to teach her something. And in taking up awareness she also discovered the power and necessity of personal responsibility. As I often say, "He, she or it is pushing our buttons, but we own the buttons."

This woman began practicing awareness in every negative situation in her life. Following the rest of the four strategies she learned how to create firm and unassailable boundaries, to honor herself in ways that made it hard for others to take advantage of her. She learned how to speak and act her truth. She left her husband, got her own place, handled her own money and lived her own life. In the end her actions initiated an awakening in her husband and they began healing their relationship. Eventually they got back together after she created strong and clear boundaries and demanded real change. Not all stories end this way, of course, but more important than the happy ending is what she accomplished as a person. It is inspirational.

A wonderful thing happens when, in the thick of our interpersonal difficulties, we are able to maintain awareness. We suddenly realize that we are not powerless. Observing our own emotions, and owning them, allows us to deeply see the possibility for change. Not going along with the ego allows us to get a glimpse of the fact that we *can* change our lives, that we are not victims of other people or circumstances. Seeing ourselves clearly for the first time, and understanding that others do not define us, but that only we ourselves can do so, is a great liberation from a terrible false belief. When we reach this understanding, we also grasp the hard work ahead, but the feeling of liberation is a true blessing.

Bhagwan Shree Rajneesh used to say "the mind can only doubt and the heart can only believe." Thinking about a difficult emotional situation or trying to resolve it by thought we often end up in doubt. If we focus instead on ways to open our hearts to ourselves and others, on having mercy, we find a certainty that is beyond thought. It allows us to let go of the branch.

Opening the heart in difficult situations takes time. We have to be patient. But each time we choose awareness we are moving away from the mind's need to control outcomes. Over time, practicing awareness, we realize that our opinion, our bit of control is not always necessary. We become better listeners; we become more accepting of consensus, and discovering resolution. We begin to discover the way things really are rather than immediately trying change them into a form that is comfortable for us. Again, we stop trying to fix everything.

If the heart is the believer, we will have to learn how our hearts work, learn how to keep our hearts open when they want to close. Otherwise we will find ourselves right back in our old fear based behaviors. Our logical, mind-centered fear encourages us to leave the path. It tells us, "This path is dangerous, I am too vulnerable here. What is my best defense?" Fear tells us we must develop strategies for coping with our difficulties, when, in fact, safety lies in letting go of old strategies, letting go of the branch and in learning how to trust in something larger.

Whether we believe in a deity or practice a religion, we can all practice keeping our hearts open to others and ourselves. This work does not belong to a particular religion or faith. However, this is the ultimate spiritual path, beyond dogma, beyond separation, beyond rules and judgments, even beyond the quest for enlightenment. Jack Kornfield states in his book *After the Ecstasy, the Laundry*, "Again, the lesson of spiritual practice is not about gaining knowledge, but about how we love. Are we able to love what is given to us, to love what is in the midst of all things, to love ourselves and others?"[11] Fear says this is dangerous. Fear knows

---

[11] Kornfield, Jack . *After the Ecstasy, the Laundry*. Bantam Books, 2000

that opening our hearts brings down all the barriers it has so carefully constructed. Truly opening the heart alters our comfortable, conditional love. Surely the murderer and the embezzler and the rapist are not included in this openhearted idea? But yes, they are: we contain or access the same ego as they do. Until we learn to open our heart to the terrible, we will have no chance of changing it or learning what it is trying to teach. The mind gets very upset about political crooks, immoral corporate types, murderers and rapists, sociopaths and other scoundrels. It wants to make them wrong and bad. It says they must be excluded from the open heart. Once again the ego has made a false statement that we can use to justify keeping our hearts closed. It tells us that opening the heart to these people is the same as condoning their actions. This is totally false; there is no connection between the open heart and condoning or indulging the negative actions of others. This is perhaps the reason that Jesus hung out with tax collectors and whores, the despised and socially ostracized. Over and over, he set the example that no one is excluded from love, from the truly opened heart and he demonstrated that love begets love.

Saying that "the heart can only believe" also means that we need to stay in the heart if we want to find belief. The trust and safety we seek are found here. If we want to believe in love, in a greater plan, if we want to understand the perfection of things, if we want to find peace, we will find it in our hearts, not our heads. This is why letting go of the branch is so important. It is often the only "way in" to the spiritual realm, as they say.

Many of us have not practiced this way of being. The river of consciousness is dammed up by logic and fear. When we let go of the branch, when we practice staying in the heart, the dam breaks open, and more awareness is birthed. Letting go of the branch is a gesture we are asked to practice over and over. Because we are ever evolving, challenges are guaranteed, but we can remember there is no destination except the current moment. In developing our awareness, we can focus on letting go of the branch over and over until it becomes less and less difficult, more a second nature. Each time we let go of the branch, we discover anew the power of love, and the world of true safety, until over time the gesture becomes our leading response to the world.

53

Once I had bad flying and height dreams. In my dreams I would be in plane that suddenly began to fall out of the sky, or I would be hanging off a cliff like the atheist, petrified. Finally, one night, when I was having the cliff dream again, a part of me said, "Go ahead and jump." I realized I was in a dream, even though the dream seemed absolutely real. "Jump?" I thought, "why not? What the hell? I am so tired of being scared to death up here. I'm going to do it." I jumped, and to my surprise, I found myself flying. As I flew I discovered that my belief that I could fly kept me up, and when I doubted my ability to fly, I began to descend. I flew around for a while and then just let myself fall. Nothing happened. Since I jumped off that dream cliff, I have never had a bad flying or fear of heights dream again, but I have flown in my dreams many times.

It is a typical spiritual paradox that we will not discover our ultimate safety until we embrace our fears. Like the atheist hanging above the abyss, before we let go of the branch we might experience some terror. We jump into our fear with no guarantee that we will fly. Only faith in our ultimate safety allows us to jump. The jump is the definition of courage, of faith. We let go of the branch and fall, or maybe, like the dreamer, we don't fall. In making the choice for jumping, for letting go of our old fear based patterns with no guarantee, we learn to develop trust and faith in the perfection of all things. This perfection usually lies at the frontier of our experience. Going into that frontier takes us into a new world, a world in which the truth is revealed to us without our having to figure it out. We are heroes journeying into the unknown, the only new place we can travel. How powerful is this letting go? Jack Kornfield says of the enlightenment experience, "Although the experience is special, it does not happen to a special person. It happens to any of us when the conditions of letting go and opening the heart are present, when we can sense the world in a radically new way."[12]

When we practice awareness, there are many places we would rather not go, and it seems so reasonable to raise a barrier to unpleasant or fearful experiences. But, to fully enter awareness, we have to let go of the branch. We drop into faith, and we discover that, regardless of what is happening in us and around us, we are

---

[12]Kornfield, Jack . *After the Ecstasy, the Laundry*. Bantam Books, 2000

fundamentally safe. This discovery is grace. Our life opens up before us. We are waking up.

Getting Lost in the Story
Dealing with the Tyrannical Mind

Sometimes it seems impossible to stay with awareness. We get back in our bumper car and say, "The hell with it." We indulge ourselves in the events that are occurring around us. I call this common phenomenon "getting lost in the story." The story is one of the strongest forces that pull us out of awareness. The story is the playground of the ego. Getting lost in the story often indicates we have abandoned personal responsibility. The moment we get lost in the story, our life experiences give up their teaching value. We move out of learning, and often, back into victim mode from creator mode.

We can tell when we get lost in the story. We want to know things like: "Who did what to whom? Why didn't so and so do that? Why did I ever think that was a good idea? If she hadn't done that, everything would be fine. It isn't fair and why me? They are a bad person for doing this to me," and so forth. We want to fix or change things. We become consumed with ideas and thoughts about what happened and how we could have prevented a disaster or caused something better to happen. We analyze. We gossip. We make suppositions. We focus on other people's behavior and how that could have made things better or worse. We find ourselves justifying our anger or hurt with perfect reason and precise logic. When we are lost in the story, any unpleasant feelings we are having are easily seen as the result of someone else's behavior or outside circumstances. In short, we have relinquished our power to our ego.

If getting lost in the story sounds familiar, it is because this is the way most of us live. It's the bumper car lifestyle again; the way we encounter and deal with uncomfortable situations. Sometimes when we gossip, we become lost in other people's stories. "If I were him, I would have...." If the lives of neighbors and friends are not enough, we have the popular soap operas and TV series in which to lose ourselves. Here we can become lost in stories about fictional characters who are totally lost in their stories. Fantasy chasing fantasy; it's all part of the bumper car ride.

Getting lost in a story is easy and, even when we understand that there is nothing to be gained from dropping out of awareness in this manner, it is so easy to slide back into this pattern. We are so used to being in the world this way.

In order to stay focused on what our life is trying to teach us, it is very helpful to become aware of the moments in which we become lost in the story. As soon as that awareness arises we can remember that we have a choice. We can either continue staying lost in the story, indulging our emotions and allowing our ego full control, or we can choose to expand our awareness to embrace the whole. This expanded picture includes our own part in the story, our feelings, our own culpability, our role and our responsibility as a participant. It includes watching as well as experiencing our ego. We also can view what is happening to other participants in the story. We can do all this without getting lost in judgment or blame. With this choice we are back in full awareness, in the bumper car but simultaneously watching the whole show. This choice for an expanded awareness often means ignoring the dictates of the ego, and letting go of imperatives that try to drag us back in, such as being understood, being right or being completely heard. Letting go of these seemingly desperate needs can be can be quite challenging. The rewards, however, are immense. Freeing ourselves from the tyranny of the ego is a major life goal, especially if we desire to live with less fear and greater freedom. Learning to avoid getting lost in stories is an important exercise that allows us to watch the ego at work rather than to accept its imperatives blindly.

Stories occur through time so that there are really three different types of stories: the past story, the present story and future story. And each requires a different strategy for regaining awareness.

The *present story* is the story that is happening right now, right in the moment. There are two fundamental varieties:

conversational and *confrontational*. In the conversational story, we get lost in a story we are sharing with someone. They might be gossiping about someone or we might be joining them in judgment or blame about some group, as in a political or religious conversation. Getting lost in conversational stories is easy. Often we don't even notice it happening. We think it is innocent enough to chat about others and make opinions, but these stories can be harmful and are often filled with conjecture, judgment and untruths. Sometimes they are malicious. Most of us would not want to be a subject of gossip ourselves, and gossip is often harmful to others, perpetuating judgment and bad feeling. Gossip is an escape from our own life, our own difficulties, and it is seldom compassionate in the true sense. Judgment often masquerades as compassion and over-care. The moment we become aware that we have been invited to gossip or see ourselves offering these stories, we can choose simply to stop. If someone is sharing gossip or opinions, they won't go on talking for long without our participation. Gossip loves fuel and often needs it to keep going. By not adding fuel or energy, we are doing the subjects of gossip a favor, and we are choosing not to become emotionally wrought up and distracted about things outside of our realm of action.

Political conversations can also turn acrimonious and so provide a good practice arena for not getting pulled into the story as well. If, in the midst of a political discussion, we notice we are getting judgmental and riled up, it is a good time to pull out. Pulling out of these kinds of stories can be difficult but becomes easier with practice. Also, if we know someone is adamant about their political views and we don't share them, we can deliberately avoid talking about politics. It is possible to have good friends who don't share our political views. Some of my friends and I even joke about having different views. We don't go into political discussions: philosophy "yes," politics "no."

In a *confrontational* story someone has yelled at us or called us names or disturbed us in some way. We may have been insulted or have just been the recipient of rude or unskillful behavior. We may have just learned something hurtful. We may feel threatened or demeaned. We get lost in the confrontational story most of the time because we feel attacked. Our dignity has been impinged upon and we question our safety. We want to attack back, defend ourselves or withdraw. These stories are of two kinds, those perpetrated by friends and relations and those perpetrated by people we don't know.

It is important to prevent present confrontational stories from becoming past stories. These stories, especially those perpetrated by friends or relatives, fester and can take up a great deal of energy and time. They can sabotage our best efforts to act kindly. They can be a continual source of fear. We need to learn how to respond to perceived attack while endeavoring to process our feelings as quickly as possible to prevent the accumulation of resentment or sorrow. We can do this by moving to awareness as soon as possible.

The confrontational story is usually harder to deal with than the conversational story. We often get trapped in the confrontational story by the belief that we must respond skillfully in the present (see Action chapter, *Say It Later*). When we don't respond in this way, we judge ourselves, and this becomes another enchanting ingredient in the story. Actually, there is no law that says we have to respond immediately. If we are feeling especially emotional, it is often more skillful to withhold a response while simultaneously staying aware.

There are three useful phrases that I sometimes call "the three spell breakers," that help us to break our enchantment with the story and can keep us from getting lost in the story. The first is, "Being right isn't it." Being right is a big escalator in many interpersonal conflicts that get out of hand. Being right often seems critical to our very survival, but is usually surprisingly unimportant. However, the ego thinks being right is *very* important. It says that when someone doesn't take our view, they don't understand us, and it turns this lack of understanding into an attack on our values and dignity. If we think about this when we are not in the midst of a "being right" situation we can see that whether someone else thinks we are right or not is actually not important. If someone doesn't take our view, it really doesn't matter. Everyone is entitled to his or her view. This does not mean we do not create boundaries to prevent behavior that is harmful to us; it means we can let go of what Buddhist teachers call "the anguished imperative" to be right, to have the last and most important word. We are not devaluing ourselves by this. We do this by understanding that other people are free to enjoy their personal opinions. We can take the view that disagreement is not threatening. If we find this difficult, we need to ask, "Why is it so important to me that my view be the only one standing at the end of this encounter?" In reality, not having to be right, allowing others their opinion, no matter how crazy it may seem to us, is a huge release, a letting go that we can feel intellectually, emotionally, and physically. It is a nice gift to oneself.

The second spell breaking phrase that helps us when we don't want to become lost in the story is, "This person (use their name) is acting X (angry, upset, annoyed, disdainful, insulting...fill in the blank) and I'm OK." This helps us to avoid self-judgment and self defense loops and to remember that there is no connection between their aggressive or unskillful behavior and our basic, good self. Their attack or opinion does not constitute the absolute truth. Furthermore, we are not responsible for their behavior; the way they are acting belongs to them. We are not a bad person if they do not like us or are critical of us. Often we forget this when someone attacks us in any way. This is not to say we should be insensitive about other people's feelings and issues, or that we never act insensitively ourselves. The point is that we do not have to take their, perhaps unskillful, behavior as a personal insult.

Often our reaction to perceived attack comes out of the unconscious. The phrase, "...and I'm OK" is a conscious response that short circuits egocentric reactions. Doing this in moments of interpersonal stress has a powerful effect over time. By using this affirmation we block the ego's desire to react negatively and reinforce itself. Over time this desire loses strength.

I have been helped by this phrase many times. For instance, sometimes Babbie gets angry at me and immediately I feel upset (I'm judging myself). I go to my bad boy space. I feel small and vulnerable. Or, I start to get lost in the story and get angry. I want to attack back or defend my actions. When I am aware this is happening, I tell myself, "Babbie is really (upset, angry, disappointed) with me and I'm OK." Her opinion about my behavior can even be right, and I may need to make some personal changes, but, if I go to guilt, I will begin feeding the ego, and end up trying to defend myself or I will run away hurt. Remembering that I am a loving and kind person, right at the moment of conflict, helps me to be present for her anger, perhaps even to validate it. She may be angry or upset and I am still a loving person with a good heart. I know I can and do act unskillfully and that's OK (remember having mercy applies to oneself) as long as I take responsibility and make change. This is not a method for avoiding responsibility for our own unskillful actions. We are still encouraged to review and take responsibility for our unskillful behavior and to speak our truth at some point.

Not getting lost in the story, remembering that we are ultimately safe, even in the midst of painful emotional conflict, and avoiding impulsive reaction, all create a safe container for the situation or confrontation. This makes it more possible for others to speak their truth. Not feeling safe to speak the truth and not being heard are major relationship issues that creating safety in this manner can ameliorate.

An understanding of the ways of the self-judge is helpful here (covered in more depth in *Polishing The Mirror*). Not only is the self-judge the source of all our judgment of others, it is very sensitive when someone else picks up the gavel and points it at us. It is usually the self-judge that is at the bottom of our unskillful reactions to perceived attack. Even though we may not be conscious of it, the self-judge is often a leading tyrant in our inner world. To understand how this works simply ask yourself, "If I felt fundamentally good about myself and had excellent self-esteem, would a personal attack really bother me?"or, "If someone said something about me that I knew was completely wrong, would it bother me?" It is when we do not feel good about ourselves that we are most sensitive. Thus, when we are attacked and we react harshly, it is often because our inner judge agrees with our attacker! The perceived attack triggers our self-judge and this makes us even angrier. If we were warned in advance that someone was mentally ill, and then we met them, and they verbally attacked us, how would it affect us? Probably not so much.

For our third spell breaking phrase, we can remember the powerful teaching from *The Course in Miracles*: "All unloving behavior is a cry for healing and help," which encourages us to apply mercy as soon as possible. All three of these phrases cut the legs out from under the ego before it can jump up on its self-justifying soapbox.

When anger is our first reaction to a present story, it is important to keep it from moving to rage. While it is natural to feel anger, it is not always practical or helpful to manifest it immediately if we cannot communicate it authentically, i.e. without judgment or blame. Once unskillful anger is let loose, it gets very hard to keep from getting completely lost the story and becoming over emotional.

In his book *Emotional Intelligence* Daniel Goleman quotes the work of University of Alabama psychologist Dolf Zillmann who made a study of what he called "the anatomy of rage and anger." Zillmann states, "A universal trigger for anger is the sense of being endangered. Endangerment can be signaled not just by an outright physical threat, but also, as is more often the case, by a symbolic threat to self esteem or dignity; being treated unjustly or rudely, being insulted or demeaned, being frustrated in pursuing an important goal."[13] The ego goes instantly to red alert.

Zillmann discovered that one of the most effective ways of defusing anger is to "challenge the thoughts that trigger the surges of anger, since it is the original appraisal of an interaction that confirms and encourages the first burst of anger and the subsequent reappraisals that fan the flames."[14] And what could be a better challenger than mercy?

Sure enough, Zillmann discovered that by changing our first impression to a more compassionate view we can quickly cool anger and prevent rage. We can remind ourselves, that the unloving behavior that is being directed at us is a result of our attacker's lack of skill and their ignorance. People who repeatedly act inconsiderately or unskillfully, who need to be right all the time, or who often seem angry, are often simply ignorant of any better way to act. Mercy also allows us to give them the benefit of the doubt. Perhaps they are tired, preoccupied, upset about something else and therefore they are acting out unconsciously. Maybe they have had a bad day. Quickly coming to mercy often defuses an entire situation,

---

[13] Goleman Daniel, *Emotional Intelligence*. Bantam Books, 1997, page 61
[14] Ibid. page 62

while simultaneously completely undoing the ego's plans. And, there are always two sides to a story.

The sooner we deal with a present story, the less chance it has of becoming a "past" story and affecting our future. For most of us, past stories are the ones in which we can get really lost. Most of us have old stuff we lug around, and we would definitely feel better if we could let go of this baggage. Some of our past stories are nurtured or embellished over time and can easily be called up by current events. Other past stories remain hidden until something happens that triggers them. Past hurt, past abuse, past anger are the emotions that fill these stories. There are two ways we can keep from getting lost in our past stories. We can view them metaphysically as non-existent or we can view them as important teachers on our path whose lessons we have failed, so far, to integrate.

The metaphysical approach to past stories is outlined in the provocative and interesting book *The Power of Now*. Our past stories, according to the author, Eckhart Tolle, are products of the mind. The mind is what holds us back from experiencing the present fully. By understanding that the past does not exist, we free ourselves from a trick the mind uses to control us i.e. dragging us back into the non-existent past with past stories. Tolle reminds us that the present is all that exists, and that when the mind occupies itself with past stories it is taking us out of the present; it is actually taking over our present, leaving us without a current life. To rectify this, when we see we are going back into a tale of woe from the past, we remind ourselves that the past does not actually exist and we bring ourselves into present awareness.

This metaphysical approach is very compelling. It asks, "Why should I be upset about something that does not exist *now*?" It sounds simple and in principle it is. Tolle begins his book by saying, "I have little use for the past and rarely think of it...."[15] He has learned how to stay out of his past stories. Interestingly, like a few other great teachers, Tolle says that he experienced instantaneous enlightenment. He went to bed one night in despair and anguish and awoke the next day in an enlightened state. He says of awakening on

---

[15] Tolle, Eckhart. *The Power of Now*. Namaste Publishing, 1997, page 3

that morning, "It was as if I had just been born into this world."[16] All of a sudden he completely understood, without a single doubt, that reality only exists right now in the immediate moment.

Since most of us are not enlightened beings, and are replete with all of our conditioning and beliefs, we often find it difficult to live totally in the present. Our past is still real to us, and the concept that the past does not exist, while understandable, is more esoteric than practical. We are so conditioned to getting lost in our stories and living out of our unconscious that we find it hard to jump directly to living fully in the present, into a state of full awareness and openness. If we decide to live completely in the present, we also run the risk of denying our past. Denial is very seductive. It is the invisible abductor that carries us away from unpleasant realities and off of our path. Denial is the psychological equivalent of the fruit of the poppy, numbing us to the pain and fear that are our true teachers. When we eat the sweet candy of denial our teachers slip away, and we are unable to perceive or learn what our lives are trying to teach us. Therefore we have to be very honest with ourselves if we want to deny the past. Are we really living in the present or are we faking it, and denying our emotional pain?

Although the past is technically non-existent, and living in the past is, as the Tibetan Buddhists say, like "trying to write on water," past stories have an emotional charge because they have created embedded fears and feelings that have not been fully resolved. For those of us who do not receive the extraordinary grace of instant enlightenment, our past stories can be trials. The major key to leaving these stories behind is to view them as teachers and to learn their lessons, releasing self blame and having mercy on our past self. Very often these stories demonstrate the places we are stuck in our journey from fear to freedom from fear, from inner confusion to inner peace.

Some past stories can be big teaching tales, gold mines for personal growth and change. They can have such an emotional charge that, in addition to our personal work, we may need outside help and support dealing with them. Often they are encrusted with years and years of hurt and sub-plots making them emotionally

---

[16] Ibid. page 5.

dense and heavy. Our stories are the doorways to new ways of being. Sometimes they take a long time to work through. Patience is often required. While we take the view that there is plenty of time, we also need to continually recommit to our inner work. If we don't, we may become eternal victims of our own stories.

For most of us the work of awakening, of becoming, is ongoing. This is why it is often said that the process of enlightenment after we reach the age of 20 is the process of letting go of everything we have learned! On the other hand, because the view that the present is all that exists is fundamentally correct, we need to experiment with living in the present and being fully present as often as we can. The classical action for practicing this is meditation, stilling the mind. It also can be used as an interesting measure of our progress. On this point the Tibetan teacher Sogyal Rinpoche tells us:

> "If your mind is able to settle naturally of its own accord, and if you find you are inspired to rest in its pure awareness, then you do not need any method of meditation. However, the vast majority of us find it difficult to arrive at that state straight away. We simply do not know how to awaken it, and our minds are so wild and so distracted that we need a skillful means or method to evoke it.
>
> By 'skillful' I mean that you bring together your understanding of the essential nature of your mind, your knowledge of your various, shifting moods, and the insight you have developed through your practice into how to work with yourself, from moment to moment. By bringing these together, you learn the art of applying whatever method is appropriate to any particular situation of problem, to transform that environment of your mind."[17]

---

[17] Rinpoche Sogyal. *Samadhi: The Stages of Meditation According to the Sutra and Tantra Traditions*. Rigpe Dorje Center: Treasury of Knowledge Retreat, 2004.

Tolle wisely suggests that we work on staying in the present by practicing awareness, which is the first of our four strategies for learning what our lives are trying to teach us. "Be present as the watcher of your mind – of your thoughts and emotions as well as your reaction in various situations. Be at least as interested in your reactions as in the situation or person that causes you to react. Notice also how often your attention is in the past or future, don't judge or analyze what you observe. Watch the thought, feel the emotion, observe the reaction. Don't make a personal problem out of them. You will then feel something more powerful than any of those things that you observe, the still, observing presence itself behind the content of your mind, the silent watcher."[18]   This is a wise prescription for taking up awareness.

The "future story" is constructed in the imagination. Stories about the future are filled with conjecture and with whatever emotion wants to find an imaginary outlet. Very often these stories are products of present fear. In future stories we can get lost in tales of possible outcomes that get quite fantastic and take up lots of present energy. Our future stories are actually the easiest to work with once we realize that they are completely fabricated. The Tibetan expression that, "Living in the future is like throwing your nets in dry riverbeds" describes living in the future very accurately. There is nothing out there! This view reminds us that the future is pure fabrication. Fear around illness, scarcity, money, and being alone are typical topics of these stories. A few years ago at an event Babbie and I attended, the Dali Lama was asked was he worried about the Mayan prophecy that the world would end in 2012. He laughed and responded, "How can I possibly worry about that? I don't even know what is going to happen tomorrow!"

With future stories it is easier to access Eckhart Tolle's "power of now" because it is easier for the mind to comprehend that the future does not exist than that the past does not exist. To deal with future stories we have to become aware when we are creating them, and, right in that moment, bring ourselves back into the present. When letting go of the future it is helpful to remember that,

---

[18] Tolle, Eckhart. *The Power of Now.* Namaste Publishing, 1997, page 55

despite our expectations, things seldom, if ever, work out as planned or predicted.

The worst thing about getting lost in scary, future stories is how this affects our present experience. These stories sometime take over our emotional body, with dire fantasies turning our current state into one of worry, frustration, and inner turmoil. When we find ourselves lost in some future story, it is helpful to move our attention and focus to what we are currently doing. We can say about any future event:, "I'm not in that compartment right now" and bring the energy being used on the unknown into the known, where we can use it to affect what is right in front of us.

Focusing awareness on our reactions to our stories, on how they are affecting us, is how we begin to learn what our lives are trying to teach us. Many of these stories cause uncomfortable feelings. Staying with these feelings without indulging them leads us directly to our deeper fears, the fears that perpetuate our unskillful reactions and our acting out. Questioning these fears, finding ways to bring love into the areas of doubt that they represent, is a powerful part of our journey. Seeing our stories as gifts they is a great boon to our personal evolution. Once we are able to stop getting lost in our stories, almost simultaneously we arrive at the next important strategy for learning what our lives are trying to teach us, personal responsibility. With personal responsibility great change becomes possible.

No Room for Form

On the night when you cross the street
from your shop and your house
to the cemetery,

You'll hear me hailing you from inside
the open grave, and you'll realize
how we have always been together.

I am the clear consciousness-core
Of your being, the same
in ecstasy as in self-hating fatigue.

That night, when you escape the fear of snakebite
and all the irritation with the ants, you'll hear
my familiar voice, see the candle being lit,
smell the incense, the surprise meal fixed
by the lover inside all your other lovers.

This heart-tumult is my signal to you
igniting in the tomb.

So don't fuss with the shroud
and the graveyard road dust.

Those get ripped open and washed away
in the music of our finally meeting.

And don't look for me in a human shape.
I am inside your looking.
No room for form with love this strong.

Beat the drum and let the poets speak.
This is a day of purification for those who
are already mature and initiated into what love is.

No need to wait until we die!
There's more to want here than money
and being famous and bites of roasted meat.

Now, what shall we call this new sort of gazing-house
that has opened in our town where people sit
quietly and pour out their glancing like light, like answering?[19]

Jelaluddin Rumi

[19] Barks, Coleman with Moyne, John, *The Essential Rumi*. Castle Books 1997, page 138

Personal Responsibility

The Gateway to Change
The Foundation of Personal Power

Personal Responsibility Overview

We will be absolutely unable to learn what our life is trying to teach us without the vital strategy of taking personal responsibility. No lasting change in our lives can occur until we take personal responsibility for *where we are right now*. Until we take this position unequivocally, we will be tempted by victim-hood. Being a victim is an alluring vessel for despair and anger because it is so easy to become one. Victim-hood also offers no rewards, no ultimate satisfaction, and it creates an inner life filled with anger, sorrow and resentment. The victim is that part of us that likes to blame others and circumstances for our condition. Our victim is good at supporting blame and judgment with reason. As a victim, our focus is the outer world, while our inner world is the place where the real attention is needed. Taking personal responsibility for our lives, and all that happens in them, forces us to focus on this inner world. Working in this world we make the energetic shifts that can change our lives and the world around us into what we truly desire.

There is a vicious cycle associated with victim-hood. At each new occurrence of an old unpleasant pattern (sometimes in a different guise) our belief in our lack of power is reinforced by history. "Oh no, not again!" we say. The rut seems ever more real. Sometimes we feel despair, and the inability to function. The bad news and the good news are the same. We continue to attract the same difficulty until we take responsibility for what is happening. Strengthening our ability to take personal responsibility brings us into the arena of true change.

The ego is very clever at keeping us in the place of no change because change is the thing we usually fear the most. Often, we even prefer our current, familiar pain to the unknown. We find ourselves in a rut, living in and reacting to the same experiences over and over in the same way. Once, during a channeling session I attended, the entity known as "The Tibetan," Dwajl Khul, defined the rut in which we find ourselves as an "elongated grave." Many of us experience our lives as a rut. We have fallen into the grave before our time. Personal responsibility is the track out of the rut and up onto the surface. With personal responsibility the walls of the grave disappear and the power of vision is restored.

Personal responsibility is picking up the reins, and taking charge of our lives; being the creator of a whole and unique self, our offering to the world. It is the axis of all personal and spiritual growth.

The saints exhort us to know ourselves, to discover our true nature; some say our divinity. Personal responsibility is a primary key for making this happen. Without it nothing ever changes; with it everything does. As we practice personal responsibility, we also discover how it is the foundation of authentic personal power.

The Boss of Me

Personal Responsibility and Personal Power

Back in the early days of the New Age, when many of us were rushing around "seeking," some friends and I invited Sun Bear, the founder of the Bear Tribe, to Hanover, NH to give a workshop. Sun Bear stayed at our home in Vermont for a few days. He has since died. The thing that I remember best about him is his laugh. He liked to laugh, and his laugh was very infectious. When he laughed everyone else seemed to laugh too. He was a big man who usually wore a purple cowboy shirt and a fine pair of cowboy boots. He blessed the stone circle on our land on a cold, windy, winter day, and he left me some tobacco for the four directions. He was very easy going. I liked him.

We rented a room for the event in the Dartmouth College Gym. As soon as the posters were up, I received a visit from a local white man who had taken up the job of representing Native American interests in our area. He asked that our group cancel the workshop. It seemed that Sun Bear was controversial with some of the Native American community because he was teaching native ceremonies to "whites." Sun Bear had created a new tribe in the west which included white people. We did a review and discovered that not every tribe was against his work and, in fact, he was a very close friend to some of the best-known and well-respected Native American chiefs and tribal leaders across the country. Many of them approved of his work with "whites."

We went on with the workshop. We did not learn any great secret ceremonies, but at one point Sun Bear had us go outside and hug hardwood and softwood trees to feel the difference in energy;

hardwood for strength, softwood for healing. There we were, right in front of the Dartmouth College Gym, hugging trees. Of course Sun Bear thought this was very amusing, a bunch of white people hugging trees in the middle of an Ivy League campus. Thus it happened that our group actually performed one of the most ridiculed and deprecated actions of the so-called New Age, tree hugging. Most of the time, however, Sun Bear focused on teaching us the philosophy of native peoples, and one of the most important teachings had to do with power, our own power, what is often called personal power.

When we experience personal power, we feel safe and confident in our relationship with others and the world around us. We are able to speak our truth without judgment or blame, to be more authentic in our dealings with others, rather than manipulative. Personal power means we act from our center, from our truth. Personal power gives us the ability to move our life in the direction we envision. It gives us the ability to hold our shape in difficult and threatening situations.

Sun Bear taught the ancient teaching that personal power could be given away to someone or something else. When we give someone else the power to make decisions for us, or when we rely on someone or something else to fulfill our needs, we are giving away our power. A less obvious, but more common, way in which we give away our power is by blaming something or someone other than ourselves for our condition. In other words, we take up the role of victim. When we take up the role of victim, we give up the role of creator; the creator of our life. When we give away our power, we stop learning, and we stop growing. Sometimes we also expose ourselves to manipulation and control. Victim and creator cannot co-exist within us at the same time. There is no middle way here. In any part of our life in which we blame our condition on someone or something else for how we feel or what is happening to us, we have given away our power, and our personal progress is effectively blocked. Thus, taking full and unequivocal personal responsibility is absolutely necessary if we wish to experience real personal power, the power to control our own destiny.

Because we are often afraid to take personal responsibility (sometimes we actually work hard to avoid doing so), we do not recognize or experience its connection to personal power. In place of the real thing, many of us have developed a very twisted and misaligned idea about personal power. We interpret it as the ability to control, manipulate or even hurt others, and the ability to influence the material world, and people, through force. Many desire this kind of power, and our world is filled with the results of its action: emotional and physical abuse, violence, sociopathic behavior and war. Television, movies, and video games celebrate this predominant cultural misunderstanding. In the popular view, personal power is not about taking full responsibility for our condition or viewpoint and maintaining healthy boundaries. It is about invading other people's boundaries, forcing them to our will, even to the extent of doing emotional or physical damage in acts of revenge. This kind of power is viewed as a legitimate channel for frustration and anger, as a reaction to moments in which we feel we have been disempowered or attacked; moments in which we believe our dignity has come under assault. We leap to reaction without any thought that we may be personally responsible for our condition or the situation in which we find ourselves. Then, when we are made aware that we have been unskillful or insensitive, we refuse to take any responsibility. We claim even slight provocation as a legitimate cause of our sometimes harmful behavior. The pattern is the same in the micro and the macro, from individuals to nations. In our ignorance, we have woven personal power and a lack of personal responsibility together.

Genuine personal power can influence others deeply while having no need to control anyone or anything. It is a result of inner, rather than outer, action. With genuine personal power, we are able to respond to fear and fearful situations in a way that is never paralyzing. Often, even though the circumstances may be fearful or difficult, debilitating fear is absent. When we experience real personal power, we feel safer in the world; we exhibit comfort with ourselves, but not in a self indulgent or insensitive way. We are present for others but do not need to leap forward with suggestions or ideas about how they should change or handle a situation. We do not necessarily feel a compulsion to change people or the world around us. When we develop true personal power, we experience equanimity; we are at peace with ourselves.

Personal responsibility is the second of the four strategies for learning what our lives are trying to teach us. Personal responsibility is defined here as refusing to blame others or current situations (even events beyond our control) for our current condition. It is taking responsibility for our effect on the world and the world's effect on us, completely. It is taking full responsibility for who we are and how we behave.

The understanding that we give away our power each time we blame someone or something for our condition is especially helpful and useful for its corollary: when we take personal responsibility, rather than blaming others or the world for our condition, we take back our power. There is a wonderful kid's expression we used to use when another little kid was trying to boss us around. "I am the boss of me," we would say, emphatically denying their control. For many of us, it is time to go back to the days of yesteryear and start being the "boss of me" again. In the instant that we decide to take personal responsibility for all that is happening in our life, we again become "the boss of me." We are once again the shaper and creator of our life.

Of course, taking back our power by taking personal responsibility is much easier said than done. When things go wrong, it seems there are so many obvious culprits, both events and people that we can logically blame, including, of course, one's self.

Holding our difficulties as learning experiences, rather than mistakes, helps to minimize blaming and judging and, generally, the more difficult the experience, the bigger the lesson is. The view that our difficult experiences are personal lessons keeps our focus where it belongs, and where it can do the most good, on our own reactions, on our own behavior, and on creating better responses. These are the areas in which we can discover the truth about our beliefs, our expectations, and our fears. Time spent looking for lessons, rather than culprits, is beneficial and productive. This can be very hard work, and we will not always be successful, especially at first. The stories will try to suck us back in. Using awareness is particularly helpful. Noticing the moments in which we chose blame or self-pity, we can see ourselves shutting down, getting myopic, getting lost in stories of abandonment, hurtfulness, sorrow, anger and abuse. With awareness, we can see that going into these patterns and immersing ourselves in the story is a choice. We see the difference between mindless reaction and conscious response. Awareness allows us to deeply understand that blaming solves nothing and creates only more unhappiness and frustration. Regardless of how the world seems to see us, we can determine to view ourselves as students of life, learning from our experiences and moving forward.

The good news is, like physical exercise, the more we stretch psycho-emotionally, the more skillful we become in our responses. For this reason, hard times are paradoxically a weird form of grace, a place where the opportunity for personal growth is accelerated and hidden potential is often unleashed.

Embracing personal responsibility in difficult or tragic situations creates a spiritual opening as well as psycho-emotional growth and maturity. The moment we refuse to blame and judge others for our condition, we stop separating ourselves from the fear that is the source of this behavior. Accepting our own fear puts us in touch with the great ocean of fear that the world swims in. Our awareness expands. We see our fear in others. We become aware of the fear that surrounds us, and we realize how universal fear is, how it guides so much action. This realization helps us to accept that we are more like others than not, because we all share exactly the same fears. From this more conscious understanding, we are able to develop compassion, where judgment and blame once ruled. Compassion connects us with the whole. This is deep work.

Healing and developing compassion often start with personal responsibility, with focusing on our contribution to unpleasant or unskillful situations, with letting go of blame, with accepting our own fear, rather than converting it into unskillful reactions. Through these actions we take back our power to create positive change. The truth is that there can be no healing until we let go of blame and judgment, including blaming ourselves and practicing self-judgment.

Taking personal responsibility is not relegated to the realm of the dire or dramatic. More mundane perhaps, but equally therapeutic, are the opportunities for self-improvement that exist in our daily life. If we are feeling anxious and are "looping" or going through stories over and over, we can take up meditation and learn to tame or still the wild horse of the mind. If we are not in good health, we can take up an exercise program or special diet. All of us know where we need immediate work. According to Wikipedia, in 2008, 33.8% of Americans were obese with dire consequences for our health. Some of us smoke cigarettes or drink too much or gossip. It is obvious that when we take personal responsibility, when we choose personal discipline in these areas, we are creating personal power; we are taking control of our lives. We feel the benefits of our self-improvement in two ways: in the direct results we experience, (for instance in the physical area in more energy and strength, or in our personal work, in a more balanced emotional body) and in the feeling of wellbeing that is engendered. This feeling is the opposite of the frustration we feel when we allow ourselves to be a victim. Personal responsibility coupled with personal discipline is a path of true freedom from the slavery of our bad habits.

Sometimes the things for which we need to take personal responsibility are so much a part of our lives that they are difficult to see. I had a client, I will call him "Bill," who had a good sum of money and yet continued to create businesses that were marginal or failed until he created one that wiped him out. This business failure involved a sociopath, embezzlement and gross mismanagement. By any measure the disaster was not completely his fault. After first fruitlessly dwelling on blaming the manager for the obvious failures and then seeing how this got him nowhere, he began to travel inward looking for the lessons, rather than blame the obvious outer protagonists. He said he felt that, in this awful experience, there must be a huge lesson. He wasn't talking about being a better businessman. He was talking about reviewing the actions he had taken that had resulted in this crash and looking for the inner beliefs that had fostered these actions. He had to separate the actions of others from his own actions. To do this, we agreed that it would be necessary, despite the evidence, to let go of blame and judgment as much as possible, to remember that, because the business was his creation, everything that happened was related to him and was, basically, his responsibility. He asked himself why he had hired a person who did not tell the truth, who was an expert at telling him what he wanted to hear; who was, it turned out, a closet alcoholic. Bill became aware that he had a great deal of anger and judgment and was very indignant about being lied to. I talked with him about the spiritual truth that we often judge those who mirror some part of ourselves that we don't like or don't want to recognize. Our judgment of others very often, if not always, comes from hidden self-judgment. Thinking about this, he suddenly realized that he had been lying as well, but he had been lying to *himself*. He had been pretending that his heavy drinking was OK and that he was perfectly well. When he discovered the manager was an alcoholic, it all fit together. He had hired a reflection of a part of himself. He didn't notice the warning signs because they were a reflection of a part of himself that he didn't want to see. Bill had to face the truth about his own drinking, and, as a result, he quit drinking completely. The experience literally sobered him. This was a blessing that came from this experience.

This kind of inner work was very challenging. But here is what Bill discovered when he took personal responsibility for the disaster. First of all, he took the view that *he* had hired the embezzler and the poor management team. With more diligence, he might have prevented the manager from ruining the company. He realized there had been warning signs he had ignored and about which he had been in denial. But, he learned a bigger lesson.

When Bill looked at the whole business venture in the context of his personal history, he realized that it was yet another effort in a lifelong quest for approval, and specifically, approval from parents and peers. Being a businessman was an "acceptable" course; one that he thought everybody would understand and be happy about. But this path was not really his desire. For most of his life up until this big business failure, Bill had denied his creative side in order to try to be someone his parents could be proud of, someone that fit the mold that made *them* comfortable. He had to admit that this business venture was yet another of these attempts to gain their approval. The sheer size of the catastrophe woke him up from this bad dream, and he vowed to make every effort to respond to his own inner passion rather than to continue to try to garner what he finally realized was their unattainable approval. Many of us keep on trying to gain our parents' approval even after they have died! This is a very common pattern. Sadly, they are often much harder to please when they are dead as there is no chance of the "good word" any longer.

Trying to please them, (and, by extension, everyone else) by choosing a career of which they would approve, understand and therefore appreciate, had ended in a resounding defeat. But this defeat turned out to be the stuff of the phoenix. Bill would arise a new person. Not living his life for others was a good learning, a great start on a new life, but there was yet another important lesson he learned.

He saw that his pattern, of trying to be acceptable to others, included making a great deal of money. Like so many of us, he believed that in this way he would gain respect. This idea was certainly culturally acceptable. While this desire was tied into trying to please the unappeasable parents, it was also a part of his whole lack of understanding about scarcity and abundance. This misunderstanding was one of the causes of his business troubles.

Reviewing his childhood, Bill realized that he had been raised in an atmosphere in which there was "not enough." Even though his family was wealthy, the children were continually reminded to be frugal and were often told there was never quite enough. They were not allowed to eat between meals because it was wasteful. Food portions were always small, and he could never take more than two small portions at a meal regardless of how hungry he was. There was much talk about wasting things, about being grateful for what things the family had and not wanting more. In other words, there was a real focus on scarcity. Bill's childhood was filled with scarcity training. At the time of his business failure he had no idea that he had embraced this concept so completely. His desire for more was so intertwined with his desire for respect that he did not understand this part of his experience until later. As a part of his taking personal responsibility he wanted to explore his relationship with abundance. So, after the business crash, learning how abundance really works became a study of his. He developed a different, more positive outlook. He began to trust more in abundance rather than focusing on scarcity and the "not enough." He told me that he had learned what has real and lasting value.

As earlier stated, much of the time we believe the lesson is contained in the surface story. For instance, in this case Bill could have reproved himself with the obvious: "I should not have hired a liar, I won't do it again. I won't go into this kind of business again, that's for sure. I was drinking too much and I can't do that, if I want to do great things." The lessons we garner from the stories are often good lessons, but they do not always address the deep issues that are the sources of our repetitious folly and dysfunction. This is like healing the symptoms rather than the causes of a disease. Repetitious problems usually indicate an underlying lesson we keep missing. These are the critical lessons. One of the lessons Bill needed was to stop trying to please others as a motivation for work, to view abundance in a different way, but, deeper still, he needed to know how he had allowed the situation to get so far out of control. In other words, he wanted to know, not so much what was present in this situation, but what was not present. What was he missing? And, in looking for what was missing he found the big lesson that changed his life entirely, the shining gift at the heart of his tragedy. Bill saw that he had not stood up for himself, for his interest; that he had allowed himself to be manipulated; that he had accepted lies because he wanted to avoid, and was afraid of, confrontation. The element that was missing in Bill's life was the ability to feel and express anger. He could not make boundaries. People took advantage of this inability. This weakness is what lay at the heart of Bill's business failure.

Like many of my clients, Bill had no idea how to deal with anger. In fact, he believed he never got angry. He was so busy trying to be nice all the time that it never occurred to him that his lack of anger was actually a major problem. Again, we can't manifest personal power until we take responsibility for our emotions, and we can't do this until we know what those emotions are. Once we recognize them, we can then learn how to manifest them skillfully.

In order to take personal responsibility and to develop personal power, we have to be able to create clear boundaries. Possessing clear boundaries is one of the hallmarks of personal power. The ability to manifest skillful anger when necessary is a vital component of creating boundaries. Like many of us, Bill needed to understand his anger and then learn how to use it in a sensitive and skillful manner.

We deal with anger in just a few ways: we repress it (the nice guy approach that Bill used); we do a "slow burn" until we can't contain it, we anger easily, or we blow up and go quickly to rage.

83

Some of us use the passive aggressive approach, annoying others consciously or unconsciously to express our anger. Bill was "Mr. Nice Guy." People took advantage of the fact that he would never rock the boat with anger. Bill was convinced that anger was not nice, and he did not get angry with people directly. He thought anger was a sign of emotional weakness. Actually, he was so numb, so out of touch with his anger, that, by the time of his big business failure, he did not even know what anger felt like. He also believed that things *always* could, and should, be worked out in a calm, intelligent fashion.

Many of the eastern teachings I have studied make anger a bad thing, one of the *gunas* or robbers of peace and inner communion with God. Peace and equanimity have great value, but before we can experience them fully, we have to know how to respect and skillfully manifest our emotions. Otherwise, we can end up following the path of denial. The view that anger is perfectly healthy and necessary is a radical concept for many of us. Don Rosenthal taught that anger is composed of the same energy as passion, and that we can't have one without the other. Without passion, our lives become cautious, dry, and brittle.

To be skillful with our anger we need to learn how to own it and express it without judgment or blame. No small task. Don's view, that anger is perfectly normal and OK, is especially scary for those of us, like Bill, who have always felt that anger was bad.

If we have repressed our anger, the first thing we have to do is get in touch with it. We can use awareness to discover any incongruence between what we are feeling in certain situations and what a "normal" reaction might be. For instance, using awareness, we review situations that should have made us angry but didn't, or situations we keep feeling uncomfortable about for some time after they have occurred. We keep a watch for these situations as they present themselves. Someone insults us, and we feel nothing, or we might make excuses for other people's rude behavior. We might act overly polite when anger would be more appropriate. We can even use religion as an excuse to repress anger. For instance, we might think that it is unchristian to express anger. However, one of the most memorable colored pictures in my childhood New Testament was an angry Christ chasing the moneychangers from the temple.

You could say the lamb was able to get in touch with his ram. Sometimes it is necessary.

One method of denying and repressing anger, or unpleasant feelings, is to turn the energy into logical discourse; we try to create understanding. Sometimes, we will attempt omniscience and understanding and avoid feeling. We fool ourselves into believing we are objective and not subjected to unpleasant emotions, like anger. We hang out in our head trying to work things out up there, denying our feelings as inappropriate or bad. We can find our seemingly missing anger by developing awareness of the moments in which this pattern is taking place and then going deeper, being more honest with ourselves and discovering the anger beneath.

If we have developed the seemingly easier, passive aggressive system of handling anger, we manifest our anger consciously or unconsciously as behavior that annoys others, without our showing any overt anger. With awareness, and watching the feedback of some of our familiar actions, we can find out if this is one of our anger avoidance techniques. There is no doubt that, using awareness and taking personal responsibility, we can discover our anger. Our intention to do so gets the ball rolling. For some of us, our anger is a revelation.

Once we discover our anger we need to release it, and this is tricky because we don't know how to release it without freaking people out or causing damage to relationships. We may not have had much practice. Although we know that repressed anger is unhealthy, when we let it loose, we still have to learn how to bring it into the world, to let the energy flow skillfully, not to indulge in rage or let it come out dishonestly and "sideways."

Here is where a conscious approach to situations can be useful. Rather than just letting the anger fly and upsetting our relationships, we can discuss our difficulty with those who will be most affected as we practice releasing it. If we are in relationship, and have a supportive partner, we can ask them to support our investigation, by allowing us to express our anger directly for a while. Of course, as we experiment with being more skillful with our anger, it can still be scary for both the giver and the receiver, but, because we have agreed to proceed in a conscious manner, with

85

permission, much can be learned without having to get lost in the story.

Some of us come from an upbringing in which anger was not acceptable and in which being "nice" was valued highly. We will feel pretty uncomfortable as anger is released. Others of us experienced anger as dangerous (for instance, if we had an angry, scary or abusive parent) so our reaction to anger will be fear. It takes courage to begin consciously dealing with anger, especially if it is an emotion we have been denying or allowing to have total control.

If we have no experience with releasing anger, at first, we might be pretty unskillful, by blaming, judging, and lashing out. But we need to let it roll to get the feel of the emotion; to know what it is like. We may frighten and disturb people who know us: our children, our partner, or our co-workers. So, we need to let people know what we are doing. If we do this, we will be able to go forward without causing confusion, chaos and hurt. We will soon become conscious of the benefits. Often, in a family, we can use the unfolding or our true anger as an opportunity to teach our kids how to express anger skillfully as well. What works, and what doesn't, becomes painfully obvious. In my family when I started doing some "anger work" it really upset the family dynamic. For the first two or three weeks it was a wild ride as I actually reveled in the taste of allowed anger (I had an agreement with Babbie about this whole process, of course and her turn came later). Releasing anger, after a long period of repression, is quite a liberating experience. We come to understand how important our fire is through manifesting it freely for, what sometimes seems like, the first time. Finally, like a fire that has gone through a hot fast burn of ignition, our passion settles in the belly and glows nicely. As we proceed, we learn how to handle anger skillfully; to use it without judgment or blame, and how to own it.

Having our anger makes us whole. Without it, we are socially crippled. Without it, a big piece of what is necessary for living an emotionally balanced life is missing. With this practice, we learn to feel comfortable expressing anger, and this allows us to be forceful and to guard our boundaries when necessary. We feel the personal power this emotion can create. The rewards of this practice, expressing anger without allowing it to go to rage, are extraordinary.

Like many of us, my client Bill had brought what had been a useful strategy in childhood into his adult life where it no longer served him and actually created dysfunction. As a child, avoiding confrontation had been necessary. While not expressing anger had been a good strategy for survival in his father's angry world, it meant that he could be manipulated by someone else's anger, or even the threat of anger, when he became an adult. It meant that anyone could take advantage his very civil and polite boundaries. This was made obvious from his experience with the manager, who had done whatever he pleased, knowing that Bill was afraid to confront him, and knowing that Bill, like so many marks, would believe whatever he wanted to hear (some critical lies) in order to avoid confrontation. Bill's lack of boundaries was the main reason the business failed. The villain was his teacher, as is so often the case.

What is most important about this is that none of the gifts of wisdom could have occurred if Bill had not taken personal responsibility for the situation. By focusing on his own contribution to the mess and taking personal responsibility for the whole situation, he actually retrieved a huge lost piece of himself.

Not all of us, but many of us, will experience some kind of crisis in our lives: a divorce, a death, bankruptcy, or family or social problems. One very effective way to move through and beyond these difficult times is to discover the lessons present. These lessons are a form of grace, because they are perfectly made for us. They represent an opportunity for positive change, sometimes in a dreadful disguise, but opportunities of great value nonetheless, jewels in the mud. However, these experiences can only become opportunities when we take complete personal responsibility for them. When they do happen, we need to sharpen our awareness and be vigilant in our personal responsibility. Sometimes we discover, as Bill did, that an important part of ourselves is missing or buried or undeveloped and we are given the opportunity to recover or repair it.

Bill's story is a dramatic example of using personal responsibility to create personal growth, but it is not necessary to go through a big trial to make significant change. Each time we make the conscious choice to take personal responsibility, even in the smallest things, we are exercising and increasing our personal power. We are working with our demons, letting them go. We are saying "no" to the tyranny of the ego; every single time.

The Gang of Three

Personal Responsibility and the Voice of Reason

In his wonderful first book, *The Hero with a Thousand Faces*, the mythologist, Joseph Campbell, explored in depth the archetype of the hero, the part of each of us that is at the heart of our personal and spiritual evolution. Thanks to Campbell, many people have become aware of the power of myth; the way archetypes can be used for personal discovery as well as understanding the world around us.

According to Campbell, the hero is a seeker, one who moves into the unknown to retrieve a treasure, understanding or truth. Once he or she has moved into the unknown, the hero may return with the treasure, offering it to others, or may choose instead to stay in the unknown. The Buddhist's bodhisattva vow illuminates one of the hero's choices. The aspirant vows not to enter nirvana (loosely interpreted, a realm like heaven) once they have become enlightened, but to reincarnate to help others, until all beings become enlightened. The hero's return guarantees no special treatment; he/she may be greeted with praise or disdain. Christ is a quintessential hero, traveling into unknown realms both literally, the wilderness, and spiritually, embracing unconditional love, and returning with a wonderful gift for mankind, only to be crucified.

We all have the hero inside us. It is the part of us that is forever challenged to change and move forward into a newer self, often a daunting prospect because we are required to act in new ways, to drop old habits and create new ones, and to move into the unknown. The hero's path can be exciting and frightening, but if we avoid this journey, if we try to stay safe and comfortable all the time, life tends to turn dull; to lack juice and passion. We stop growing, and we live in fear of change. Learning what our lives are trying to teach us is the hero's journey. That is why familiarizing ourselves with the hero archetype and its aspects can be very helpful.

Once the hero has embarked on his journey, he usually meets an ally who gives him something that will be useful during his pilgrimage. Thus, as we decide to grow and change, and then demonstrate our intention through action, we are often greeted with just the right teacher or experience from which we receive the perfect gift that will help us in our evolution. Like the hero, we often don't recognize this is happening.

Most of us know the story of *Jack and the Beanstalk*. The modern version is a combination of a few stories from the old Appalachian folk tales known as *The Jack Tales*. In these tales, a boy named Jack always follows the mythological hero's path. In his travels, Jack usually does someone a kindness, shares his meal, or helps an old person in some way. For his kindness, he receives a little gift or a piece of advice, that turns out to be the key to his own safety and success when he later encounters giants or thieves or challenging circumstances. This is exactly how the hero myth works. These gifts can be real or symbolic. We need to keep an eye out for them, to stay aware, to look for coincidences or synchronicities.

Eventually, after having his intention tested by trials and encounters, the hero comes to the gateway into the unknown. This gateway is always guarded. The hero must get by the guard somehow. This is usually a very challenging part of the journey. Sometimes the gift he received along the way is the key. One of the most interesting observations that Campbell made in his interviews with Bill Moyers entitled *The Power of Myth*, is that, in our time, the guardian at the gate to the unknown, and therefore to personal change, is "the voice of reason." Indeed, there is usually a good reason for not traveling into new territory. As individuals and as a culture, we often know or create many reasons why we should not proceed. We often use what appears as obvious and logical as an excuse to avoid change. Ironically, the smarter we become, the more difficult personal change seems to be. The clients I have who are the most intelligent seem to have the hardest time embracing the heart and taking chances. The mind naturally loves logic and reason and likes to view the world through these two windows. Smart people have a harder time letting go of the branch. They hang above the valley clinging to reason and logic.

When our awareness blooms, we suddenly see life in an expanded way and begin to understand much more than we have before. For this reason, it is sometimes thought that awareness is all that is necessary for personal growth and healing. This idea can be a dangerous trap, because real change often requires personal responsibility and inner and outer action. And, if we use our awareness to focus on the behavior of others, or the dynamics of a story, we will make little personal progress. Many of us are already experts in these areas. But, in order for awareness to be useful for personal change and growth, it must include or better yet, be limited primarily to our selves. Focusing our awareness on ourselves, on our own behavior, expands our understanding. This focus brings us to personal responsibility rapidly. Taking personal responsibility automatically take us to the threshold of the unknown, areas that we have previously avoided and not yet explored. It is right in the moment when we expand our consciousness to embrace our own behavior that we most often encounter Campbell's guardian at the gate, the voice of reason. To gain the reward, to discover the lesson behind the story, we have to move beyond the guardian at the gate.

I have an example of how this works from my own life. Many years ago my father died, leaving behind my mother, my two younger sisters and myself. He left some money, and a great house that had been in the family for quite a while. This house was full of antiques and beautiful furnishings, and it was assumed that all of this was to belong to my sisters and me one day. I had been instrumental in arranging a trust and getting him to reluctantly sign it two years before he died. The trust saved the house and the estate from probate and disintegration.

A few years after my father died, my mother decided to stir things up a bit. My mother is the type of person who does not care how they get attention, or what the quality of that attention is, as long as they are in the middle of it. I had been working with her for some time, trying to get her to put her affairs in order as my father's had been. She pretended to play along, but nothing ever happened. One weekend, just as my family and I were leaving her place to return home from a visit, she told me that she had recently asked my sisters to mark all the furniture in the house that they wanted in order that there would be no dispute with the tax people in the future about inheritance. A quick investigation determined that my two sisters had indeed marked every single item in the house, dividing up everything they wanted between themselves without telling me a thing about it. I soon discovered that my mother had minimized me in her will as well, leaving me a smaller proportion of the estate than my sisters. It was obvious that, despite our long conversations, everything had already been arranged. All of this followed a magazine article in which the family house was featured. In the article my mother, and two sisters were photographed and featured, while my father, my wife and children and I were not mentioned at all. The article made it seem as if our family was totally female and had been propagated by Immaculate Conception. All of this, the article, the furniture distribution and the tilted will, pushed my buttons into the red zone and garnered my mother the attention she wanted. I felt particularly hurt by the will, a document that was meant to reach out of the grave to give one last blow. To me, this act seemed very mean spirited. When I questioned my sisters, I discovered that they also knew about the changes in the will.

My mother's unskillful behavior got results. I was very hurt and angry. I wrote a long letter to this effect, and then I severed ties with them. I sarcastically labeled them "the gang of three" after the famous Chinese political scapegoats "the gang of four."

I stayed angry for several months. I am sure that the anger I felt was centered as much on old angers and hurts as it was on the current situation. At first, it felt good to release my anger and frustration. We know that repressing this kind of anger can be unhealthy. I also needed the anger to create clear boundaries, and to honor myself.

But, as time went on, I noticed my anger was not diminishing. I knew that, because it was so long lasting, I needed to revisit the situation from the standpoint of personal responsibility. I was aware that I was actually growing tired of being angry. We can use awareness to be on the lookout for this important sign. When we get to this place, when we've had enough anger, when the very mention of an old hurt puts us into an angry state, it is time to make the choice to take personal responsibility.

The longer we fail to make this choice the more our anger will become a part of our whole view of life. This is the root of bitterness; the inability to move on. Personal responsibility is the surest route out of this dilemma.

So I asked myself, "Why am I still angry? Why is the anger so intense? Where did this anger come from? What is the deeper lesson for me?" I needed to review the entire situation to see how I had caused it or, if not caused it exactly, contributed to it. Did I want to do this practice? Not much. This was a trip into the unknown, I was pretty sure I was angry because of how I had been treated. What else could there be? Sure enough, the voice of reason was carefully guarding the gate. It asked perfectly logical questions. "Why should you take any responsibility for this? Look how you have been treated! You have every right to be angry! Why should you do any personal investigation when you're the one who has been humiliated and hurt? Why should you take any responsibility? You didn't start this. In fact, you deserve an apology." And then the voice of reason would review the hurt and the behavior of the "gang of three" to shore up these arguments. You see how it works. The reasoning and logic were correct, but they were keeping me from moving into the important territory where any lessons from my experience resided. Reason and logic were impeding my psycho-spiritual growth.

Taking personal responsibility for my anger meant moving beyond my perfect justifications for it and asking what its source was within me; turning the focus away from my family's behavior and back onto myself. Doing so, I discovered and then had to admit that, I was hooked on the goods: the furniture, the house, and the money. I realized that if I had not been so attached to the goods, my mother's mechanizations would have had little effect. I would have seen her action more as unskillful behavior rather than a personal attack. I saw that she had used my attachment to the place and its furnishings to manipulate my sisters and me into an antagonistic position. Taking personal responsibility in this situation, and moving beyond the voice of reason, revealed the power of attachment in my life. My mother's unskillful and mean spirited behavior became a gift. My awareness of how attachment worked in my life was expanded. I saw how this attachment also had a grasping side to it, engendering a constant desire for more, rather than gratitude for the gifts that always surrounded me. I saw how my occasional lack of from-the-heart generosity, my misunderstanding about flow and abundance, all stemmed from trying to hold onto things, or the belief there was never enough. This realization of how attachment has affected my actions became an important gift of grace as I sought to understand, trust and accept the flow and nature of true abundance.

After six months I re-engaged with the family. I had already spoken my truth about the situation to each of them (see *Say It Later*). I determined to be conscious about my own attachment and to be aware of the times when my mother set traps and to respond with new, more skillful action. Over the years, whenever she has tried to bait me with the same kind of activity, soliciting my opinion unnecessarily, I have chosen to change the subject or have not responded. I have changed my unconscious instant reaction of wanting to be helpful to a more skillful, cautious response. I had to let go of my attachment to the goods in order not to get hooked into conversations about the property and family matters. I learned about the power of attachment and the importance of not getting hooked by it, of letting go. This was a great lesson.

This story has a good outcome, and I certainly learned a great deal, but it brings up an interesting question. I didn't live with my mother. What if a person, either intentionally or unconsciously, seems to be making our life miserable and unhappy continually? What if they are unwilling to make any personal changes or take any responsibility despite our pleas? What if it is someone we see every day or someone we live with? This is a much more challenging situation.

An important act of personal responsibility in a situation like this is speaking the truth about unskillful behavior and how it affects us, letting the unskillful person know it is not OK. Sometimes when we bring someone's harmful actions to their attention, they respond by justifying their behavior, and blaming us. Often, even if they repent, there is little behavior change over time. If their behavior is habitual, and they continue to humiliate us in ways big or small, we can, for our own good, sever the relationship. Creating firm barriers is a very powerful act of personal responsibility. It is very difficult to do when the person who is treating us badly is someone we love.

Taking personal responsibility has two parts: one is recognizing that we are a part of every challenging situation in which we find ourselves and, therefore, we are responsible to some extent for the dynamics of these situations. To take personal responsibility we are required to own our actions and our feelings. When we do this, we learn the lesson contained in our stories. In my own story, by looking at my own behavior, I came to discover how my attachment to goods allowed me to be manipulated. I saw how my fear of scarcity, of not having enough, fed my anger.

The second part of personal responsibility is taking action on our own behalf; action that creates the psychological safety that allows us to grow into the teaching we have received. Creating boundaries and moving out of harmful situations are very important acts of personal responsibility. I cut my relationship with my family to honor my anger and myself and do my inner work. The work of the hero is not easy. We do not know what lies ahead. There are no guarantees. But, even though we sometimes avoid it, we usually know in our heart exactly the action that is required in the moment.

When I counsel couples, I often experience abused people trying to make excuses for their partner's abusive behavior. Once again the voice of reason is called upon, this time to excuse abusive behavior. "They are nice sometimes, really nice," people say, "and sometimes we still have fun." "They are really nice with the kids. I don't know what he would do without me. What would happen to the kids?" Why do we use the voice of reason to excuse someone who is verbally, emotionally and even physically abusive to us? For one thing, being the victim is what a victim knows. Not being the victim is the unknown, and strangely, the unknown is even more uncomfortable for most of us than an unhealthy environment. It takes a great deal of courage to travel into the unknown, out of victimhood. In the end, we need to do what is best for us, and choose to treat ourselves kindly. Putting ourselves in harm's way is unhealthy. Staying in a relationship in which we are being poorly treated is taking on the role of the victim.

As we view our part in any story, it is helpful to remember that personal responsibility does not mean blaming ourselves.

Blaming ourselves, feeling guilty, centers our focus on our bad behavior rather than the embrace of true responsibility. Personal responsibility creates change while guilt results in stasis. Guilt reinforces a bad image of ourselves, rather than acknowledging our basic goodness. We need to remind ourselves that just because we act unskillfully sometimes does not mean we are a bad person. Have mercy.

When we think of people who have acted unskillfully towards us, it is helpful to stop reviewing the stories of hurt and mean spirited behavior that arise. They take us nowhere. There is little to be gained by continuing in the hope that others will change their behavior. Often, the change we hope for may not happen in this lifetime. Waiting for others to change is often another way we avoid personal responsibility.

We need to be aware of the anguished imperatives mentioned earlier. Sylvia Boorstein, in her book *Pay Attention For Goodness Sake*, reminds us that the Buddha taught, "Suffering is the extra pain in the mind that happens when we feel an anguished imperative to have things be different from how they are. We see it most clearly when our personal situation is painful, and we want very much for it to change. It is the wanting very much that hurts so badly, the feeling of 'I need this desperately,' that paralyzes the mind. The I, who wants so much, feels isolated. Alone."[20] This often happens when we want a relationship to be other than it is. By letting go of the need for others to change, and dropping the anguished imperative that things be different, we experience the relief provided by the wisdom that everything changes in its own time. We gain a less encumbered perspective from which to begin our practice of personal responsibility.

To review: By exercising personal responsibility, recognizing our contribution to the events that shape our lives, reflecting and taking new action; by letting go of our anguished imperatives, and creating important boundaries, we take back our personal power. The road is not always easy. We are often required to make difficult choices. Asking for help is important, but in the end, we walk our

---

[20] Boorstein, Sylvia. *Pay Attention For Goodness's Sake.* Ballantine Publishing Group, 2002, page 50.

path alone. If we hide or run away from our personal challenges or if we allow ourselves to be turned back from the unknown by the voice of reason, we will keep arriving at the same old gate(s). We will recognize the gate by its guardian, who will say the same reasonable things he has said before. Meanwhile, on the other side of the gate, some wisdom awaits us that is particularly ours, an important part of the way forward. Over time, the continual, courageous action of moving through our personal gates and into the unknown will become the treasure inside all the other treasures we encounter, the deep realization of our own fundamental safety, the source of real inner peace and equanimity.

Polishing the Mirror
Saying Goodbye to the Judge

The big snake in the garden we call Earth is judgment. It's the snake that is keeping us from experiencing paradise, and it is so much a part of our lives that if we all hissed every time we made a negative judgment about something or somebody else, or especially ourselves, all we would hear all day would be a great hissing noise. Judgment is the greatest cause of trouble, harm and discord in the world, and there is no destructive force as intractable as righteous judgment. Despite all its drawbacks, and all the pain, suffering and misunderstanding it causes, our world is completely enchanted by judgment. As we begin to learn what our life is trying to teach us, we also begin to see that, when we take up judgment, we are avoiding personal responsibility and stopping our personal and spiritual progress dead in their tracks. If we are serious about personal responsibility and manifesting personal power, we will need to learn to free ourselves from the sticky web of judgment. Learning how to eliminate our judging nature is a very positive contribution to everyone.

When it comes to judgment, we are vigilant about seeking opportunities for its expression. We judge constantly as we go about our day. We judge covertly, keeping many judgments to ourselves and, when we feel safe, we judge overtly, sharing our judgments with others. We judge other drivers, we judge religions, we judge people's clothing, we judge their ideas, we judge people we see in the store, we judge smokers, we judge non-smokers, we judge alcoholics and drug addicts; we judge politicians. The list is endless. And, of course, we judge ourselves.

The second we choose judgment, we close our heart and close the door to compassion. Not only do we help create a world that feels unsafe, unforgiving, and unloving, we simultaneously diminish our own sense of safety. Judgment reinforces the view that the world around us is full of alien ideas and people who are different from us. As we take up judgment, the world seems confining, brutish and unforgiving. We use judgment to project our own fear onto the world, and that fear is reflected back onto us. Others respond to judgment whether it is spoken or not. Our judging causes others to contract, to defend, or to attack back. It engenders a fearful, cautious atmosphere. Obviously, by releasing judgment, we benefit every person with whom we come in contact. When we stop leading with judgment, those around us feel safer; they let down their guard a bit and are able to be more open. We become better and more appreciated communicators. The rewards of letting go of judgment are immediate and great.

Ridding oneself of a judging nature is extremely liberating. With awareness we discover that judgment takes up a great deal of our energy, both in its creation and in its maintenance, holding on to our positions. Because judgment is such a tight and contracted energy, we find, as we release it, we are more opened and relaxed, less stressed. Each time we choose to keep our heart open, rather than to judge, we can feel this energetic shift. Judgment has a direct relationship to fear in that, as we practice letting go of it, and opening the heart, many of our personal fears drop away. We find ourselves living a much more forgiving and accepting life.

Once again, we use awareness as a starting point for this liberation. Becoming aware of our own judgments, as well as all the judgment in the world around us (without judging the judgers), is the first step. We need to be vigilant and watch for the subtle ways that judgment arises in us and in the world. Once we have attuned our awareness, we need to take personal responsibility for our own contribution to the merciless flow of judgment. We reflect on each individual judgment and learn what it has to teach us about ourselves. We can choose this approach, as opposed to giving these judgments energy and expanding them. If we are accustomed to judging things or people easily, without thinking, this will be hard work at first.

When the topic of judgment as a negative or unskillful behavior arises, the mind and the voice of reason often protest. "But we need judgment; how can we survive without it?" Judgment often disguises itself as being protective and sensible. "If I don't judge murderers, my lack of judging will make more murder possible. If I lack judgment I may get murdered or hurt." This thinking represents confusion between judgment and discernment. We need to be able to discern what is good or bad for us, and to avoid the embodiment of what we sense as dangerous. In every city, for instance, there are dangerous areas we should avoid. Avoiding them is smart, but this does not need to include judging the people who live there or their poverty.

In Neale Donald Walsch's interesting, worldwide best seller, *Conversations with God*, we are told,"'Rightness' or 'Wrongness' is not an intrinsic condition, it is a subjective judgment in a personal value system."[21] When we speak of judgment, we mean casting our pejorative and negative opinions, our subjective values onto people, ideas and objects. It is one thing to notice something and another to judge it. It is helpful to separate the two. Noticing that someone is overweight, without personal opinion, is quite different from the voice that says, "Look, what a fat slob that person is!" Because we stop judging murderers does not mean we hang out with them, or that we approve of murder. A wise man is said to be able to judge the deed without judging the doer. We can consult the heart at any time. Rumi said, "Consult the heart even if the legalist has issued you an opinion. Show the legalist's opinion to that discernment so that it can choose what suits it best."[22] For Rumi, the heart is the source of true discernment.

When we become aware that we are judging, we have a stark choice. If we ask, as our judgment enters our awareness, "What is the condition of my heart right now? Is it opened or closed?" and if we find that it is closed, we can choose to open our heart and end the judgment. Just like that. Contrary to our ego's ideas, the open

[21] Walsch, Neale Donald. *Conversations with God*. Hampton Roads Publishing Company, 1996, page 48
[22] Helminski, Kabir (edited by), *The Rumi Collection*, Boston & London: Shamballa, 2000

heart is not weak. It is wise and strong. It is the source of our courage, the voice of our own true self.

As we let go of judgment and open our heart we need to remember to let go of all judgment, including self judgment. Judging ourselves for being judgmental is a distraction from opening our hearts. We are still sitting in judgment; we have simply changed the object of our judgment. While it is often tempting to stay with our quick and easy judgments, opening our heart when judgment is present is like opening a door with rusty hinges. We apply the oil of mercy to the hinges and we work the door, back and forth as much as possible. Eventually it opens with less effort and our heart is accessible more quickly.

By connecting with the heart, we practice awareness that does not move into judgment. We grow accustomed to using our discernment. We find that we do not need to judge people at all. Each person has his or her own path. We can let them go in peace.

The good news is that we can rid ourselves of most of our judgment through a simple understanding. Our judgment of others is, more often than not, a reflection of self-judgment and of personal fears. For this reason Rumi called judgment "polishing the mirror." Lo and behold, when we judge others and their behavior, the source of our judgment is very often a hidden part of ourselves that we dislike, or a part we are missing, or a part with which we feel uncomfortable, or a part which is incomplete, or a part which desires more for ourselves, a part which is feeling scarcity and need.

This understanding illuminates the importance of personal responsibility as a practice for letting go of our judging nature. When we become aware that we are judging someone or something ,we can take personal responsibility for our judgment by acknowledging that its source is within us, and that our outer judgment is a but reflection of an inner condition or fear. We turn the spotlight back onto ourselves, focusing our awareness onto the source of our judgment, back to the place where change is possible. This opens a great doorway into personal discovery and healing. Imagine what a different world we would live in if each of us took personal responsibility for our judgments and used them for self healing.

When we are judgmental, we can expand our awareness to witness our own state. Are we feeling discontent? Sad? Hungry? Is our energy low? Are we experiencing unspoken anger or fear about something else? When we feel these emotions, judgment seems near the surface. Sometimes our judgment reflects a discontent that seems to have no conscious source.

Using awareness to consciously let go of judgment when we are feeling any of the above creates an automatic response over time which eliminates our instant and unconscious judgment. We can focus on moving out of the discontent rather than changing it into judgment. As Chokyi Niyma Rinpoche states in *The Natural State of Happiness*, "Discontent ruins every chance for happiness and well-being."[23] One powerful way of moving out of discontent is to develop a practice of gratitude, being grateful for things around us, seeing our present personal abundance clearly and rejoicing in the abundance of others.

So, the usefulness of judgment comes, not through its exercise, but through our awareness of its presence, and the discoveries about ourselves we can make when it arises. Here the strategies of awareness, personal responsibility, inner work and action are very helpful. To review: Using our awareness, we notice how much judgment is present in our lives; we see how much negative and destructive energy is involved; how much work it takes to support the edifice of judgment. Then, rather than letting judgment dominate us, we decide to take personal responsibility for our judgments, to see them as reflections of our own fear, our own emotional pain; our self-judgment. In this way, we turn the light back onto ourselves; we go within and do our inner work, discovering the sources of our fear and judgment, accessing mercy and creating understanding within. Then we take new action in the world by changing our reactive patterns, being vigilant and refusing to energize judgment when it arises, learning to open the heart in place of judging. Further, we take up other more powerful and loving ways of engaging the world (such as the practices outlined in the Action section of this book). Just as Yogananda advised his followers, we "replace bad habits with good habits."

---

[23] Rinpoche, Chokyi Niyma. *The Natural State of Happiness*, The Best Buddhists Writing 2008, Melvin McLeod and the Editors of the Shambala Sun, 2008, page 13.

Often we experience judgment in the day-to-day chatter of our peer group. Some of these judgments are spoken and some are unspoken. We might say for instance, "How could anyone be so stupid?" or we might imply through story that someone was stupid. In order to make our gossip interesting, we often center it around the shared judgments of the group, so that, when we give up gossip, we simultaneously give up the quick judgments that are pejorative and harmful to others. When we find ourselves starting to gossip, and we become aware that a phrase like, "Did you hear about....?" or "so and so said...." is about to float out our of our mouths, we can run the story through our judgment alert system first. "Is this a positive story about someone or something or a negative story? Do I really need to get attention in this way?" By stopping the story before it comes out; by letting it go, we liberate ourselves from the talons of judgment. As a bonus, setting the example of not joining into judgmental conversation discourages others from doing the same.

Gossip is often connected with low self esteem, as if by judging someone else we concurrently elevate ourselves. We may be seeking peer approval. If we find ourselves continually being seduced by gossip, it might be useful to review our level of self esteem using mercy.

Another form of casual, often accepted judgment. happens when we are with a group of people with whom we share some passion about an idea, like politics, philosophy or religion, and, through our "acceptable" judgment, we close our mutual hearts to others. Within the group we feel safe to utter judgment and to support others in their judgment. From this mutuality, a certain pleasant camaraderie is often created, and we may think we have gained a measure of emotional safety. What is the cost of such judgment? If the judgment of one person is harmful to the welfare of all, then the judgment of a group or an organization can be even more divisive. Consider that religious wars rely on this type of judgment. Eckhart Tolle tells us that unconsciousness is more pronounced in the collective than the individual.

When we judge a person or news or politics harshly, we experience, not only our judging, but stronger emotions that indicate deeper, more fearful beliefs are operating. Our conscious response is the same as with any other judgment. We have to take personal responsibility, turn the light back on ourselves and do our inner investigation. Because of the emotional content, working with our harsh judgments is more challenging, but the rewards are greater as we encounter and work with fearful beliefs that have been unpleasant, long term companions.

When we feel strong judgment and fear, when we want to attack, when the ego is in full force, there is a powerful question from the Emmanuel's channeled material we can ask ourselves. "What would love say now?" In other words, if I were to choose love now, rather than judgment, how would I be acting or responding, to this situation? What would a loving response be; what would understanding and compassion look or sound like? How would I feel? Asking ourselves, "What would love say now?" helps us to envision new and more loving ways of being in the world. Actually choosing love allows us to experience this. The moment we feel ourselves going to judgment; we can choose change by enacting our vision of an openhearted response. This choice breaks the old reactive patterns.

It is useful to reflect more on our similarities than our differences; to keep foremost in our minds and hearts that we are all, basically, alike. We all experience the same fears; we all act out, we all do stupid things from time to time, we all make mistakes, hurt other's feelings, say the wrong things, and act unskillfully. This understanding is the foundation for compassion and is therefore very powerful, but, in the thick of judgment and anger, it is often very challenging to keep it foremost in our minds and hearts. Naturally, the idea of similarity is not something our ego likes to acknowledge, and it works hard to keep up the wall of differences and separation, to keep itself "special." When it comes to judging the worst offenders, the tyrant and the sociopath, we can remember that we too have a dark side, the seeds of a Hitler, Stalin or Mao, just like the rest of humanity. We can remember that what we are judging, even in these extreme cases, resides within us. The deeper our fears, the more unsafe we feel, the more severe our reactions to people and events will be. If our power comes from judging others, and being skillful at invoking fear and judgment in others, then, as we exercise this power, we become more and more isolated from love, more and more a servant of fear, until we lose touch with our humanity. This descent often begins with small judgments and grows. Our choice not to act out of judgment, not to fuel it and become more adept at manifesting it, not to indulge our ego, is what distinguishes us from the budding tyrant.

When we look at our judgments as reflections of our self-judgment, and as reflections of our own fears, it is important to understand that the reflection is not always exact or literal. For instance, we may judge someone's free spirited behavior and consider them morally loose. This does not mean that we have hidden loose morals. Why the judgment? In this case, perhaps what drives the judgment might be our own unfulfilled desires. We may hold ourselves tightly and be unwilling or afraid to experiment in the way the people we are judging do. Here our judgment has arisen through a jealously we have not admitted. We take a high moral tone, and yet we have the same desires as those who we are judging. But, we have not dealt with these desires in the same manner. We are alike, but we have chosen different paths. They indulge. We restrain. No need to judge them.

Babbie has an interesting practice that helps her to see our similarities and to experiment with her judgment. If she judges me, or some action of mine, she makes a note of it and watches for it in herself. She reports that usually within the next twenty four hours she will find herself making the same or very similar action. This is a humbling and useful practice that demonstrates how we are all so alike, as well as how we "polish the mirror."

She also taught me to make a distinction between a person and their actions. As soon as we began bringing up our kids she taught me to be careful not to accuse them of "being" a negative behavior. Instead they "acted" a certain way rather than being defined as being that way. For instance, they might have "acted in a selfish way", but they were not described as "selfish." This understanding helps us to respond to people as "unskillful" in their actions rather than making them "bad." Remembering the expression, "judge the deed not the doer," helps us to maintain respect for someone's dignity, honoring their core self, their basic goodness. It allows space for change and honors possibility.

As well as working with our outer judgments, we can contribute to our own emotional health and well being by letting go of what Don Rosenthal often described as the "merciless rider;" the constant judgment of ourselves. Since most judgment begins with self-judgment, vanquishing the merciless rider is an important part of our inner work.

When we first become aware of self-judgment, we might be alarmed at its quantity. All day long, from the moment we arise until we go to sleep at night, the voice of the merciless rider talks in our head, judging us. We often find we are by far the most severe and rude judge of our own behavior and ourselves. When we are vigilant, using awareness, we can catch these judgments as they are occurring. Often the judge is telling us that, not only are we bad or unskillful, but that we need to change.

When change does not occur, guilt and shame are piled onto the judgment and, just as they are not useful for creating lasting change in others, they are not useful when applied to ourselves. The antidote for all this is mercy. In fact, this is a great place to use our mercy practice. Every time we become aware of the presence of the merciless rider, we can challenge it, reminding ourselves that we have basic goodness, that our heart is in the right place and that we can create change. When self judgment arises in our relationships, we can use the practice of "And I'm OK" (see later section) to have mercy for ourselves. Once we are accepting of the way we are, we can begin the process of changing our unskillful behaviors. Mercy allows us to be patient and kind with ourselves as we seek change, rather than judging our every action or trying to be perfect. We sometimes act unskillfully and we can change. Have mercy. To Christ's admonishment to "do under others as you would have others do unto you" we can add, "do unto yourself as you would have others do unto you." There is nothing selfish about releasing judgment whether it is self judgment or judgment of others.

Self judgment is such a part of our outer judge that, as we let go of it, simultaneously, the outer judge fades away and a whole new world opens to us. Instead of habitually focusing on our differences, we can work to create union through the understanding of our similarities. Instead of greeting people with fear and judgment, we can become more open hearted. Being in the world becomes far easier. Applying mercy to others and our self is like taking a deep, refreshing breath.

Letting go of self-judgment can be one of the great spiritual and emotional battles of our life. Many patterns are quite deep, implanted in our childhood and taken as gospel. Some days it is hard to replace judgment with mercy. When this happens is may be a sign that there is a deep inner area that is calling out to be healed. We can ask for help from teachers and counselors. We can pray. Most importantly, we need to remember that we can change.

Accessing mercy is also very important for those of us who seek perfection. I was shocked when my eleventh grade English teacher told me that I was too much of a perfectionist, and that it was hurting my writing. I had no idea I acted in this way, but I am very grateful that she brought this into my consciousness. She cracked the curse. I had been brought up to be a perfectionist. Perfection was expected; it was imperative. Like many others, I had parents for whom I never could do well enough or be good enough. The result was that I over-tried. I became a perfectionist. When I was in fourth grade, my parents told me what a bad student I was. Years later, I found my report card from that era. It contained all B pluses! But, I remember how badly I felt at the time. Over the years, I took a long trail ride with the merciless rider.

We perfectionists judge ourselves cruelly when we make the slightest error, and we are highly sensitive to the judgment of others. Our perfectionism causes us to measure and judge other people's efforts as well. Even though we are often very competent in an area, we may never feel good enough about our efforts, and we remain fierce in our quest for perfection. To some degree, we all dance with this fear that tells us over and over, if we don't do something just right, we are fundamentally bad or not whole in some way. We tell ourselves we have failed when we have actually done a good job or made a great effort. With our perceived failure in hand we try harder to make things perfect. We perfectionists are like a person holding onto a carrot for dear life when they are slicing it. We need to realize that we can loosen our grip, hold the carrot lightly and be equally as effective. So too, we can loosen our desire to have things be perfect and still be extremely competent. Neither our desire for perfection, nor our fear of failure, is what makes us competent. The greatest competence comes from practicing good attention and finding joy in what we are doing.

When we replace perfectionism with our love and understanding of a task, with our inherent curiosity and interest, our results are just fine and the process is more enjoyable. Perfectionism relies on the self-judge to determine the value of action. Rather than celebrating our skills and our unique contributions, perfectionism spends its time judging our shortcomings.

Therefore, if we are letting go of the self-judge, we need to let go of the "perfect" demon. In exchange we embrace flexibility, which in turn allows our more creative and intuitive self to emerge. This self is far more enchanting, useful and powerful than Mr. Perfect. Great athletes work hard, but the greatest athletes are easy and natural with their talent. Often these athletes are called "natural" athletes because they don't look like they are even trying. Even more interesting; they often have their own unique form. Babbie's mother was a "natural" athlete. When she won the women's tennis trophy at her club, she challenged the men and won that trophy too, and then she hurt her hip and took up golf. In a year she had a scratch handicap, a perfect game. She never seemed at effort. She never was down on herself or judged herself for a bad shot. We are not all "natural" athletes, but, when we try to be "natural" people rather than "perfect," the results can be astounding and, no matter what the results, we are far more relaxed in the world.

Judging can take up a great deal of our time, our energy and our lives. Letting go of judgment is like a balloon lifting into the sky. Our life becomes less stressful as we stop looking for people and things to judge. No need to worry; the world goes on without our contribution of judgment. There is still plenty around! As we do the work of taking personal responsibility while showering mercy on ourselves, compassion fills the void that judgment leaves behind and we lighten up.

The Good Medicine
Without Which It Will Be Difficult

A sense of humor is one of the most important attributes we can possess or achieve in life. I am often grateful for a humorous perspective and for those who can generate the genuine laughter that is so healing. Having a sense of humor and being a thoughtful person are often companion qualities. True wit, when kind, is a flash of wisdom. Being able to see the whole picture and not getting distracted by the emotional details, is what allows us to find humor in tough situations. A sense of humor frees us from total seriousness, can expand our vision and open the heart. With a sense of humor we can hold life lightly, and sometimes in even the most difficult situations, we can see the ironies that keep us from falling into our stories completely. Humor can be like a great balm in times of trial, releasing us from worry and hurt as we view our condition more gently. It is also a sign of a healthy emotional body.

My father died in the hospital at three in the morning, my mother and I rose early that day and prepared to make plans for his body. We decided to visit the undertaker and ask him about cremation. We arrived at the funeral parlor at around nine o'clock, and the undertaker was apparently asleep. We were told to wait. We waited in a gray room that had no windows and was full of caskets. Most of the lights were off. It was a grim space. We were seated on two small uncomfortable chairs in front of a small desk. Finally the undertaker appeared. He was bleary and unkempt. One of his shirttails was out, and his glasses were dirty and askew. It looked as if someone had literally dragged him out of bed. I forgot that some undertakers are people of the night. He was not happy. As soon as we told him that we wished to have my father cremated he began pitching us on various caskets. When we politely told him we were not going to have a traditional burial and asked him about the procedure for cremation he became rude. The combination of the lost revenue on the casket and the graveside service, plus being awakened while the sun was up, caused an abrupt change in the polite manner common to his profession. He forged into hard sales, making more attempts to sell us a casket, despite our firm no thank yous, and he tried to make us feel guilty about wanting cremation. When we made it clear we were non-buyers, he became curt. When we asked him what happened to the ashes after the cremation he said, in a surly tone, "They just sprinkle them on the rose bushes around the crematorium." Overlooking this insensitivity, we told him we would like to have the ashes and he said, "OK, they will be put in a box and sent down." I asked him what kind of box and he told us, "It will be a cardboard box... like a shoebox." My mother was getting upset. I said we would prefer to keep the ashes in something nicer than a shoebox until we disposed of them. What would he recommend? Reluctant and grumbling, he got up and found a book containing some urns. My mother and I looked through the book, and I asked him, "Is this all you have? These things all look like ice buckets!" My father loved his cocktails so the remark had more meaning for us than for the undertaker, and my mother and I cracked up laughing. His misunderstanding face made the whole scene even more comical. What a relief! After all the tension, waiting all night as my father lay dying, and then having to deal with the rude undertaker, we were blessed with the refreshment of humor. It was a balm.

Developing a sense of humor is an important component of personal responsibility because a sense of humor is an attribute of balance and personal power. The ability to see the humor of our personal condition is a fundamental basis for all great humor. To do this we have to turn our focus inward, look at our own stories and find the humor in many of them. This is an act of personal responsibility that releases us from taking ourselves too seriously. It engenders personal compassion and releases us from separation and judgment. I have noticed over the years that the best teachers have a very healthy sense of humor, and are quite at ease with light, self-deprecation.

Of course humor can be used in destructive fashion as well, attacking others for their beliefs or lifestyles for instance. That is why it is good to focus on the humor in our own lives as starting place. There is plenty of pejorative humor in the world, of course, but the humor we are describing here is the humor that finds entertainment in our mutual, human condition.

The kind of humor we want to manifest is compassionate, since viewing our own condition as the shared condition of others is the basis for compassion. This is perhaps one of the reasons so many Tibetan Buddhists are renowned for their humor and joy. We recently attended a talk by the Dali Lama. At the end of the talk he was asked, "What do you think about the Mayan prophecy that the world will end in 2012?" He laughed and answered, "How would I know anything about that? I don't even know what is going to happen tomorrow!"

Like judgment, humor that is racist, or focuses on other people's peculiarities, pain or suffering upholds the framework of separation. We can never go wrong with self-humor, or humor about our mutual condition. This kind of humor allows us to hold ourselves more lightly; to see the lessons of life without pondering them to death. There is a time for humor just as there is a time for seriousness.

But how do we develop a sense of humor? We grow into it. While there are helping environments, a sense of humor is often an indicator or barometer of our inner condition. As we develop mercy for ourselves, we naturally become more flexible and open. As we take personal responsibility (with mercy), we begin to understand our similarity to others. As we let go of judgment, we become less serious, and we begin to see the humor in things much more clearly.

This is not something that is taught in school. In fact, the kind of humor that we find in our schools is often cruel humor made at the expense of others. Once we are more relaxed and open how can we enhance our ability to laugh at all the irony in life and at ourselves? Our environment is an important part of this ability. If we are brought up in a home in which humor is regarded as an important part of life we may appreciate it later in life. My father was a great joke teller. Telling a good joke or a captivating story and getting others to laugh is an art form. You have to remember your lines, say them in just the right way, and have good timing. Just listening to him sometimes was instructive. My Uncle was also a great storyteller and joke master, a great public speaker in fact. At one time he was the President of the National Grain and Feed Dealers Association, the largest agricultural organization in the country then, and he often had to speak in front of large audiences. He knew hundreds of parables and allegories that he could apply with laughter to any situation. Although he lived in the Deep South, I never heard him tell a racist joke. All his humor was focused on our shared conditions, false beliefs and foibles. He would often start off with the statement, "That reminds me of the man who...." And you would know that you were about to hear a funny teaching joke. He was a very kind man and his jokes were kind. Of course, it is not necessary to be able to tell a good joke in order to have a good sense of humor or to be able to see the humor in things.

Before we can see that things in the world are not as serious as we often take them to be, we have to stop taking ourselves so seriously. It is our own beliefs, our own seriousness that shapes our view of the world. Buddhists contend that there is no solid self, that the self is a construction of our mind. Mipam Rinpoche tells us that, "The Buddha saw that we try to make ourselves into something real and unchanging when our fundamental state of being is unconditionally open and ungraspable - selfless."[24] What we call the ego is the part of us that constantly struggles to make ourselves into "something real," a person defined by well-entrenched opinions and beliefs. Our consciousness work questions this creation. When we are conscious, we are aware that if there is any true part of us, it is that which is outside of us noticing, what Rumi calls the "true consciousness core." We become aware, that although we appear to be inside this creation, we are outside as well looking on. We discover over time that our nature is changeable and changing, not solid. This vision allows us more flexibility as we let go of the need to hold ourselves rigidly in the ego's model of who we are. When this happens, we can view ourselves with more humor because we have let go of taking our self, which perhaps doesn't really exist

---

[24] Mipam, Sakyong . *Turning the Mind Into an Ally*, Riverhead Books, 2003, page 12.

except as changing interpretation, so seriously. When we let go of the all-important persona we have created, we connect with those who share a similar understanding and we can laugh together about our condition.

If we hang around with people who like to laugh, we will get the good medicine. If we hang around with very serious people, life will naturally seem serious. We are influenced by our sangha, those with whom we choose to associate. Creating a balance between seriousness and humor is an important function of being whole and having personal power. Wise men often find life more amusing than glacially serious.

Not all laughter has to do with a sense of humor. Sometimes we find things funny that really aren't, and we laugh at inappropriate times. Nervous or inappropriate laughter can be a psychological and emotional escape mechanism. We laugh in order to escape some emotional discomfort or fear. We can use our awareness to notice when we do this. Many times I have encountered people in my workshops who could not handle the serious and more profound interactive exercises. They often begin to giggle uncontrollably, and I sometimes have to ask them kindly to step out for a while so that the rest of us can experience the solemnity of the moment. I have experienced this myself when I feel embarrassed about some action I have taken, and Babbie points it out to me. I am aware that I sometimes nervously try to laugh it off. When I see myself doing this, I realize she is somehow pushing a button in some deep, incomplete area, some place where I feel very uncomfortable. I make a note of this and tell myself, "Time for some inner work."

If we are serious most or all of the time, then life becomes dry and brittle. There is no juice. In this state we spend a great deal of time sorting through and reviewing all of life's problems. Our vision becomes limited because we are trying to think our way out of our problems and are not allowing our creative nature any space. Sometimes, if we could just step back from our problems, we would be surprised to see that many of them are not as important as we have come to believe. A sense of humor helps us keep this focus and is a part of our creative nature. By allowing us to view things less seriously, to hold them less tightly, a sense of humor frees up our creative abilities and lets in new choices and solutions.

One of the ways we can exercise personal responsibility is to look at the places in our life that we consider very serious indeed. Why do we grasp these areas so hard? What are we afraid of? Can we accept, or at least review, another viewpoint? Just as nervous laughter alerts us to areas of deep discomfort in our life, "deadly" seriousness indicates the areas we are holding in fear.

This happens, for instance, when we define ourselves by our religion or our work, or when we get too serious about politics. It happens when we lose our compassion for others who have different beliefs. What are we afraid of? Are we actually threatened by others beliefs? Most often the answer is "no." Often we are suffering once again from the "anguished imperative," the desperate need to have something be different than it is. People of other faiths should take up our faith. People should understand the importance of our work, or people should see that our political party has the only right ideas for solving our social problems. We are often "serious about this!" Humor then is also a form of faith. When we hold things lightly, we let go of the need to control everything, to have things be a particular way. We trust the plan; we trust the dance, letting the Great Spirit, God, the Universe or the elegant patterning do the work.

When we take ourselves too seriously, we are not much fun to be with, and we end up attracting people who are not much fun to be with either. This is the wrong prescription for balance and harmony in our lives. When we are too serious sometimes we need to let go of the anchors that are holding us, and move into new waters. Why are we so serious about something? Why so judgmental? Why so strict with ourselves; so merciless? As we focus on our similarity to others we can let go of these tyrants. We begin to see how often our seriousness is misplaced, how silly we all can be, even ridiculous.

None of this means we cannot keep our serious friends, our religion, our job, or our political party. It means we can learn to hold them more easily, rather than holding onto to them for dear life (an interesting expression). If, when we begin to hold things more lightly, others may respond to our personal change saying, in effect, "This is not OK." We may have to let them go and make changes for

Be Yourself H —

the sake our own health and wholeness. In *Conversations with God*, God tells Walsch, "If there were such a thing as sin, this would be it: to allow yourself to become what you are because of the experience of others."[25]

Humor is also powerful because it is a vulnerability practice. Accepting our own vulnerability is a profound act of personal responsibility. It is courageous and is an important part of developing true personal power. When we allow ourselves to be vulnerable, we are acting on and strengthening our belief in our own safety, while simultaneously creating an atmosphere for others that encourages their vulnerability. This can be a big relief for those who are holding onto their self-judgments tightly. Revealing the humor of our own condition in the presence of others allows them to feel safe with us. They feel more freedom to be who they are, rather than whom they think the world wants them to be. Laughing at our common foibles is a powerful relaxant and uniting force. It is a balm. It is good medicine. The effect of a group laughing is exponential, the more people laughing, the stronger the medicine. Sometimes a line in a movie strikes a funny spot in the collective audience and we find ourselves laughing together at something that isn't even that funny. My good friend Peter developed a whole humor weekend workshop. He presents it to some very serious people in college departments and on hospital staffs. I admire his courage! He will take on any group and, when people are finished with the weekend, they feel wonderful and light. He always gets straight A's. His ability to create laughter and get others to share in the joy of humor is a rich gift.

Remember that we can also use our awareness of the level of humor in our daily lives as a barometer to indicate the lightness or heaviness of our inner condition. When we are easy with ourselves and less self-judging, we tend to manifest more humor. When we are worried or perplexed or angry or self interested, our sense of humor is diminished.

---

[25] Walsch, Neale Donald. *Conversations with God.* Hampton Roads Publishing Company, 1996

117

Studies indicate that laughter and humor are amazing cures for many things that ail us, both physical and spiritual. Here is a list of the health benefits: Laughter relaxes the whole body. It is a great stress reducer. They say that laughter has a lasting effect. Laughter gives the immune system a lift by decreasing stress hormones. Laughter is good for the heart and cardiovascular system. You even get an endorphin rush from laughter. And sometimes, when things are really grim and sad, it is laughter and humor that save us from despair and self-pity.

When we learn to hold things lightly, and are able laugh at ourselves we bring balance and ease into our lives. We are taking a draught of the good medicine. On our own or with others, there is nothing like it.

NO FEAR!

Understanding the Ocean in Which We Swim
Personal Responsibility and Fear

Once we understand that personal responsibility is a major component of personal power, we become able to maintain personal power. If we all understood this dynamic and began to take personal responsibility, we could move our world from the domain of fear to the domain of compassion and understanding. We would move the world away from constant blame and judgment. In fact, if only a small percentage could do this, we might make the move.

Perhaps nothing represents our misunderstanding about personal power more than the "NO FEAR!" signs and bumper stickers that used to be so ubiquitous. All across the nation, pickup trucks, semis, hot cars, and even skateboards, cruised a dangerous and unforgiving world with these stickers prominently attached, as if, by simply attaching this sticker to our transport, we could magically banish fear. When we understand the true nature of our relationship to fear we will understand that NO FEAR! is actually an announcement that means "HELP! I'M REALLY AFRAID". Whether we put a "NO FEAR" sticker on our car, or we feel the need to carry a gun or knife, we are often completely unaware that we are acting out of fear. We have bought into the big myth that fear is something to be vanquished, overpowered, or magically banished. We might have a secret vision of ourselves as one of the special people who can do this. Often, we believe that vanquishing fear requires violent and fear-filled action.

The persona many of us associate with personal power is a Goliath, huge and strong and overpowering; a force to be reckoned with; a force that strikes fear into the heart of others: Rambo, Darth Vader, the violent cop, the destructive master of martial arts, the ruthless business man, the clever and calculating rich man, and the fast gun. Many of us spend our lifetime trying to become a copy of these archetypes, trying to manifest this kind of power. Ironically, those of us who do gain this kind of power are actually frightened or numb, and, no matter how big an outer show we make, we live in fear. In this lifestyle one is required to maintain constant vigilance in order to guard and maintain their status. Living in constant fear of losing power takes a great deal of energy and time.

As we discussed earlier, we believe that personal power is a force for overcoming others and controlling events, for shaping our world and the people in it so that they conform to our personal desires and agendas. The ego tells us that, to achieve these ends, we must be strong and forceful, domineering, overtly or covertly. It tells us that it can lead us to safety when, as Don Rosenthal often said, "It is the voice of fear itself". It tells us to take advantage of others and their weaknesses before they take advantage of us. This is a vision of the fierce competitor and the big winner. The world of law and politics and big business is built around this vision. This model of personal power is the cultural norm, but, spiritually and realistically speaking, it could not be further from the truth.

We do not have to go far to see how this version of personal power manifests and is continually reinforced. It's not subtle. Television and the movies are filled with images of people gaining the upper hand through violence and intimidation. Violence is celebrated over and over again as the ultimate solution to problems. The world is continually engaged in countless wars. Yet the person who can create understanding, or manifest compassion or loving kindness in difficult and fear filled situations, is the true person of personal power. As long as the fear-based model is the principal male model of personal power there will endless unnecessary suffering.

Social anthropologists point out that this adolescent behavior, and ignorance, is the product of a culture that lacks reverence for age and wisdom, and that celebrates youth in its place. Many American males are locked into an adolescent model that has spread around the world through media, advertising and imperial adventures. This lack of genuine maturity and wisdom is having a tremendous impact on the world. Older and more balanced indigenous cultures are being overwhelmed by the American ethos and its youth worship. But there has always been another way. Throughout time, older cultures have honored and delineated the transition from boyhood to manhood through ceremonies of initiation. We see some of this in the Jewish celebration of the Bar Mitzvah but, for the most part, modern western culture has no such cultural mechanism.

Today, many young males are left in a perpetual state of adolescence, with very few places to turn for a model of wisdom, much less true personal power. Fathers are distant or absent of abusive. Television shows and movies have replaced the father, the uncle and the elder as the source and model of how to be and act in the world. Because these shows are designed for entertainment, they celebrate and pander to fear and sexual urges in order to draw the largest audience. They focus on competition and survival; the dog eat dog world.

The culture has created a model of personal power for a woman that is no less false. It has little regard for feminine intelligence or wisdom, unless it is attached to beauty. As a general rule, it seems that, to be a television newscaster or commentator, a woman must be pretty or sexually appealing. Many older women, who could act as guides for young women, are lost in trying to stay perpetually young. Personal power for women is represented with being attractive to males, staying thin, looking good, being witty, but not too smart or too competitive. There are women who pursue the aggressive male model of personal power too, and, in this model, motherhood and the feminine are sometimes seen as weaknesses.

Meanwhile, many parents spend their lives lost in the "not enough," working more and more just to feed their families and pay their bills. Children are cast adrift in the world with mostly media images for behavior models that mix easily with the cultural model of fear-based power. A part of this adolescent model is, of course, that someone else or something else is always to blame for our personal, or even our national, shortcomings and difficulties. Again, we often fear that which we don't understand, and this fear becomes the basis for separation and disharmony.

War, violence, and manipulation demonstrate complete ignorance about the nature of personal power and also constitute a misunderstanding and misuse of fear. Rather than using fear as a teacher, we react to it like lemmings, reacting in often accepted, unskillful and non-compassionate ways.

While it is important to understand what personal power isn't, we need to know what true personal power is and how it manifests. What are the qualities of those who possess it? One definition of real personal power is the ability to live without fear as a constant companion, and to maintain equanimity when others are immersed in fear. Since the world is swimming in fear, living outside of the great immersion is a significant milestone in personal and spiritual growth. In order to do this, it helps to understand some of the dynamics of fear.

When we understand that fear is a messenger, coming and going in different guises, and we start to observe and listen to it, we discover that that there are three fundamental types of fear, each one manifesting in a slightly different way. One key to achieving personal power is to become aware of these three levels and to work with them consciously. As we do this, we begin to recognize how deeply fear influences all of us, and again, this understanding helps us to access compassion.

The first type of fear is made up of our daily fears, the "merciless rider." These are the omnipresent fears to which we frequently react. "What will people think?" "They don't like me." "I don't have enough money." "What if they don't like my report?" "I need those people's good opinion." These can be dealt with using the four strategies for learning what our lives are trying to teach us: awareness, personal responsibility, inner being, and action. First we become aware of these fears, and then we take personal responsibility by accepting that we are the source of these fears and not what is happening in the world around us. When we do the work of inner being we can work with one fear at a time, investigating its source, our beliefs and finding ways to replace it with love. Inner being practices, such as meditation, are powerful aids in this work. Then we take action, bringing forth new behaviors to match our budding understanding. Our daily fears are very responsive to inner work. Because these fears are so predominant, they actually lend themselves more easily to investigation and change, although some of them may have deep roots and many levels. Working with these fears, learning what they are teaching and then letting them go, brings a great deal of peace and real emotional relief into our lives. Stress is greatly diminished. Imagine not having the merciless rider of self-judgment as a constant companion. The release of fear is not something that happens in a sudden flash. We keep working on our personal set of fears, and one day a familiar fear-causing pattern arises, and we suddenly realize that we are no longer feeling fear. We are simply observing the pattern. We experience a moment of inner joy and new freedom.

The second type of fear is collective fear, the fears we all share. Of course, some of us are more focused on one variety than another. Often, it seems that we are put on earth expressly for the purpose of working with one of these fears. These fears are sometimes harder to discern. An example would be Bill's childhood fear, the fear that disguised itself as very acceptable politeness. In order to stay safe from his father as a child, Bill created the Mr. Nice Guy, Mr. No Anger, and the Mr. Polite Persona. Fear for personal physical safety and fear of anger was so deeply embedded into this persona that he didn't recognize it. It took a big shock to wake him up from the "nice guy" dream. Taking personal responsibility for his condition allowed him to finally see that his avoidance of anger was causing his inability to create boundaries and speak the truth about his feelings, which in turn was the cause of many of the problems he was experiencing in life. He had to acknowledge his fear in order to make changes around it. As we acknowledge and work with these deeper fears, we release at a deeper level and experience ever more safety. Fear of starvation, loss of shelter, loss of means, physical injury, sickness and violence are examples of our common fears. When we investigate each of these, it is interesting to discover what beliefs we have about each of them. Sometimes these beliefs are actually fantasies, and our fear is groundless. Sometimes our fear is invisible until we investigate, as Bill's was. But, once discovered, we can work with it.

All of us need to work with probably the biggest fear in the category of collective fear, the fear of death. Fear of death is a powerful fear we all share at some level. It is commonly regarded as the ultimate fear, the source of all our other fears. Essentially it is the fear of non-existence. Coming to terms with this fear creates very deep levels of safety (for more see *Hanging Out with Yama* in the Action section of the book).

If we learn how to work with the first two types of fear, when the third suddenly arises, and it arrives quickly, we are more prepared to deal with it. This is our instinctive animal fear, an adrenalin rush. This highly energetic rush is built into our body to help us survive physical attack. Coming from deep in the amygdala of the limbic brain, this instinctive "flight or fight" response is still occasionally necessary for survival. It is hard wired and will, perhaps, always be with us. While we cannot control the sudden arrival of this fear, as we become more accepting and knowledgeable about our other, more controllable fears, we learn to rapidly acknowledge this instinctive fear when it arises and respond skillfully to it rather than react blindly.

My experience working as an emergency medical technician provided me with interesting insight into this kind of fear. Police, EMT's and firemen frequently deal with life threatening, critically time-sensitive, conditions and, sometimes, their own survival is threatened. When I first started working as an EMT and ambulance driver, I lived close enough to the station that I could drive down and join the rest of the crew when there was a call. I snapped my red light onto the car roof, turned on my siren and rushed to the station. My adrenaline started pumping the minute I was called out. Radios, strobe emergency lights, and sirens all contributed to an adrenaline rush. I found this chemical rush unpleasant and distracting. I felt I performed better when I was calmer. I developed the practice of calming down and breathing on the way to the station and, in the ambulance, on the way to the call. To be of the most service I needed to get the rush under control until it was no longer an issue. Each time the tones went off on my beeper, I felt a moment of electricity, but, over time, I was able to respond to this more skillfully and I could calm myself, slowing my heartbeat and thinking clearly. As we develop personal power, we are able to abide with fear rather than avoid it or indulge it, and, over time, we learn to release it or diminish the reactions it calls forth, so that, even when our deep primitive, physical fear, the fight or flight mechanism, arises, we are able to see it for what it is and exercise reasoned action rather than unconscious reaction.

A feature of true personal power is the equanimity that derives from a lack of the "anguished imperative" to have one's way or have all our desires fulfilled. This does not mean one does not argue a point or take a position or that we do not have desires. Sometimes our personal power is not enough to overcome obstacles. Gandhi wanted India to remain a nation of Muslims and Hindus living together, working in harmony. He was unable to persuade Nehru, and Jenna, to stop the partition of India into two separate states, but there is no doubt that he had great personal power.

Those with true personal power are often willing to let truth succeed or fail. It is not as important to be right as it is to be heard. The most important thing is that the truth be present. In the action section of this book, we learn about authentic communication, the ability to communicate one's truth without judgment or blame. This ability is often found in a person with true personal power. To such a person, what is most important is that their truth be clear. Once this has occurred they can rest. Therefore, sometimes ironically, they are often not as deeply attached to outcome as some others. Because a person of personal power has a high degree of understanding and respect for the fears and passions of others, they are able to consider these fears and work with them, rather than simply reject them as the ego model of personal power is want to do. We can remember that the source of personal power is personal responsibility; we are working with our own feelings and reactions rather than making someone else wrong for theirs. Because a person with real personal power is not desperate or fearful about outcome and is able to honor other people's opinions, they are less threatening and can often influence others powerfully.

Gandhi's life illustrates perhaps the most important aspect of true personal power: the ability to choose his truth in the face of fear. When the British confronted Gandhi with threats concerning his own safety and the safety of his followers, he went forward unarmed, fearlessly taking the high ground. His devotion to the manifestation of truth, and what he believed was the best outcome for India, through non-violent protest, often put him and his followers in collision with those who believed in the power of violence, intimidations and brute strength. To this day, his model is used to create lasting change, to bring wrongs to consciousness without violence. This is the powerful gift he brought to us all. He called on the best in his enemies, rather than the worst. This too can be a part of our vision of true personal power. Not only can we be understanding and patient listeners, but we can call forth and expect the best from others. We can appeal to their basic goodness, rather than feed our pejorative attitudes and beliefs. Gandhi, armed with integrity and belief, confronted an empire and was influential in driving the British from India.

With personal power we are not concerned about overcoming fear, but more about acknowledging it and honoring whatever it is bringing to the situation. Gandhi's attitude after he had spoken his truth was basically "I will do what I have to do, and you do what you have to do." His work was often a process of bringing consciousness to situations in order to demonstrate a higher and more compassionate truth. When others are in fear, a person with real personal power is able to open the heart and demonstrate safety, but not by denying the fear others are feeling. Rather, they create an atmosphere of expanded possibility that can influence others profoundly.

The fearful mind asks, "What about our physical selves?" Does the choice for love mean we will always be safe in physically dangerous situations? Of course not. Many people who have had personal power and who have had the ability to create a field of safety for others in dangerous situations have died. Many prophets and saints have been killed. Many people who have had the personal power to demonstrate expanded possibility, who have called on the best in others, have died. Martin Luther King is a perfect example.

We can summarize the qualities that are found when a person manifests true personal power. Again, they are not what the ego would have us believe. We find: personal responsibility, patience, compassion, the ability to listen deeply, the ability to speak the truth without judgment or blame, respect for the fears of others, the wisdom of love, vulnerability, an ease with our own challenges and difficulties (often manifested through a sense of self humor), and, of course, the ability to bring love and tranquility to situations fraught with fear. The person with true personal power does not feel compelled to save anyone, or to teach or preach. They show us the path through their actions and deeds. They demonstrate the "field of possibility." It is in this manner they show us the way.

It is evident that I am compelled and inspired by the idea that we can live our lives with a different and wiser relationship to fear. Much of the fear that is a constant in our lives can be calmed and diminished when we take fear as an ally and do our personal work. As we drop our own fears, as we operate less and less out fear and more and more out of love, tolerance and understanding, we begin to manifest more personal power. We make room for wisdom. While the qualities set forth above are an important vision we can embrace, personal power is not something that we gain overnight. Because we have been conditioned to avoid fear, and have grown up with separation, each of us has developed unskillful and reactionary habits and coping mechanisms we have to deal with before we can fully experience this extraordinary way of being. And, of course, even as we develop personal power we sometimes experience old fears at deeper levels. This is part of the plan. We grow level by level. As soon as we master one level we are presented with the next, and on we move, developing awareness, and taking personal responsibility for our condition, time after time. We are peeling off the accumulated layers of beliefs that no longer serve us. We work with our inner being and take new action in the world. Paradoxically, and contrary to our instinctive avoidance of fear, working with our fears expands our understanding and knowledge of our intrinsic safety. Fear is a deep river for many of us. Some float on the river forgetting they are floating, denying fear, others drink heavily of the river immersing themselves in constant fear. We can use the river to transport us to greater levels of understanding that aid us in developing personal power. Our journey takes time and patience. With mercy as our ally, we keep working with the four strategies, and, as time passes, personal power begins to blossom naturally. True personal power is the possession of those who can manifest love and understanding in the most difficult and trying situations. It is the extraordinary domain of the lover.

The Man with the Inexplicable Life
Trust and Following the Heart

Islamic mysticism is called Sufism. Its practitioners are called Dervishes. The Dervishes teach by telling wonderful stories. One of my favorites is the Sufi tale called *The Man with the Inexplicable Life*.[26] Rajneesh, the so-called "golden" guru who some feel gave "guruism" a bad name, was undeniably a brilliant teacher and speaker, despite some of his other more flamboyant and dubious activities. He once gave an extraordinary satsang on this tale. I have memorized this tale because it is so inspiring. It is a beacon I carry with me. Rajneesh claimed that all we need to know about the spiritual life is contained in this one story. He called it "one of the greatest stories," and "incomparable." We not only learn from this tale that the ultimate personal responsibility is following the heart, but that the path is illuminated as well.

> *There was once a man named Mojud. He lived in a town where he had obtained a post as a small official, and it seemed likely that he would end his days as Inspector of Weights and Measures.*
>
> *One day when he was walking through the gardens of an ancient building near his home, Khidr, the mysterious Guide of the Sufis, appeared to him, dressed in shimmering green. Khidr said: "Man of bright prospects! Leave your work and meet me at the riverside in three days' time." Then he disappeared.*
>
> *Mojud went to his superior in trepidation and said that he had to leave. Everyone in the town soon heard of this and they said: "Poor Mojud!*

---

[26] Shah, Indries. *Tales of the Dervishes*. E.P. Dutton & Co., 1970, page 155

He has gone mad." But, as there were many candidates for his job, they soon forgot him.

On the appointed day, Mojud met Khidr, who said to him: "Tear your clothes and throw yourself in the river. Perhaps someone will save you."

Mojud did so, even though he wondered if he were mad. Since he could swim he did not drown, but drifted a long way before a fisherman hauled him into his boat saying: "Foolish man! The current is strong. What are you trying to do?"

Mojud said: "I don't really know."

"You are mad," said the fisherman, "but I will take you into my reed hut by the river yonder, and we shall see what can be done for you."

When he discovered that Mojud was well spoken, he learned from him how to read and write. In exchange, Mojud was given food and helped the fisherman with is work. After a few months, Khidr again appeared, this time at the foot of Mojud's bed, and said: "Get up now and leave this fisherman. You will be provided for."

Mojud immediately quit the hut, dressed as a fisherman, and wandered about until he came to a highway. As dawn was breaking, he saw a farmer on a donkey on his way to market. "Do you seek work?" asked the farmer. "Because I need a man to help me bring back some purchases."

Mojud followed him. He worked for the farmer for nearly two years, by which time he had learned a great deal about agriculture but little else.

One afternoon, when he was bailing wool, Khidr appeared to him and said: "Leave that work, walk to the city of Mosul, and use your savings to become a skin merchant."Mojud obeyed.

In Mosul he became known as a skin merchant, never seeing Khidr while he plied his trade for three years. He had saved quite a large sum of money and was thinking of buying a house, when Khidr appeared and said: "Give me your money, walk out of this town as far as the distant Samarkand, and work for a grocer there."Mojud did so.

Presently he began to show undoubted signs of illumination. He healed the sick, served his fellow man in the shop during his spare time, and his knowledge of the mysteries became deeper and deeper.

Clerics, philosophers, and others visited him and asked: "Under whom did you study?"

"It is difficult to say," said Mojud.

His disciples asked: "How did you start your career?"

He said: "As a small official."

130

"And you gave it up to devote yourself to self mortification?"
"No, I just gave it up."
They did not understand him.
People approached him to write the story of his life.
"What have you been in your life?" they asked.
"I jumped into a river, became a fisherman, then walked out of his reed hut in the middle of the night. After that, I became a farmhand. While I was baling wool, I changed and went to Mosul, where I became a skin merchant. I saved some money there but gave it away. Then I walked to Samarkand where I worked for a grocer. And this is where I am now."
"But this inexplicable behavior throws no light upon your strange gifts and wonderful examples", said the biographers.
"That is so!" said Mojud. So the biographers constructed for Mojud a wonderful and exciting story – because all saints must have their story and the story must be in accordance with the appetite of the listeners, not with the realities of life.
And nobody is allowed to speak of Khidr directly. That is why this story is not true. It is the representation of a life. This is the real life of one of the greatest Sufis.

When we first meet Mojud, he is living a safe, secure, and comfortable life. Many of us think we will find safety in the tenured position, the job with built in salary increases, the all-important benefits and some potential for advancement. We seek the life without risk. We think things like, "If I just had more money, or if my job was totally secure, all would be well."

In this sense, when the tale opens, it looks like Mojud has it made. As an inspector of weights and measures, he has a safe, secure, much sought after government position. His job represents the risk free life so many of us seek. But what happens to Mojud can also happen to us. Rajneesh tells us: "The word 'mojud' is beautiful. It means two things. Literally it means; one who is present.; one who has an inner presence, who is aware, who is alert, who is conscious. And the second meaning comes from the first: one who lives in the present, who is present to the present." Before he begins his journey then, Mojud is aware.

As Mojud is walking home through the park, Khidr, the mystical guide of the Sufis, appears before him dressed in shimmering green. Notice this "call" happens like a flash, in a second. This is often the case with a spiritual understanding or revelation. Mojud is just walking through the park, maybe thinking of dinner or going bowling with his friends, when he suddenly becomes aware of a deeper call. He has a sudden realization that his life needs to change, that there is something more, something missing, a further place down the path, if you will.

Shimmering green is color of the heart chakra. Green represents peace. The mystical guide of the Sufis is the heart, the seat of peace. Mojud's heart is suddenly calling out to him. Maybe he has the perfect job and lifestyle, but he is aware his heart is not in it. We notice that Khidr calls Mojud "man of bright prospects." This reminds us that at any given moment we all have bright prospects; we have the power to make good choices. We are not what we do. There is never a moment in which we cannot choose the ultimate form of personal responsibility, following the heart as it seeks the truth. Following the heart and understanding what happens when we do, what obstacles we may encounter, what help we might receive, are the central themes of this amazing tale. This story is beautiful because it is a simple map of the journey into consciousness, the journey toward the life that is our heart's desire, the life for which we may actually exist.

Rajneesh taught that "the heart can only believe and the mind can only doubt." When we hear our doubt, we know that the mind is voicing fear, and we are not following the heart. Just as Joseph Campbell taught that the voice of reason keeps us from discovering the unknown; so following the heart is often a path into the unknown. We want to experience ourselves as spiritual beings, but the mind with its fine arguments, its voice of reason, holds us back. Mojud is the quintessential hero. By following his heart, he puts aside the mind that doubts, that says, "Keep the good job, the reputation, the money, the security." He ignores the fearful response we know so well. He lets go of the illusion of safety; he lets go of control. The story demonstrates the important understanding that the heart, like love itself, is unequivocal. We can't bargain with the heart. It asks for our full will and intention.

Like the people of the village, we would probably think Mojud was crazy for quitting his secure job. If a neighbor of ours, who worked at a secure position for a big corporation, suddenly quit his job and became a professional caddy because he loved golf, the tongues would wag. Mojud quits his job. Already he has demonstrated his intention and taken the first step on the path of the heart. Soon other gossip replaces stories about crazy Mojud. This is good to understand; that the peer opinion we so often fear is fickle, always looking for new sources to judge. Thus the decisions about our own life that we make for the good opinion of others are built on a false foundation. These opinions are more often based on a collective fear that our action has triggered than the truth about our condition. Because others would be afraid to do what Mojud is doing they judge him. It disturbs them, but they soon forget about Mojud as other gossip arises. When we choose a decision from the wisdom of the heart it is often this way. We cannot always expect others to support our decision, and very often quite the opposite happens; we are derided. The choice for following the heart is often a lonely choice. After all, we are the only one who can follow *our* heart. The opinions of others; whether they agree with our choice or not, are not important. Our heart does not need the minds of others to direct it. Mojud ignores the gossips.

If Khidr is a guide, he must have someone to guide. Who are the followers of Khidr? We call them "seekers". Mojud is a seeker, but what are we all seeking, as we follow the river of life with our hearts? We are seeking the truth, and in this tale Mojud is following the wise intuitions of the heart to find it. Like Mojud we must follow the heart to discover who we really are, to discover our divine self. Spiritually speaking, this is what we are here for, what our life is trying to teach us. This is the path.

In three days' time, Mojud meets Khidr by the river and is told to tear his clothes and throw himself in the river. Interestingly, Khidr offers no assurances. "Perhaps someone will save you," he tells Mojud. This is one of the most important teachings from this tale. Following the heart, seeking the truth, always requires that we make a leap of faith.

When we first embark on the path of the heart, there are no guarantees. Of course the ego wants guarantees. It wants the risk-free path. This is why, so often, when we are pulled toward spirit, we find it very difficult to let go of the familiar, solid, ground of our current experience. We try so hard to limit our risk, to make sure we will be safe, that we find it nearly impossible to leap off the cliff (as Khidr instructs Mojud) and therefore, ironically, we can never discover that we are always, truly safe. The deep knowledge of our basic safety is one the biggest rewards of taking risk, but true safety can never be experienced without the leap of faith, without trusting in something greater than the self. We will not arrive at the nature of our own safety through logic, through the mind. But, of course, we all keep trying. Note that there is no one on the cliff selling books about how to jump in the river, or giving lessons and counseling. Mojud must make the jump without help, all alone. Remember, Khidr is not actually a physical presence either. He is a metaphor. Mojud is a man on a solo journey.

Why does Mojud tear his clothes? This is a common gesture of mourning. Right at this point he is leaving his past behind. Tearing his clothes is a purging, a letting go. We are allowed a moment of grief, a last farewell, as we make this fateful transition; then, into the river, and a new ball game begins.

Mojud makes the required leap. The leap we can all make and make many times. The leap itself becomes a practice. Once I took a job in marketing and sales at a software company. I found that, although I was making it work financially, I was not enjoying my life. I lived the American way, maintaining debt to maintain my lifestyle. I was very tired of living in debt. Our house was a huge debt anchor and, because I traveled a fair amount in my job, I didn't seem to be spending much time with my family. When I was home, I spent most days going to, coming from or being at work.. As a result of the personal work I was doing, my inner life was changing, and I saw that my reality wouldn't change until I gave up my current life, my attachments to the past, to others' opinions, to what I knew. I remembered the story of Mojud. I decided to jump in the river. I told my family we were going to let go of the house and with it all the accumulated debt and start over. I quit what had become an unpleasant job, a job that definitely was not following my heart, and focused on the change, on jumping into the river.

It was hard for all of us to leave the beautiful place we lived, the house that we had built with our own hands. It was the only home my children had ever known. The mind had plenty of reasons to doubt the letting go: people's opinion, credit difficulties, leaving a very beautiful place with no immediate home in which to live. Fortunately, most of our kids were already out in the world. We had a big mortgage. I made the arrangement with the bank to give them the property without contest. We had the sad task of emptying our house. It seemed endless. I remember I was the very last one to go. I stood in the kitchen where we had shared a thousand meals and wonderful times, and I realized that the house meant nothing without us. A long time ago somebody had told me that a house was not a home. They were certainly right. It was simply a shell. I closed the door and never went back. The decision to let go of that life was one of the best I have ever made, even though it took a few years for our lives to settle into a new groove. I had no idea what I was going to do, but my heart called for me to stop the life I was living, a life I had created like so many, to meet the expectations of others.

Like Mojud, I jumped into the river with no guarantees. I hesitated on the river bank, for sure, but I jumped, and I believe that if I hadn't I would not be alive today. There was grief and sadness but also intention.

My current life is much less stressful than the old one. I have time for beauty and work that I love. Many of the trappings the consumer world offers have no more allure. Life is simpler. I feel more peace in my life. I do not feel the necessity to prove anything to anybody. I am able to do a lot of service work that I love. Right now, I am sitting on a mountainside in Panama writing this book. Outside the window it is a beautiful warm, peaceful blue day. I am provided for, but I had to leave my old world behind and jump in the river to get here. I am blessed in the most miraculous way by having been given the support and help I needed all along the way. I am blessed that Khidr appeared, to show me the leap of faith. My hardships and difficulties became the compost for a completely different life. Will I have to jump into the river again? Maybe so.

Mojud jumps in the river and is saved by a fisherman. "What are you crazy?" the fisherman asks, and Mojud replies, "Perhaps I am." This is the classic mystic's answer. Crazy? Following the heart? Perhaps following the heart, seeking truth, we appear crazy to others, but, once we leap, it is hard to go back to the old risk adverse life. By normal fear-based standards we are crazy. The mystic falls in love with life, life just as it is; duality begins to fade.

135

The fisherman discovers Mojud's talents and puts him to work teaching his family how to read and write, while some days he has Mojud assist with the fishing. When we jump off the cliff we are never sure what talents we have that will be called upon. We are not really "looking for a job." Mojud never thought he would be living as a fisherman-teacher. Since I left my old business life I have been a computer teacher, a carpenter, a property manager, a teacher of interpersonal communications, an ambulance driver, an EMT, a builder, an investor, a hospice volunteer, a workshop leader, a counselor and a consultant and a better father. We like to know exactly what is going to happen next in our life. But taking what is offered is often the hallmark of the heart follower as we discover when Mojud moves through his life. Rumi describes the world as "flowing towards me." If we are awake; if we stay aware as much as possible, watching the symbolic, watching the patterns, keeping our heart open, we see that life is always flowing towards us and we accept the gift. We worry less about the future, remembering that it doesn't exist, only this flowing towards us in the present exists. When we take the path with heart, it is hard to fit us into a box, to label us. Sometimes others feel uncomfortable with this. Are we crazy? Perhaps.

One night at the fisherman's house Khidr appears again and says, "Get up now and leave this fisherman, you will be provided for." This is different from his early statement, "Perhaps someone will save you!" What has changed?

When we decide to take the leap of faith we discover our true safety, thus Mojud in his heart now knows that he will be provided for. He obeys immediately, without hesitation. In itself, the certainty that he will be provided for, is a great blessing, a tremendous reward. If we trusted that we would be provided for what would we do? Would we keep on with the life we are living? Mojud trusts his inner voice. He has handed over control to Khidr. He is following the flow of life not trying to control it. This is an interesting journey.

Mojud leaves the fisherman's house and, in the morning, finds himself on the highway to the marketplace. A sheep farmer hires him for the day and is so impressed with his abilities that he offers him a job. He becomes a shepherd. He is content, but, after a couple of years, Khidr appears again and tells Mojud to leave the farm and proceed to the city of Mosul to become a skin merchant. This job description may not mean a lot to us, but, in many cultures, a skin merchant is the lowest position in the social strata. Mojud does not hesitate and moves to the city. Here he becomes a successful merchant, and he is about to build a house and settle down when Khidr instructs him to give up his money, go to distant Samarkand and work for a grocer. Sometimes, when we decide to settle down and join the crowd, our heart pulls us away just as we are about to settle in. We are often tempted by old ideas of security; it is not always easy following the heart. Mojud leaves Mosul. Nothing is linear about the journey into consciousness, and we may be required to make the leap of faith many times; to make many changes. There is no path more challenging.

About this time in his life, Mojud begins to show undoubted signs of enlightenment. He heals the sick, and his knowledge of the mysteries continues to grow deeper. Mojud has metamorphosed into a healer, a wise man. We note he still works in the store, however, making his daily bread and serving his fellow man as a humble clerk. To be a wise man and the healer was not his intention. In the old traditions, a true guru makes his own way, not asking for money for his spiritual help, or building shrines to himself.

The pundits come to make discovery, to put shape and form to his enlightenment, to co-opt it for their own purposes, but, when they ask Mojud how he has arrived at the place of wisdom, they are disappointed with his story. He hasn't studied with any great teachers. Instead, he recounts for them the many ordinary jobs he has had. His spiritual progress is inexplicable in common spiritual description so they make up a story to suit their listeners to cover over his inexplicable life with a story that suits them.

Mojud's spiritual journey was following his heart, his inner guide, seeking the truth. Doing this he became a wise man. Like Mojud, if we want to follow the heart we need to be alert to what the heart is saying, to what love is saying; to follow this inner guide.

No one speaks of Khidr. Why? Because Khidr belongs to every man. He lives within. He is invisible. He is a voice. What is that voice saying? By the time Mojud took the job as store clerk he was a true lover. Staying in his heart, listening for love, he became a true saint. He came from the heart, he lived in the flow of love, he could heal the sick, and "the mysteries became deeper and deeper." He lived the ordinary life extraordinarily.

How long has this story been going on? How long has this choice been set before us? From Normandi Ellis' beautiful collection of interpretations of ancient Egyptian funerary poems *Awakening Osiris, The Egyptian Book of the Dead* we read the poetic words of an ancient Egyptian written perhaps 4000 years ago. The italics are mine.

Becoming The Craftsman[27]

"What can be named can be known, what cannot be named must be lived, believed.

This way to the cliff edge! Jump to know the unknowable!

I speak of the creator and the creation, the ordinary life lived extraordinarily.

Mojud's jobs were the ordinary jobs, his life seemingly ordinary on the surface. Christ was a carpenter, the Buddha, born a prince, chose to live as a wandering monk. Gandhi created an ever more simple life. Mother Teresa did her work as a simple nun.

I work for the sake of working. The joy of creating is the joy of forgetting everything else.

No concern about salary or prestige here.

I lean into life. My tongue is fire; my breath is wind. The spirit spits from my mouth.

We are all connected to spirit. Celebrate your passion.

I speak of a chain of events where making leads to making, action to action, love to love, where the beginning began so long ago we find ourselves always in the midst of it.

Life flows towards us. Again, Rumi says," for sixty years I have been forgetful, but not once has this flowing towards me ceased or slowed!" Stay aware. Remain alert. Experience the great gift that is your life.

There is no rest. The act is now.

---

[27] Ellis, Normandi. *Awakening Osiris, The Eygptian Book of the Dead*. Panes Press 1988, page 162

The flowing never ceases. The opportunity is now. We are all men of bright prospects. We can jump off the cliff right now!
In your lives you will make children, make peace, make errors, you will make trouble, you will dance under the sun and moon. As long as you live you will create life. You will rise and fall many times. It is like the making of a good loaf of bread. You will be nourished."
You will be nourished by your life, by your action, by your choices. You will be cared for. You are safe.

There is no greater act of personal responsibility than following the heart. Many of us are so embedded in our jobs and our lives, in the activities of our children, in our sports, hobbies and activities, that we are unaware this choice is always nearby. When, or if, we discover its existence, we may persuade ourselves that, with all we are doing, following the heart is not possible, we are too busy. Perhaps we will persuade ourselves we are noble in some way, perhaps a voice will tell us that we are sacrificing our heart path for the benefit of others. But how can this be? Have others asked us to do this? Is this a valid request? Are we not all served when the heart followers come into the world? With this one precious life to live can we really say "no" to our heart?

We can ask for a vision of what following the heart would truly be like for us. What would we need to let go of right now, and what would we need to bring in? We can sit quietly in our heart vision and let it grow. We can understand the obstacles. And if the path isn't completely clear right now, it is coming towards us; the doors open in sequence. We can always open the first door and take the first leap. Our intention to know our path is the shining beacon that will guide us to it. We can be prepared, so that when we are out walking one day, and we meet Khidr, we will recognize him and we will know what we have to do.

Inner Work

"A world lives within you.
No one else can bring you news
Of this inner world."

John O'Donohue

Inner Work Overview

As personally responsible individuals, it is up to us to find the teachers, practices and teachings that will aid us in overcoming obstacles to our own spiritual growth. For each obstacle we meet, each dysfunction, each fear, there are practices and understandings that can aid us in dealing with and transcending these conditions. Some of these practices we can develop ourselves from our own intuition and inner knowledge; others are classic, passed down through time, to be learned from friends and teachers and books. We are always learning. We are always in process. We are always creating our life. We are always becoming. When we do this with clear intention, we gain wisdom.

The resources of our inner work keep us grounded and steady in the difficult times when our outer world is chaotic, and we feel discouraged. Our inner work suffuses our life with purpose. When we take personal responsibility in hand, we often make discoveries about ourselves that we have been avoiding. We come to see clearly the areas in which we need to work and, with practice, we develop the inner resources which help us to replace past ineffective and dysfunctional patterns with new skillful ways of being. Inner work here means the development of our inner world, the world of context and realization, the world of belief. Our entire life passes through this world, whether we acknowledge its existence or not.

The Secret Garden

Discovering the Real World

As our awareness expands through daily practice, we often discover that there are some definite changes we would like to make in our outer world; changes that we believe would make our lives more fluid, peaceful and easy. Simultaneously, we become aware of how difficult or impossible some of these changes seem. We might feel overwhelmed by the many challenges they seem to present and powerless to create solutions to our dilemmas. When this happens, we can console ourselves with two truths: first, we can't eat the whole elephant at one sitting, and, crazy as it may sound, it is often fruitless to focus directly on making these changes. If the patterns in our lives that are not working have not changed by now, then they are probably not going to respond to further worry or interventions. We can take a deep breath and let go of the frontal assaults, or the ten easy steps that seem to work for a short time before we drop right back into our old patterns.

Spiritual progress seldom originates in our outer world but comes from deep change in our inner world. Action that is born here can create true and lasting change. The name for this action is "inner work."

The elephant is our life, the big story, a piñata filled with many smaller stories. These stories sometimes consist of unpleasant emotions and ongoing unskillful and reactive behaviors. These are the pieces we want to change. They are the parts of our lives that don't seem to be working very well, and the parts that are so deeply submerged that we haven't discovered all of them yet. Awareness is like the blow from the bat that breaks open the piñata. Suddenly, a great deal is revealed. When we take personal responsibility for our part in all these stories, we reframe them as lighthouses that, in time, will guide us into perfect, waiting harbors in our inner world, harbors containing revelation. In this sense, our stories are not what is really happening. In themselves, they are not so important. Rather, they are messengers from, and reflections of, our inner world. In Caroline Myss's book *Anatomy of the Spirit*, she describes the journey into consciousness as learning to see the world in a symbolic rather than literal manner. Our stories and experiences are filled with symbolism and pattern. They are our perfect personal teaching tales, and each tale calls forth certain reactions and responses we can use to do our inner work. Some of the tales are deep, filled with layers of meaning, while others are less intense, easier to understand and comprehend. It is a wonderful "on board" system.

What can we learn about ourselves from our dysfunctional and unskillful behavior or our unpleasant reactions? What can we glean from the symbols in our stories? What can we learn from the ways we hold the world; from the relationship that isn't working, the money that isn't coming in, the discomfort we feel when someone speaks to us in a certain way or takes a certain action that affects us deeply? What can we learn from our unease and our disease? By now, we understand that these are all stories. Instead of trying to tackle all our problems at once we can choose to deal with them one at a time. Working with them one at a time is not just easier but more effective. Often one change in our inner world has a domino effect, collapsing other internal edifices of similar structure. We do not have to exhaust ourselves trying to change the world, or as the Taoists say, "trying to push the river." Inner work is exploring ways to voyage inward; discovering the causes shaping our outer reality and learning how to unearth and let go of beliefs that are not working. We learn how to dance and parry with fear until it becomes a powerful ally. We learn how to still the mind, to access equanimity until experiences float before us as patterns, as teachers.

Not all inner work is rational and direct. It is not all a head-trip or mental investigation. The results of reflective practices such as meditation, yoga or going on a retreat often have subtle, but powerful, experiential effects, changing the way we respond to life, rather than acting as specific rational interventions and fixes. Other practices such as conscious connected breathing (learning how to use the breath therapeutically) allow us to enter into the full and direct experience of our emotions, to experience ourselves more clearly and meet our demons face to face. Through inner work we discover the keys to true change.

Inner work takes time. To do this work it is necessary to develop patience with our selves and to quiet the anxiety that often attends our desire for change. It helps to go easy, to embrace the belief that there is plenty of time. This is not work that always provides instant gratification. We can be encouraged by the fact that opportunity for change occurs only when we are ready; so there is no need to rush. Much of inner being work is preparation, simply getting ready.

We sometimes use the exigencies of the so called "real" world as an excuse to avoid our inner work. What we usually mean is the tangible and material world, the outer world of oft-repeated and familiar cause and effect. But the real "real" world is actually our inner world. This is where all our reactions and responses to the outer world are born. These reactions and responses completely shape the story of our life. This actual real world is the sometimes strange, and often confused, world of our personal belief system, our deep core reality. Inner work is the exploration of this inner world, learning to understand how it creates the outer world and then, through discovery and practice, altering it, piece by piece, into a space of peaceful equanimity that first influences, and then becomes, our experience of the outer world.

As stated earlier, with awareness we often make the discovery that we are not manifesting what we truly desire. It is through inner work, exploring our inner world that we discover, often for the first time, that which is blocking us, as well as that which can remove the blockage. Sometimes the paths we have chosen so far don't work because they are so incompatible with our true nature that they never will. We try to fit the square peg in the round hole to satisfy others, often completely unaware that this is happening. We sometimes sabotage ourselves. Then we wonder why things are not working. This happens especially when we are securely buckled into our bumper car, when we encounter emotions and fears that are unpleasant and we deny them or placate them unskillfully. Many of us lose contact with our inner world. We forget who we really are, and lose touch with our fundamental selves. This is a lot like losing your compass in the wilderness; although you are free to wander about, it's much harder to find your way.

Many of us do not know our inner world exists and we simply act on autopilot whenever discomfort arises. Emotions pop up, which we do not bother to identify, and we desperately try to cope with them by acting out or running away. We have spent so much time avoiding the inner world that many of us have lost or forgotten the way in. The doorway is not very alluring, actually, it can be frightening to some extent, and, since it represents the unknown, we avoid it. Our inner world can be a scary place, filled with emotions and thoughts we would rather ignore or that we feel ashamed of having. Avoiding personal responsibility and staying lost in our stories keeps us outside of this zone. Being and acting unconscious is, after all, the norm. However, the moment we take up awareness and personal responsibility, living in ignorance of our inner world becomes unacceptable, if not impossible. And, almost immediately, we want to make changes in our life. We want to straighten things out. We have embarked on a journey into consciousness. It is difficult to turn back.

So how do we go about this exploration? The story, *The Secret Garden*, written in 1910 by Frances Hodgson Burnet, is a perfect allegory. When her parents die in an epidemic in India, a young, very self-centered child is sent to live on the remote moors of England with an uncle who she has never met. Life is boring at her uncle's huge and remote hundred-room mansion out on the windswept, treeless moors. She seldom sees her uncle. He travels a great deal, and they live far apart in the huge house. At night she hears crying, but the staff denies that there is anyone else living in the mansion. Maybe it is the wind.

Bored and lonely, she eventually takes to the outdoors. Her health, which had been sickly, improves as she experiences fresh air and exercise. Walking around the huge estate garden she comes to realize that there is an area that is walled in with no apparent entrance. She has heard of a secret garden on the property and has seen a bird flying over a wall to an area she determines must be the location of this garden. One day, she discovers an old buried key and she surmises that it must be the key to a long locked door in the garden wall. Her curiosity is piqued. She becomes determined to find the way in. She has also made another discovery; the crying she has heard is that of a boy, her cousin, in fact. He is more spoiled than she is and is also, it appears, a cripple.

Eventually, she finds the door, hidden behind tangled growth, and, using the key, she enters the secret garden. It has long been neglected, and is full of tangles and weeds, but she can tell that there are beautiful plants and rose bushes in all the weeds. She decides she is going to tackle its restoration and, to the surprise of the staff, she asks for a set of garden tools. She enlists a local boy who is deeply in touch with the natural world, and secretly they work in the garden. As the garden becomes more and more beautiful she physically blossoms. She loses her spoiled nature. She gets her cousin into a wheel chair and he comes to the secret garden to help too. In the end, many people are healed by the transformation of the secret garden and by her selfless work.

Like the forgotten secret garden in the story, if we have not tended our inner world when we find the key to the door (awareness and personal responsibility) and first enter, we often discover a tangled and confusing environment. The discovery can seem overwhelming; we can't weed the whole garden at once. We begin to improve the garden, area-by-area, weeding, cutting away old useless growth and then nourishing the plants we have freed from the weeds. Like the young girl, we seek help, usually from those familiar with the nature of the inner world. As we do the work on our inner garden we become more whole, freeing our divine nature and basic goodness from the weeds of neglect, applying the water of self-nourishment. Eventually we find ourselves in a completely different world than the one we always thought was the "real world." In this new world we walk with less fear and more freedom; we begin to benefit others by "demonstrating possibility," the possibility of change, the possibility for harmony, the possibility of a world of more compassion.

To do this work takes time, and our culture wants change to be instantaneous. We want the magic pill that cures all our problems in one swallow. But, our difficulties are often layered and, because it is necessary to remove one layer at a time, there is no way we can weed our entire inner garden in a flash. We need to be patient and practice self mercy when old, unskillful behaviors suddenly arise. Alas, there is no magic pill.

Like the girl in the secret garden, we discover that it is handy to have some tools, as well as helpers, for this work. We need to learn tools that can help us to map, and shape this realm. These tools will be the understanding and wisdom we gain and the practices that we pursue. Our helpers will be our teachers. To enlist these aids, we will need to develop discernment, the ability to choose the practices and teachers that will benefit our particular situation. We will always need to remember, that although revelations and teachers can be helpful, only we can do the work. It is also very helpful to understand what nourishes supports and makes our inner work possible.

Keeping the Garden Watered

Developing Deservingness

If feeling guilty or selfish about taking time for ourselves prevents us from focusing on our personal issues and nourishing ourselves, how will we ever do the inner work that is so critical to changing our outer world? In order to take this precious time, we need not only to appreciate its value, but also to believe in our own intrinsic worth. We are required to move beyond anything that is limiting our self-esteem, and to let go of self-judgment. Again, we need to embrace the view that we are, in essence, divine, or as the Buddhists say, that, like everyone else, we have "basic goodness" at our core. This is easy to say, but truly embracing this view is not always so easy. Nevertheless, once we realize and accept this truth, it will seem obvious. This acceptance is a very important sign of our spiritual progress. Like most things spiritual, the path to full self-acceptance is very personal and most often takes time and patience.

It helps to remember that we are a part of the whole, and not separate. And that our individual self is the part of the whole over which we have the most control and for which we are totally responsible. It is through our own lives that we can bring goodness and mercy into the world. It is helpful to remind ourselves of this good purpose when we begin to doubt our worth and the value of our contribution; when we begin to withdraw from our personal work. It is obvious that the work we do on ourselves, the positive changes we make, the slow but inevitable release of fear, benefit everyone around us and indeed, the whole world. Far from being selfish, our inner work is an important contribution to harmony. As an ancient Egyptian funerary poem simply states, "to live in harmony is a beginning." This was written 4000 years ago and yet our world still finds itself short of the beginning.

Inner harmony proceeds outer, and the harmony of individuals is required for the harmony of the whole. To change the world we must change ourselves. Each of us has plenty to do. And, we are each given our own perfect path.

How can we discover our basic goodness or essential perfection, our "OK"ness? One powerful way is to develop the practice of speaking to our self in the language of these true conditions. We nourish and enhance our self-esteem by talking to ourselves in a loving and supporting manner, replacing the voice of the inner judge, the "merciless rider", with the voice of the heart, the voice of wisdom and compassion. For many of us this is like learning a new language. We already understand that mercy is the antidote to judgment and self-judgment. When we view our actions with mercy, we simultaneously let go of low self-esteem because compassion for our self is one of the highest forms of self-honoring. By speaking kindly to ourselves and holding ourselves gently, we acknowledge that we are worthy. Acknowledging our worthiness actually brings it forth. It grows, not as an arrogant or conceited condition, but into powerful self-acceptance. The good news is that, as we develop true compassion for ourselves, we are developing it simultaneously for others. We begin to see our condition reflected in the world around us. Seeing our similarity keeps us humble and connected as we begin to see how we are essentially one.

Self mercy is a completely conscious inner gesture, a sacred practice. When we become aware of the voice of self-judgment we consciously choose a different voice, a voice that is patient, kind and understanding. This is a literal choice that soon becomes a wonderful habit. We repeat the gesture over and over until it becomes second nature. So, when we hear the voices of guilt and shame and self judgment, we don't dwell on them by going into the stories that they are sure to present: "You did it again. I'm so stupid." "What will so and so think?" or similar old stories that arise like weeds. Instead, we immediately change to the kinder voice in our head that says things like "I see that my action was unskillful, but it does not mean I am a bad person; I know that at heart I am a good person. I can do my inner work and make discovery about this kind of unskillful behavior so that I change it; I can learn to manifest my loving nature more." These phrases are examples. We can choose whatever kind, merciful and supportive statements we wish. Learning to speak kindly to our selves is an extremely rewarding practice that reduces the stress caused by self-judgment while creating a safe and nurturing inner being to replace our self-judge. Without awareness, specifically the awareness that we are judging ourselves, the rewards of this practice would never be ours.

If we doubt that the foundation for inner work is compassion for self and self-honoring behavior, we need only remind ourselves that the opposite approach, feeling guilty or judging ourselves has never really worked. When we hold ourselves more lightly and regard our actions with more humor and compassion, we experience our difficulties and ourselves in new ways. Much that has been hidden begins to surface, areas that we felt unsafe to consider, or that we have always judged begin to reveal their true nature. They reveal the fear(s) that feed them so that, finally, we are able to see what is really happening underneath all of our awkward and unskillful behaviors. These areas become teachers and allies. To go back to a garden metaphor, the ground of compassion is the place where the seeds of change find nourishment, not in the dry, hard soil of self-judgment, personal rules and self-regulations.

Some of us are still under the illusion that taking care of ourselves is selfish and somehow non-caring of others. We have been brought up to believe that doing for others is more important than doing for ourselves; that these actions are mutually exclusive. We may have been taught that we are supposed to sacrifice ourselves for the greater good. Many of us spend a great deal of time volunteering in so-called "selfless" endeavors. This is certainly appropriate diction because the true self is not always present for our service work. Instead, the persona of a noble contributor is doing the work. There is nothing bad about this. Being kind and considerate of others is a good thing. It is civility. When this kindness and consideration is rooted in compassion, rather than in a sense of duty or social responsibility, it is more authentic. It can be sustained in more adversarial conditions. It is rooted in the natural and deep love that comes from the experience of self-mercy. It is not an idea but a reality. In our family we changed a traditional phrase in our mealtime grace from "make us ever mindful of the needs of others" to "make us ever mindful of the needs of others and ourselves."

To believe that helping others in this world precludes self-nourishing behavior is a common misconception that leaves a trail of burned out caregivers in its wake. Compassion is the deep understanding that we are all alike and all equally worthy of love. If we do not spend time discovering who we are and understanding and accepting our own fears, how can we do this with others? If we are not able to nourish ourselves, we cannot nourish others deeply. Through compassion we experience the wisdom that allows us to be at ease in difficult or unusual surroundings, and we are able to demonstrate the "field of possibility" for others.

Many of us, including many teachers and healers, are trapped in what is known as "the savior mentality." This condition is often a sign that we may not be taking care of ourselves. When we take up the role of savior, we are busy working to save others, to fix things, to assert our view, sometimes to change a situation in order to make ourselves more comfortable by being in control. To make this dynamic more difficult, there are many who want to be saved, who want someone to tell them what to do, who are definitely not interested in taking up the work of personal responsibility. For every savior there are usually many "savees".

Often, when we are trying to be the savior, we have forgotten, or have not yet personally experienced the truth that the world is evolving perfectly, that the big plan is good, that we are all safe. When we doubt our own safety, we often project our doubt on the world by trying to help others. Or, when we see others in a condition we fear, we try to save them. So, unfortunately, very often when we are busy being the savior, we are not experiencing our own safety, rather we are subtly pandering to our own fear. Ironically, although we are making a loving gesture, we are operating out of fear. Saving others can become a form of the "anguished imperative" to reshape and subtly control the world in a way that alleviates our own fear. As we accept the world just the way it is and our place in it, and, as we manifest compassion for ourselves, we are simultaneously released from this "anguished imperative." We let

154

things simply be the way they are, and we demonstrate that this is fine. We hold the safe space.

Discovering our own safety is one of the great rewards of inner work and, with this discovery, we can let go of the need to fix everything, a major energy drain for many of us. This is a huge relief.

The belief that self nourishment is selfish is also based on the belief that there is not enough love to go around, not enough for others and ourselves at the same time, and yet nowhere can we find proof of this. Who says so? Do we doubt the size and scope of love itself? We remember Rajneesh's statement that, "the mind can only doubt and the heart can only believe," and we can see that, when it comes to self-nourishment, the mind is definitely doing the doubting. If we remember to ask the question "what does love say now" we will always find our heart ready to appreciate us. We are as worthy of love as everyone else in the world.

It is important to remember that the self-love we are talking about here is not a form of self-admiration. It is not self-aggrandizing, or self-indulgent. It is not narcissistic. It is self-accepting, self-appreciating, and self-nurturing. It is quiet and not pretentious or even obvious, yet it is purposeful and conscious. It is the same love we are learning to share with others.

Often people object when we take actions for our own benefit because we are moving away from their beliefs. They can become upset when the synchronous nature of our former mutual behavior is terminated or disturbed. They feel disoriented as we change any behavior pattern they have come to expect from us. Sometimes we have to be courageous in order to break away from old patterns that others use to make sense of their world. Some folks will drop away. When we replace these old patterns with new and more powerful ways of being that include, for instance, self nurturing, we are creating a new field of possibility, and we attract new friends and companions who are sympathetic to our work. We are offering others a view of a deeper spiritual reality.

There is a very concrete action that accelerates our manifestation of love and compassion for ourselves, and helps us discover our own safety. It is one of those wonderful things we often don't see that are right in front of us. In the next section we talk about action, the fourth component of learning what our lives are trying to teach us, but because awareness, personal responsibility, inner work and action are so woven together we need to jump ahead into action for a minute. As we shall discover, in order to manifest the conclusions and solutions of our inner work, we have to take a concrete action. One important action that is very necessary and rewarding is taking time for ourselves. This can be difficult at first, especially if we are not used to it.

Like most important or vital actions in our lives, the moment we decide to take time for ourselves we will encounter what Gurujeiff called the "second force." Almost immediately a second force will appear to test our resolve. Since inner work often requires a degree of self-time, and, because we have been taught that this is selfish, it is not unusual for contrary demands to arise whenever we decide to experience self-time. These demands usually seem very important, in fact equal to or more important than our self-time. Their importance will be supported and confirmed by our peers. Examples of the second force, in this case, are: time with our spouse or kids; time doing some form of volunteer work; time hanging out with our friends; or extra time at work. However, if we follow the second force and relinquish our self-time to these sensible, acceptable demands, we will never be able to achieve what is possibly the most important work of our own life; the work on our inner world. Therefore, we sometimes have to be courageous in order to make the difficult choice to take time for ourselves. Because this is not a common practice in our world, we will usually meet with resistance. But, each time we make the choice, we discover the rich rewards of self-time; the deepening experience of our self and clearer understanding of our place in the world, and the choice for self time becomes easier.

In order to create self-time, willpower is usually required. For many years when I took my personal retreat, Babbie used to grumble and tell me why I should not go "this year." There was always something of seemingly equal importance, like a kid's special game, an illness, or a long delayed task. I know that she was also motivated to curtail my self-time because she felt uncomfortable with me being away for a week. Even with my knowledge of the second force, and the knowledge that my time away benefited her as well as myself, it was always hard to resist her. I love hanging out with her more than anything else, so her entreaties and logical arguments became a powerful second force. Yet I went, and I was always rewarded with new perspectives and the deep inner joy that comes from being by oneself, especially in nature. In my retreats I renewed and deepened my connection with spirit. I battled with my demons and hung out with my angels. The action of taking time for myself fully revealed to me the importance of self-nourishment. Without this time, I would find myself running on half filled or empty batteries.

Sometimes, again because we believe that self-nourishing behavior is somehow selfish, we find that it is often easier to love and appreciate others more than ourselves. In this regard it is useful to learn how to receive thanks and praise. When we throw kind remarks off with comments like "oh you look nice too," or "not really," or "it was nothing," or "so and so really did all the work," we are missing a good opportunity to nourish ourselves and exercise self esteem. Don and Martha taught Babbie and me a little consciousness tool they call "receiving practice" that helped us to learn to accept our own beauty and goodness and to nourish ourselves. Whenever one of us avoided or rejected a compliment, the person giving the compliment would say, "receiving practice" and we would stop and consciously let the compliment sink in rather than throwing it away; then we would *truly* thank the other person. Taking this conscious action also demonstrated how unkind we often were to ourselves. After doing this for a while we found that receiving compliments with grace became the norm, so that, now when we receive compliments from anyone, we automatically let the compliment in and give thanks. This is not just a good practice for building worthiness; it is a gracious practice as well, returning thanks for kindness. We are not talking about receiving flattery, which is a deliberate attempt at manipulation, but receiving genuine appreciation.

Far from being a selfish thing, the act of self-nourishment, of self-discovery and self-mercy is the great beginning of compassion and unconditional love. We are clearing away the ego's carefully fabricated blockages. We are tending and watering the garden. We are entering a new realm in which love is allowed to flourish, and grow.

The Power of Vision

When we follow the way of the visionary
we are able to make the truth visible.

Angeles Arrien *The Four Fold Way*

Another way we can nourish our garden is by enlisting vision. Doing vision work, with David Gershon and Gail Straub at the Pathworks Center in the Catskills one year, impressed upon me the power and importance of creating our lives from vision. Not having a positive vision for our lives, a guiding inspiration, is one of the reasons so many of us feel lost in the world, ungrounded and disconnected from meaning, from our truth. Gail and David had a very integrated vision, a part of which was spreading their work, and at the facilitators' workshop, they taught their entire vision workshop to the participants.

Once David had a vision of people moving the Olympic torch around the world and he made it happen. The torch began at the UN and ended there. It was a great feat of organization and hard work. He was completely driven by his vision of bringing many different people around the world together in a joint positive outcome that celebrated humanity.

Working at the Omega Institute, I was impressed by the vision of the founders and their allies: Stefan Rechtschaffen, and Elizabeth Lessor, and major contributors such as Ram Dass, Tom Valenti, Skip Baccus, and Garret and Elizabeth Sarley. Their vision and hard work continues to attract thousands of people. The vision of Amrit Desai created Kirpalu, a well known yoga and personal discovery center in western Massachusetts. The bible says, "Where there is no vision, the people perish."

The lack of vision seems to be a current human condition. According to eastern religions, we live in the age of Kali Yuga, sometimes referred to as the "iron age." This is a time of strife, discord, and contention. Change is hard or sluggish. We react to violence with violent solutions, creating more violence, to poverty with scarcity thinking and austerity measures causing more poverty. We try to "fix" problems with old tools, rather than envisioning a new model and tapping into our creativity. Thus, we keep using the same solutions over and over. When a leader has even a small vision many people immediately react with interest and support. We are starving for vision as we beat against the wall of the status quo with the same old battering rams.

It is amazing how incomplete and shallow our vision for ourselves can become when we fail to ask or answer one very important question. "What do I really want in this life?" The truth is that many of us lack a clear vision for ourselves; we are not in touch with what we really desire, what is deeply satisfying. If we sit down and really think about this, we often discover that what we really want it is not what we usually think we want, or that which we have simply accepted. If we ask most people what it is they really want in life they will often answer with something material or a changed outer condition: "If I had a little more money; something for the kids; if we could just buy a new place; if so and so would just change their behavior." We all share these kinds of desire. I call it "longing for the one thing." We focus on "one thing" that we are sure will change our life or make us happy. We say to ourselves "If I just had that I would be happy." But we usually discover, when we acquire or achieve the one thing, it doesn't do the trick. Longing for something different should not be confused with having vision. David taught that once we have created a clear vision we do not need to dwell on it constantly, rather trust that it will occur. We let go of the anguished imperative that it must happen.

The concept of "the perfect stranger" is an example of a misleading vision. Many of us, when we grow tired of our primary relationship, when we see it has a tiring pattern of constant unpleasantness, or when it seems to have lost passion, begin imagining the perfect stranger, someone we will meet who will sweep us back into love and intimacy. Rather than working on our current relationship, taking responsibility and learning how to deepen and revitalize it, we fantasize about a person with whom we will be compatible forever. The perfect stranger will attend to our every need, never complaining. They will understand us perfectly. Some people try to find this person over and over, having affairs, getting divorced, always searching for a person who doesn't exist.

We waste much energy longing for the one thing when often what we really want is something completely different. Going out into a more perfect future takes us out of the present, and, when we leave the present, we leave all opportunity to find what we really want, right where it is, in the moment. What we truly desire is an inner state not an outer condition.

I have often done "the one thing" vision of life, fantasizing about something that I am convinced is imperative for my happiness. This seems harmless enough, but, when I see myself doing it often, and I apply some awareness, it doesn't take me long to realize that I am feeling discontent in the present for some reason. When we become conscious that we are longing for the one thing, like the perfect stranger, we can turn this awareness into the discovery about what is bothering us *right now*. While the one thing changes from time to time, it is the intensity of longing for it that demonstrates our desire to leave the present. We can ask ourselves, "What's really going on?" The reality is that if we cannot experience equanimity and accept our condition in this moment, chances are that we will experience the same discomfort in some imaginary future. Everything important is happening right now. The work is now. We often lean heavily into the future at the expense of the one and only present.

There is an inner practice we can implement when we become conscious that we are longing for the one thing. This practice helps us to remember what it is we really long for and not confuse ourselves with the distracting symbols we have chosen to represent it. It helps keep our vision clear. We do this in order to remind ourselves of the deeper values that underlie our surface obsessions. When we experience "longing for the one thing" we envision our desire fulfilled; then we ask, "And then what?" or "What will I feel then?" Often the mind comes up with another desire very quickly and when we envision it fulfilled, we ask the question again "And then what?" or "How will we feel then?" Pretty soon we see the nature of our desire, how one desire leads to another, and, as we drill down through our superficial desires, we get closer and closer to the real treasure. What we discover is that what we really want is inner peace. We want to be loved and accepted for who we are right now, with all our bumps and bruises, our anger, our unskillful behavior. We want to experience compassion and the dissolution of judgment. We want to feel the release of a subtle, ever present tension. We want to experience understanding. What we want is to be centered, calm, and compassionate. We want less fear in our lives and to experience equanimity in the face of any difficulty. Perhaps we cannot define it exactly, but we also want to be in connection with spirit. We want the joy and happiness that these things bring.

We are the only person who can provide all these core pieces for ourselves. Sometimes we are so far away from our core values that we have forgotten what they feel like and how good life can be. We find ourselves viewing everything with caution, experiencing our life as a continual task of risk avoidance and we take the hand of cynicism easily. We are a long way from our center, from spirit, from the place where the real action happens. But, when we drill down through our material desires, the behavioral changes we seek in others, or our daydreams about the future, we discover that what we truly want is not material at all, and that it is something we can only find in the present moment. It is actually a relief to realize that what we truly deeply desire can't be purchased and is not provided by others. Once we realize that "the one thing" actually represents an inner state, an emotion or feeling, that outer symbols are not a substitute for inner conditions, we can begin the rewarding work of bringing these emotions and inner conditions into our lives.

It is not just a rewarding practice to envision ourselves actually experiencing the inner state that we truly want. The essence of vision is feeling. In other words we need to bring in the feeling and the emotional tone of a fulfilled vision in order to allow our vision to generate reality. Accessing these feelings is an important way vision can sustain us. It is powerful. Using vision we can move towards that which we desire rather than away from that which we do not desire. Moving towards a positive objective is more inspiring and easier to sustain than moving away from a negative state. Thus creating a sustaining and deep vision of ourselves experiencing the states we truly desire is the wise beginning of our inner work.

Because the deep desire in our inner world for peace and love often conflicts with the reality of our outer world, we live in the tension between the two. If we take the time to clear the mind and breathe deeply for a while, we can actually feel the release of this tension in our bodies. In meditation the release is even more profound. This tension also results from our constant worry about the future and the past; our absorption in our own stories and those of others, and the dreadful feeling that things are never quite right. A strong inner vision of peace and personal safety helps calm, often-imaginary, inner storms.

How powerful are the stories that take us out of our inner guiding world? One interesting statistic concerns top executives who work in big corporations. A large percentage of these people die within two years of retirement. Retirement for them turns into a death sentence. They become so lost in the story of their position, so identified with their role, that, when it ends, they actually die shortly thereafter. Perhaps if they had learned to meditate, bringing themselves into present time and had developed a rich inner life, they might have been able to transition into another lifestyle rather than dying. These practices may have sustained them during and after all the very important hustle and bustle was over.

Love and compassion are the treasure the wise seek to bring into their lives and the world about them. All the treasure we seek through the misleading material symbols of happiness in the outer world already lie within. If we spend time learning how to manifest them in inner gesture we will see them come to expression in our outer world. If we wait for everyone else or everything else to change, we will never experience our own evolution. Taking time to envision ourselves, as we truly desire to be, and referencing that vision, often helps us to keep on track when we feel frustrated by the world around us. It keeps us in touch with what has real meaning in our lives. Our vision can be grounded in daily spiritual reading, sitting practice, and hanging out with like-minded people.

We will have to learn how to welcome change if we want to do inner work. This is a big one. The Buddha taught that change or impermanence is the only permanent condition since it is obvious that everything is constantly changing. Suffering occurs when we try to resist this truth and become attached to rigid ideas and material things including the idea of a separate self. There is nothing wrong with having things; it is the attachment to things that causes our suffering, our unhappiness, as we try to make the impermanent permanent, a hopeless task. Once we become aware that our real goal is inner peace and harmony, there is no need to go on trying to fill this longing with outer goods. We can find the core conditions we seek, the life we envision, right at home through our inner work. When our inner world is harmonious, we live in harmony with our outer world. What we need comes to us as it does for the lazy mystics in Rumi's poem *The Night Air*.

> *"Mystics are experts in laziness. They rely on it,*
> *because they continually see God working all around them.*
> *The harvest keeps coming in yet they*
> *never even did the plowing!"*[28]

They are lazy because their inner connection to God, and harmony, is paramount. Lazy means that they are not engaged in traditional striving. They see the harmony, the elegant patterning. Their trust is deep and the harvest keeps coming in!

One of the realms of existence described in Tibetan Buddhism is called the hungry ghost realm. The inhabitants of this realm have tiny mouths and huge stomachs. They can never get enough to eat. They are symbolic of our time. We have embraced the suffering of the hungry ghosts. It is the ocean we swim in, our materialistic society. Shopping, like alcohol, is a sanctioned addiction and, like other addictions, it is in large part a deliberate distraction from our discontent, the very place where the clues and solutions for experiencing more equanimity and inner peace lie. In order to stay happy we have to keep buying new things. We have to feed our habit. Over a surprisingly short time, each new thing becomes old,

---

[28] Barks, Coleman with Moyne, John, *The Essential Rumi*. Castle Books 1997, page 30

loses its initial appeal and we need another buying fix. Some indigenous tribes had a ceremony that reminded them of how unimportant the acquisition of materials goods was. In these "potlatch" ceremonies a man would give away all his processions. He would set everything out and other tribe members could come and choose what they wanted. He would then acquire what he needed at other potlatch ceremonies. In this way, tribal members did not become too attached to the idea of personal processions, and yet they always had what they needed.

It helps to carefully and honestly review what we have been seeking in the life we have chosen; to look and see how fear has shaped our life and to envision something more deeply satisfying. Why do we have the job we have? Why do we live where we live? Why have we always done what we do? Many people who ask themselves, "Is this the life I really want?" sometimes find that it isn't. Creating a vision of a different life, more satisfying and more true to our inner values is the first step in moving toward that different reality. When we feel trapped in our life, we are often bereft of any vision for ourselves.

The good news is that the work of changing the inner world, of improving our psycho-emotional condition, does not rely on changing outer conditions first. This is a very popular recurring myth that is a big part of our socio-economic myth. Rather than trying to change outer conditions we can view them as reflections of an inner world that is not fully accepting of life, just the way it is, right now. When our inner world is accepting of life the way it is right now, it can accept the moments that seem risky; dangerous; uncomfortable and, instead of avoiding our own becoming, we let it transpire. We develop the flexibility that allows us to gracefully make changes in our outer world.

In order to manifest mercy for others and ourselves, it is helpful to take the Buddhist notion that unskillful action or unwise livelihood is simply the result of ignorance. Another way of saying this is that millions of us don't know anything else but the life we are living. We hurt others; we create war and suffering because we don't know any better. We believe that all the answers lie in the world around us, and, that by changing that world and controlling it, by shaping it into what we want, we will achieve happiness and peace.

That this has never worked is utterly obvious, but what do we do instead? We develop awareness; we take personal responsibility for everything in our personal world; we do our inner work, and we take new and more skillful action.

When we take up personal responsibility rather than blaming and judging, and then begin to explore our inner world, we will most likely encounter the question, "What do I do now?" The tools we have long used, our coping mechanisms, are of no use in this arena. Often they were created to avoid our inner world and the type of practices we will be taking up. One of the answers to this dilemma is to become educated in new ways of being and acting, to discover applicable perennial wisdom, and to take up practices that facilitate realization and understanding. To do these things it is important to develop our discernment, the ability to separate the true from the false, in teachers and in teachings.

Dissolving Boulders
Developing Discernment

With awareness and personal responsibility we begin to have a much more accurate and unfiltered picture of what is shaping our life experience. However, these two strategies, in themselves, do not fully create change. In fact, without inner work and action, they might even create frustration. If we want change, we will need to do some inner work, exploring of our inner world in order to discover what beliefs are actually creating our present outer world. A major goal of inner work is changing, at a deep level, the beliefs that shape our life. It is acknowledging the gestures and actions we take within ourselves that are often hidden from others. It is about changing our view. Mapping and understanding our inner world, and our beliefs and fears, is an on-going task in our spiritual evolution.

When we use the four strategies in a linear manner, we arrive at inner work after we have become aware of and have taken personal responsibility for that which angers, disturbs, confuses, frightens, saddens or hurts us; anything that effects our serenity. By being aware of what is happening, and taking responsibility for our reactions and feelings, we often discover that there are more obstacles to inner peace than we might have suspected. Fully acknowledging that these are "our" obstacles, we use inner work to discover ways to eliminate, change or replace them. We then take outer action based on these changes. The result is that, over time, we experience a gradual transition into a personal world containing less fear and an expanding equanimity.

Once, in a channeling session, Djwal Khul, the entity known as "The Tibetan" said, "As you travel down the path you will encounter boulders that block your way. You can go around or over the boulder, many people do. But the next time you come down the path the boulder will still be there." A friend of mine when hearing this story recounted an actual experience he had while building a road on the side of a steep hill. A massive boulder could not be moved because it was too big. It could not be broken into smaller pieces due to dynamite laws. It was in the middle of the planned and approved road. No one could figure out what to do. Finally, it was decided to dig a huge hole in the road and push the boulder into it with backhoes. This was done, and then the boulder was covered over with dirt and the road continued. "We got rid of the boulder," he smirked, relieved and proud. But in reality, it was still there, waiting for erosion to reveal it again. Sure enough, it arose in the next torrential rain.

While we all have strategies that can take us around the boulders or bury them, it is much more effective to dissolve them. Inner work is the place where this happens. It is here that we break up the boulders, our rigidly held beliefs, and deal with our unacknowledged fears so that they we can move on. As long as we use avoidance strategies and coping mechanisms, we are going to feel either fear or emotional discomfort when we come down the path and encounter a familiar old boulder.

There are many paths and systems for doing inner work, for breaking up the boulders, for clearly identifying and dealing with our inner demons and for creating changes. We might decide that one great path has everything for us, or we might create an eclectic mix of practices depending on our temperament. No matter what course we choose, it is helpful to ask, "What is it I am really seeking?" Using this question we can create a more expansive and inspiring vision for ourselves. As we learned from Mojud, this vision comes from the heart. We can ask this question and simply wait. We will always receive an answer. This question helps to shape our search and the answer helps with our discernment, a critical facility we need to develop or acknowledge. When we are looking for teachers, or answers, we will need this discernment to keep us on the right track. A good teacher or guru can teach us many things, but we can also give away our power to them, rather than maintaining personal responsibility for our lives. Giving away our power to anyone or anything can be tricky and even dangerous. This is what the hundreds of people at Jonestown did when they committed mass suicide. Their teacher instructed them to give up the precious gift of life and they did so. The followers desperately wanted to believe his message and to believe that they were making the right move in following him. They gave away their power to him. There are ministers and teachers who use punishment, recrimination and shame to keep followers in line. Others condone or practice inappropriate sexual acts. Others are in it for the money. Without discernment we can become sucked into one of these paths and, rather than dissolving our obstacles, we allow others to use them to manipulate us. Perhaps we are lonely, and we are seeking fellowship, or we just want to be with a focused group. Webs await us. If we are not conscious of our own inner motivation we can be swept away. Pinocchio's trip to Pleasure Island is a classic example of this phenomenon. If we are not discerning, we too can be turned into donkeys.

The question never actually is, "who" we are seeking. It is always "what." No matter how famous or grand the teacher, no matter what we have heard about them, we need to focus on the teaching. It is our responsibility to determine how much fear is present in the teaching, to know our own motivation well, to stay in touch with the vision emanating from our heart. Is the teaching consistent with our vision? We need to remember that all teachers, even the most sublime, are actually only messengers. We have to be very discerning and mature if we end up involved in a group that is evolving into a cult of personality. This can occur even without the intention of the teacher. We will be required to separate the true from the false. We will have to be careful about giving away our power. Although there are organizations and teachers who ask us to give away our power, we are always at choice, regardless of the path we choose. Even priests can choose to leave the priesthood and monks and nuns can walk away from their orders. It is our life. Choice is the gift and the challenge.

Paths that require us to give up everything to a church, or to a master or deity, often teach that, in return, that figure will take care of us. "Wouldn't this be nice," we say, "the Master will make all my choices for me." We throw away personal responsibility. "Look at all the others doing it," we might say. A comfortable cocoon is formed. All we have to do is behave and think as we are told, and we will experience approval. We may gain a measure of spiritual pride and preen ourselves with our goodness. Chogyum Trungpa had a phrase for this behavior. He called it "spiritual materialism." Ironically, if a teacher is not tasking us appropriately, if we are just following certain rules, our spiritual growth dries up.

When we have chosen a wise and good teacher we may be inspired, at some point, to move on, to resume our individual path. "Killing the guru," is an old phrase that means once we have received the teaching, we let go of our reliance on the teacher. Until we take personal action with what we have learned from our teachers, the information is only theoretical. We kill the guru and go our own way. This can be difficult if we have fallen in love with the teacher, or have become obsessed with the teachings. It does not mean we throw away the teachings we find useful and truthful. It means we have to get out in the world and take action based on what we have learned without leaning on the teacher.

Intuition is a very important part of discernment. Many of us have not developed our intuitive nature, or we don't trust it, and yet intuition is often a better guide than knowledge. Rumi taught that we must consult the heart, that which is inside us, not outside, in order to discern the truth. When something doesn't feel right, chances are something isn't right, at least not right for us. Of course we might encounter something disturbing that we need to work on personally, but we can also come across teaching and actions that simply do not jive with our truth, such as a teacher who indulges in judgment or non-loving behavior. If this is an ongoing pattern with this teacher or path we may want to move on, regardless of what others are doing.

An intuition can arise very quickly, and so it is often overlooked or ignored in our risk adverse, careful, analytical, and very rational world. Sometimes intuition can seem irrational. The heart operates in a different fashion from the brain. It communicates with the outside world in an immediate manner. Stephen Buhner in the preface to his book *Sacred Plant Medicine* states: "When the electromagnetic field of the heart entrains with the electromagnetic field of any other organism, whether human, animal, or plant, there is a rapid download of information from one organism to another. Although this information download is in a language of its own, it is not in words. In one sense, the transfer of information can be thought of as a direct conveyance of meaning without having to use words. This information, as researchers have found, flows through the heart first, and is then routed to the brain through direct heart/brain connections for further processing. In order to maintain the information, we convert it into usable form. A translation process occurs, much like the one our radio receivers provide when they convert radio waves into music. However, in human beings the process is much more complex. From its store of sensory data, memories, experiences and knowledge, the brain constructs a gestalt of the information flow. Thus the translation can appear in many forms: a series of visions, sounds, images, feeling, tastes, words, or smells. Often the form in which the translation emerges is shaped by the culture in which the individual person was raised. The important thing is, again, not the form that these translations take, but the meanings within them." He later states, "In the end, what becomes clear, when we reclaim the heart as an organ of perception and cognition, is that we have been colonized by a particular kind of thinking. And this particular kind of thinking, naturally engendered when we locate consciousness in the brain, reduces our expression of perception and thought."[29] If this is true we need to use and trust our heart impulses more, and be open to more input than our rational constructions. Listening to our intuition is a good way of doing this, and it is especially important and helpful when working with other humans, and when we are choosing teachers.

When we go on the quest for the truth, for a fuller and more satisfying life and we encounter new teachers and teachings, we need to apply as a litmus test the question, "what do I really want or need and will this work bring me toward it?" We can ask this question over and over. While some paths may be great for others, they may not really suit us or pass our personal litmus test. Since many teachers and their students are enamored with their particular path, there is sometimes pressure, subtle or gross, brought on the

---

[29] Buhner, Stephen Harrod. *Sacred Plant Medicine*. Bear and Company, 2006, Page xx.

new seeker to take up the "one" path. In order to break up our boulders we are required to develop discernment about what tools work best for us, and to check regularly to see if they still do.

One of the best ways of developing discernment is by experiencing different teachers and teachings. While we may find one path that is especially useful and attractive, there may be other teachings and practices from another path that can also be helpful. For this reason, any path that says it is "the only path" limits our experience, spiritual flexibility and clouds our discernment. If, after wandering the workshops of the world and experiencing many teachings, we find a path that works for us, we will know that our choice is grounded in our broader experience.

In order to develop discernment, it helps to be open to and respectful of different teachings. If we are too skeptical or too guarded we may miss an important piece of wisdom or experience. We may be in fear and not willing to jump off the cliff. We will probably have to jump off a few times to see if a path is right for us. In other words, we will have to trust teachers and teachings in areas in which we have not had experience. However, once we have jumped we can review our experience and apply the litmus test. Is this helping me? Is this true for me? Am I certain this is what I need?

To develop discernment we have to become good listeners. If we feel the need to be right, if we want to jump in with our opinion all the time, if we find ourselves constantly challenging a teaching, then we may not learn much. On the other hand, we need to ask good questions from time to time. It is not a good idea to accept a teaching blindly.

As a workshop leader I have encountered many skeptics. Sometimes they can be very disruptive, and deliberately so, but skeptics often ask very important questions that allow me to see whether I am on or off the right track. Their questions sometimes show me areas that I need to enhance or change. Skeptics often ask questions that others are afraid to ask. When I answer these questions they often benefit the entire group. Sometimes, when doubters gain understanding about the work being presented, they become the strongest advocates of the work. Within groups, everyone has a different type and style of offering. If another participant is disruptive and it annoys us, we can always go to awareness and take personal responsibility for our annoyance. Who knows what we will discover? In any case, wisdom arrives in many forms. The court jester often brought the greatest wisdom to the court through silly rhyme and indirect accusations. Wisdom can arise anywhere and anytime. We have to be present and ready for it. We can also choose to challenge other's ideas with our own.

Some of us keep jumping from workshop to workshop, from teacher to teacher, like rabbits. We try out new ideas like sampling different candies and then, when the more difficult work begins, move onto another path. It is important to experience different teachers; it enhances our discernment and often increases our understanding by offering new and different perspectives. However, this kind of jumping around can also be an escape from doing our inner work. We can get so absorbed in new ideas that we fail to go inside where the work is really needed.

The Omega Institute offers over 300 workshops in the spring, summer and fall on their campus in Rhinebeck New York. It is a place where one can get a lick of many spiritual and personal growth ice cream cones. Omega has a wonderful bookstore, filled with every kind of book about every kind of psycho-spiritual or metaphysical path you could desire. In the bookstore some people buy a stack of books one day and are back the next day for another. The knowledge they are buying can be so dense that to fully understand and integrate it would take years. What is it they really want? They may want what we all desire every now and then, the easy ride out of pain or suffering or fear through some teacher's special system or a new interpretation of a religion. But alas, this seldom happens.

Many of our fear patterns are very deep and will not respond to superficial understanding or manipulation. To deal with our boulders we often have to travel deep inside and explore what can sometimes be a scary inner world. Rather than running away we need to move towards our deep, and often misunderstood, fears. Through the realizations we encounter by going deep we gain wisdom, something more than knowledge, about our condition. This wisdom opens up new possibilities and solutions that seem to suddenly and magically appear. Taking action on these answers alters our outer world, dissolves the boulders in our path, one by one. The measure of our evolution is what happens on each trip down the old path. We may suddenly notice that we are not reacting to an event in the same frightened or emotional manner as before. For instance, we are in presence of something that used to cause us immediate fear and we no longer have that reaction. This is one way we are able to see and feel our emotional and spiritual progress clearly.

There are many spiritual and psycho-spiritual paths, and therefore many ways of doing our inner work. As we seek guidance, we need to be aware that there is no "right" way. Remember the expression "being right isn't it!" There are many adaptations of teachings and many teachers, some famous and others not. Fame or glamour can, in fact, be a big distraction. No one way is right. The idea that only one way is correct is promoted by some organizations and religions, but this often ends in separation and judgment, the antithesis of wholeness and the holy. Often when we choose to be followers of the "one path" we share a false sense of security derived from our like-minded attitudes, and our conviction of our particular "rightness." This sense of security, based on having all the answers, attracts us when we are spiritually lazy and a bit too eager to give away our power to an authority figure or sect.

Any organization or religion that is preaching difference and separation is feeding on fear. Spirituality is about union, about our commonality, about the whole, about the truly holy, about learning to remove the obstacles to loving others, rather than encouraging us to see others as different, as inferior, as misguided somehow. I believe that inclusion is the most basic test of any path. How inclusive is the teacher, are the teachings? Because spirituality is about letting others find their own paths, we are encouraged to make room in our hearts for those on other paths, including those who are experiencing "the only way" and "being right." Again, rather than proselytizing our spiritual beliefs, we can live them in order to demonstrate the possibility of living on earth open heartedly. And, when our beliefs don't work we will get feedback!

Another idea that is helpful is "don't throw out the good with the bad." There are many teachers with whom we can disagree about some of their work and embrace other parts as wise. There are many teachers whose personal life seems inconsistent with what we

174

feel a spiritual teacher's should be like. Rajneesh, the "golden guru," is a perfect example. He was a brilliant teacher, although his own behavior and personal life were sometimes bizarre. In outward appearance he was a materialist. Remember his twenty or thirty Rolls Royces, his jet, his estates around the world? He was reputed to have had odd sexual appetites. These things did not deter from much of his teaching. Many people learned a great deal from him. If we required him to be a saint, we would have thrown the baby out with the bath water. We will need discernment to see what part of a teacher's message is self serving and what is true wisdom. Chogym Trungpa, was a brilliant Tibetan Buddhist teacher, and was very instrumental in bringing Tibetan Buddhism to western awareness. His books are extraordinary. The fact the he was an alcoholic did not seem to affect his teachings. In the past I used to love to listen to Ram Dass's talks. In the old days he was usually stoned whenever he spoke in public. The information he put forth, however, and his sense of irony and humor, were marvelous. And so it goes. With discernment we learn to take what seems right for us and leave what doesn't without judgment. Rather than throwing out a whole teaching because we don't like the teacher or his organization, we can harvest the pearls. There is no real rule that says we must embrace the whole teaching, although sometimes needy organizations and teachers will make this rule.

Before we try something new we may want to know the teacher a bit. Do they walk their talk? Are they real lovers, or are they lost in their own knowledge and overly eager to share? Do they listen well? Who are they as a person? Many charismatic teachers have a dark side. Which side is most influential? What can we learn from both sides? Is the teacher teaching union or separation? Do they make others bad or wrong? Some teachers create dependency; some students need to learn the drawbacks of dependency. We are all moving forward at different paces.

Money was not a requirement for participation in Sant Mat, a spiritual path Babbie and I followed. The guru had his own business, a good-sized farm in India. He made his own money. He believed that spiritual advice and information was free. When there is a focus on financial contribution, and solicitation, especially if it is forced on us, I consider a path very carefully. At the very least we should try to discover that for which the money is being used. Does the guru drive a Rolls Royce? That may be OK, but what does it have to do with the path?

Here are a few questions that can activate our spiritual discernment:

How is the information presented? Is the teacher angry much of the time, sometimes? Does the anger serve some purpose or does it represent work he or she has yet to do? What is it about this teacher that pushes our buttons? Is this our stuff? Does it bring up things we need to work on, or is it simply not good for us? Is this a loving message or are there subtle undercurrents of blame and judgment? Am I looking for a parent figure? Why do I want an authority figure in my life? Am I giving away my power now? How about the people in the organization? What are they like? Do they follow the teachings? Do they bicker? Are they truthful? Are they kind and loving? How cult-like is the group? Is there an attempt to create forced community, to make me join the group? A sense of humor is an important gauge. Does the teacher take himself or herself too seriously? Can they laugh at themselves? How much vulnerability do they manifest?

The biggest filter we can use in our seeking is to watch for the depth and presence of compassion, and to watch for the presence of judgment. To keep this filter active we need to stay aware and present. The manifestation of unconditional love and compassion (as opposed to just being talked about) is the measure of efficacy of any spiritual path.

As we encounter new beliefs, it will also be important to gain an understanding about our current belief system. We need to know if and how our belief system is serving us before we begin to replace parts of it with new material. We need to explore our shadow world.

Who Says So?

"So much human behavior is habitual – And behind every habit is a belief – about people, life, the world. We act from the premise that if we can know our beliefs; we can then act with greater consciousness about our behaviors. Examining beliefs can become a compelling process."

Margaret J. Wheatly \ Myron Kellner-Rogers
A Simpler Way

The question "who says so?" is the key to the heavy doors guarding a land of unparalleled fantasy, our belief system. When confronted with a behavioral absolute, or a personal, relentless law, asking, "who says so?" can take us on interesting tours through the back halls of the mind, where the ego and fear make their deals with the high representatives of this fantastic land. When activated by the will, the question "who says so?" becomes the relentless seeker of truth that cuts through the soft and fleshy world of pseudo-comfort we are trying to create for ourselves. This question cuts to the bone, to the understanding of beliefs that create our personal world view. With this question, we are asking what are our belief's credentials for creating our lives? "Who says so?" wants to know if our beliefs are serving us, or if we are serving them?

We do not ask "who says so?" meekly. We ask this question with belligerence, rabid curiosity and suspicion. We demand an answer that must work for us personally, and work for us now, in present time. Asking "who says so?" is a noble act of personal responsibility.

Why would we want to activate an ongoing, relentless search through the often busy, sometimes silent, hidden archives upon which our life floats? Why not leave this stuff alone? Most of us do just that. However, if we want to learn what our life is trying to teach us, we are going to need to understand how our inner world interprets information from the outer world. If we are interested in seeking the life that flows, that is flexible, expansive and open; the life that embraces change and fear with equanimity, it is necessary to discover the beliefs that are not working in our lives, to honor them and to let them go, as well as to understand what beliefs are serving us. One would think our beliefs would be obvious and transparent; however, many are so familiar, so accepted, or are so well disguised, that they remain invisible.

Our belief system acts like a big filter. It determines how we experience our life. Our reactions to this filtered experience then determine the results we are getting from life. These results are run back through the filter again. We live in a constant flow of interpretation and reaction. Since we are reacting to filtered information, understanding how our filter took its current form and how it operates is useful and important. It can give us important clues for creating change.

We create our primary filter in childhood as we begin to make sense of the world. Once childhood is past, our primary filter is largely in place. Although our belief system constantly filters information (sensory, intellectual, emotional) our conscious mind does not interfere very much in this process, but simply accepts the filtered data as reality. It is switched to "automatic."

The way most of us learn is through "filter shock." Occasional, upsetting events disrupt our filter and we are forced to adjust it in hopes of being able to deal with future disruptions of a similar nature. These are the few times we fool with the system. Filter shock is an extremely slow and painful way to learn. As in the bumper car, we live our lives at effect, awaiting the next disruption, and hoping we won't get hit again, always trying to find a safe course, never questioning our mode of transportation, never reviewing the filter.

While a passive filter alters information it is receiving to preset patterns (fixed beliefs), an active filter adjusts itself to incoming data. It is flexible, often modified and continually updated. Because filtered experience is our reality, when we create a more flexible, active filter, our reactions become this way; our worldview becomes more spacious and open. The filter of experience is one of those wonderful metaphysical paradoxes; it is both us and not us. It can be said that changing the filter is us "becoming." To use another computer metaphor, when we modify the operating software of our filter system, turning the switch to "active" we simultaneously begin to experience more flow and flexibility.

Once we understand how our filter works, and what beliefs constitute our own filter, we can make changes in it that radically change our lives. We learn how to introduce beliefs that serve us, rather than hinder us, on the path to personal freedom. The question, "who says so?" is a key to the operating system.

Knowing "who says so," what beliefs we have inherited or accumulated, is an important aspect of discernment and consciousness-raising. The investigation initiated by the question "who says so?" has the power to de-crystallize entrenched beliefs and create the space and flexibility necessary for our creative self to flourish. The passive filter of fixed beliefs sublimates our active creative nature. Creativity needs an active filter, a flexible and responsive belief system. We all have a creative nature that wishes to be exercised. When that nature is active we are living the life we are meant to live, we are not hemmed in by an unconscious, fixed belief system. Julia Cameron, the author of *The Artist's Way*, a book about freeing our creative nature tells us, "It is said that moving toward our creativity is moving towards our divinity."[30]

Beliefs become crystallized when we apply them to every situation without doubt or reservation. Welcome to the Land of Ism. In the Land of Ism we find the provinces of Fundamentalism, Communism, Totalitarianism, Militarism, or Fascism, to name a few. In the Land of Ism we try to feel safe through narrow mindedness, myopia, separation (we and they), righteousness, judgment and prejudice. We hope that by labeling everything we can control and understand the world. Black and white are our favorite colors; we see the world in this way. In Ism we act like donkeys with a linear

---

[30] Cameron, Julia, *The Artist's Way*. Julia Cameron, 1992

plan. We can become so inflexible that we can even deny the reality of our own experience. "I don't believe in anger, I believe in pacifism, so I never get angry. What I am feeling right now (anger) is not anger." In Ism we do not ask the question "who says so?" We do not ask, "Is this so in my experience?" We simply accept what we have been told by outer authorities. We often gather with others of like belief in order to uphold our limiting beliefs, to support each other's ignorance and inflexibility.

In the so-called "New Age" lexicon, people like to talk about "false beliefs." This is usually a term used to describe a belief that does not work, or the term is used pejoratively to imply a belief is wrong. In reality there is no such thing as a "false belief." A belief is either active (we are currently acting out of this belief) or inactive, chosen or not chosen. If we have a belief and we act from it, for us it is a true belief, regardless of the poor results it may bring. We are all anchored to many such beliefs. To say they are "false" beliefs is to judge our choices. Like most judgment, this type is counter-productive. We try to push away from these beliefs, and their results, rather than taking the time to discover what they are trying to teach us. It is as if we think we will learn our lesson by recognizing and then labeling them. Unfortunately, this usually doesn't work. It is typical to say we have "scarcity" beliefs when we seem to have money problems and then simply call these "false" beliefs, but this changes nothing. It does no good to paper over the beliefs that may be the source of our difficulties with affirmations. To the contrary, if we have not integrated the lessons we were meant to learn from scarcity fears first, affirmations about abundance won't help. We can be very good at wallpaper jobs, reciting affirmations, covering our real doubts, but in reality, we are experiencing acting from our fear rather than the solid ground of our truth. This distortion causes a great deal of disappointment. An affirmation cannot substitute for a true and deep belief. We need to discover and investigate the beliefs that no longer serve us before we can exchange them for a new belief.

Asking "who says so?" begins an investigation that very often takes us to the source of our beliefs. When we honor the sources of beliefs that no longer serve us, by manifesting compassion and mercy for all involved in the creation of the belief, we are able to integrate the real lesson and move on to new beliefs, beliefs that are creative rather than reactionary. We take the view that there are no mistakes, only learning experiences, and that we are fundamentally good no matter what beliefs we have had in the past, no matter how ignorant we have been. This is not always easy to believe! But, it is true nonetheless.

One of the reasons a rigid belief system is so difficult to live with is that it does not accept change. Thus we often apply beliefs that worked for us in the past to our present circumstances with drastic results. A clear example is a childhood belief system trying to function in adulthood. By using the question "who says so?" we question our entrenched beliefs. We discover their sources and then question their authority and replace them with more useful beliefs.

There are three tasks associated with the question "who says so?": identification, qualification and ratification. Identification means we identify the source of a belief. Qualification means we investigate the source's qualifications. If the qualifications are specious, then the belief could be specious, could be built on sand and we let it go: Hitler outlining the steps for manifesting compassion, for instance, or many politicians as a source of ethical opinions. Ratification means we look at the belief itself to see if we really buy it, to see if it works for us, to see if it has been true in our own experience; to see if it works now, regardless of the source. We also need to see if the source of a belief was derived from an isolated experience. Does it work all the time? Asking our belief system "who says so?" is asking it for verification of its right to act as the operating system of our psycho-spiritual self.

There are three categorical answers to the identification task: somebody, everybody and nobody. It is important which answer we receive because each answer calls for a different response. Of course we may get more than one.

When we run a "who says so?" identification check and the answer is "somebody" it might reveal a parent, a teacher, a cleric, a friend or someone we don't know well or even someone we have seen on TV. "Everybody" means that our belief is part of a group consciousness. "Nobody" is as strange an answer as it sounds, and indicates we have created the belief to serve some part of ourselves we may not recognize. Or, we may just be experiencing a little craziness.

When we identify that "somebody" is the source of a belief, we need to look at his or her qualifications. Questions we might ask are: "Did this person practice and fully embrace this belief? Did they demonstrate its effectiveness? Did it help them to maintain a core value, for instance, living in present time, inner peace, love, equanimity, patience or compassion?

An example: I have had many clients who live their lives in response to the uninvestigated belief that hard work and only hard work brings success. They feel guilty when they were not working, but hard work has not necessarily created abundance and joy in their lives. Often the opposite would happen, as their intimate relationships fell apart and they had less and less time for family and friends, let alone self-time. They became frustrated because they had convinced themselves that the hard work they were doing was a sacrifice they made for the family. They felt unappreciated when the family complained about them never being home. Why didn't the family appreciate their hard work? In most cases, when they asked, "Who says so?" it became immediately obvious that this was a very old belief that had been drilled in by parents (somebody), and their culture (everybody). In other words, from another generation with a different set of circumstances and world view. Their parents were often the authorities on the value of hard work. My clients had unconsciously taken on their beliefs. I experienced this myself. My father always demanded that I be working. Every summer he insisted that I have a job and when I was home reading a book on my day off he called it "goldbricking." My father is dead, but my mother still insists that hard work always results in success and happiness, and that, if one is not successful (using her limited definition), they simply must not have worked hard enough. In these cases it is easy to see "who says so?" The "hard work" belief does not always include enjoying your work or doing what you love. While doing work you love does not exclude working hard, it places more value on the quality of experience and less on the quantity and difficulty of work. Understanding this difference is important for creativity. We are always more creative at work we love than we are simply "doing a job."

Our focus on qualification engenders pertinent questions. For example, in this case, were my parents hard workers? Had this belief improved their lives in terms of core values? Did it make them happier, safer, more loving, and, of course, did the belief work directly? Did it create prosperity for them? Sometimes the answer to these questions is an unequivocal "no!" For instance, my mother never had a job in her entire life and my father was miserable doing work he did not like. Yet, as in my case, even when we know the person is not a qualified authority we discover we have inherited the same belief.

Encountering hypocrisy and unqualified authorities can make us angry if we have been living the belief unsuccessfully and unconsciously for a long time. We might feel betrayed or even lied to. It is reasonable to be angry, but not a good idea to get stuck there. In the next chapter we will explore the phenomena of wounds. Briefly, when we get stuck in these old stories we make them into wounds. We grow attached to them as the logical reason for our failures. We might say things like, "Of course I'm screwed up. If you had parents like mine you'd be screwed up too!" We have adopted another fruitless belief! The purpose of asking, "Who says so?" is not to make the source of our beliefs wrong, but to replace beliefs that don't work for us with ones that do. We want to make personal discovery and create personal growth. We want to alter the filter. We ask, "Who says so?" to raise a question that begins a path of discovery that we hope will end in a new and more workable belief. A belief that worked well for someone else may not work for us. We need to find out why and make changes.

Asking "who says so?" begins as an investigation that often ends in forgiveness for those from whom we have inherited a personally limiting belief. It is helpful to stay open-minded and open-hearted as we explore. Staying open-minded means that, even when we discover that the "expert" is not qualified, we will still see if we can use their belief or a part of it in any way. Staying open-hearted means we need to generate mercy for ourselves if we feel angry or guilty because we have unconsciously been using a limiting belief for a long time. We also need to find mercy for the originators of the beliefs we have inherited that do not work for us. Naturally, when we take up their beliefs there is a chance we will experience

the same frustrations. We can see the mutual difficulties we have encountered. From this mutual suffering an opportunity for compassion and forgiveness arises. Compassion and forgiveness help us to let go of victim status and stop blaming the originator of the belief for our condition, no matter how logical or tempting this may seem.

This mercy and compassion component of the discovery of "who says so?" is pragmatic as well as kind. Until we can integrate or release the emotions attached to an old belief it will be hard for us to ground ourselves in a new replacing belief. Instead, we will always be working, in some part, against the old belief, ironically giving it energy and influence. The release of old beliefs can sometimes be difficult. The good news is that sometimes, when we ask the question, "who says so?" sudden realizations arise that speed up the belief change process.

After we have checked the qualifications of those from whom we have inherited a belief, we move to ratification. Perhaps for someone else a belief does work. Does that mean it will for me? Getting back to the "hard work" example: When we try to ratify someone else's work belief (ethic) can we do it? We may not mind working hard, but the ease and grace, the elegance, the enjoyment with which a task can be accomplished may be more important to us than the level of difficulty or time needed. It is well documented that joy and ease is engendered when we find "right" work. With "right" work (work we love and enjoy) we can work almost effortlessly all day. Putting hard work above "right" livelihood doesn't work for everybody. Often, for those who believe in the primacy of "hard" work, work is envisioned as a chore, something unpleasant that has to be done or overcome.

Sometimes when we ask, "Who says so?" we get the answer "everybody." Beliefs embraced by the crowd do not necessarily have more authority than those of an individual. For example, in many fundamentalists groups everybody in the group subtly agrees that anyone not in the group is wrong somehow or is going to hell. My own experience is that there are many kind and loving people who are not all in the same group. Is love and compassion expressed by a Sufi Saint any different from that of a Christian Saint, a Buddhist, a Jain or a cab driver or store clerk? Nobody has a monopoly on love.

The belief that the group is exclusive and its members are superior to others is obviously incorrect.

It is just as important to investigate "who says so?" when we get the "everybody" answer. Everybody can be a pretty large crowd, and that can cause us to doubt our beliefs! Just because everybody says so doesn't make something so. As for qualification, what everybody believes is often very inconsistent with what everybody does. For instance, everybody may talk about love and peace, but not everybody makes them a practice. Often, when "everybody says so" fears are lurking just beneath the surface. Common accepted beliefs are often born out of group fear.

When everybody "says so" it does not necessarily negate a belief, but it is an indication that absolutes are present and absolutes are, obviously, rigid. Rigid beliefs, by their nature, tend to be exclusive rather than inclusive. Group beliefs need special scrutiny because of the tendency toward exclusion. Generally speaking when everybody says so we need to be wary.

The most fascinating response to "who says so?" is "nobody." It is interesting how often we receive this response. The "nobody" answer means we cannot identify where we received this belief. When the answer is "nobody," it often means that we have created a belief that serves a more hidden part of our ego. We have fabricated or made up a belief. The subconscious is, perhaps, ever so subtly manipulating our belief system to make it conform to what it wants. By asking "who says so?"we can catch it in the act. There is something a little bit crazy about the "nobody" answer. As for qualifications "nobody" has none, and for this reason it is much easier to change such a belief. There is less work to do than in the case of a "somebody" or "everybody" answer. We can replace a "nobody" belief with one that works.

Never-the-less, "nobody" deserves the same fair trial for ratification as "somebody" or "everybody." Does the belief work for us or is it blocking our progress or causing discontent?

Identification, qualification, and ratification give us a map to the source and nature of our beliefs, but as long as our discovery remains simply an intellectual understanding we are still surfing, skimming the surface. We can remain in this unhelpful place, confusing understanding with integration. In this situation we understand the beliefs that are not serving us but fail to move beyond them. There are two reasons for this. First, we simply do not know how to move beyond or integrate the belief; we don't know what skillful action to take. And, second, there is a part of us that would like to keep the belief alive. We pay lip service to change, but we still avoid it; we live in our wound because we are comfortable there; afraid of change. This is a very common form of stasis.

Exploring beyond "somebody," "everybody," and "nobody" we make a very important discovery. Like the wizard of Oz hiding behind the curtain, *we* are the one who is controlling the fire breathing demons of "somebody," "everybody," and "nobody."We are always the person who ultimately "says so." Because, once again, we are personally responsible for our beliefs no matter where they originate. Asking "who says so?" helps us to identify and then let go of old beliefs which are clouding our ability to really comprehend our own responsibility. We are able to see this clearly as we refocus. We are peeling back the layers. As we create new beliefs and become aware of their impact on our lives, we also reaffirm that, in the end, we are the one responsible for what we believe. Asking "who says so?" is a practice that enhances our discernment and at the same time exposes many of the limiting beliefs by which we shape our lives.

Here are some interesting ideas for a few "who says so?" inquiries, a kind of starter kit of commonly accepted beliefs.

Who says the world is not in perfect order?
Who says I should work all the time?
Who says having more is necessarily better?
Who says my kids must go to college to enjoy a full and meaningful life?
Who says their lives will be ruined if they don't go to college?
Who says I have to act nice all the time?
Who says my religion or religion is the "only" spiritual path.
Who says I have to keep on doing work I don't like?
Who says I will be happy when I just have X?
Who says I must sacrifice my whole life for my family?
Who says anger is bad?

Who says I cannot live a simpler lifestyle?
Who says I must stay in a dysfunctional relationship?
Who says hard, often unpleasant work is the only route to success?
Who says that war is a solution?
Who says I am always in danger?
Who says that love is impractical?
Who says that compassion is a sign of weakness?
Who says that I cannot find the courage to be who I really am?

Make your personal list. Remember, these are investigations not opinions. The purpose is not to create new judgments of any person or thing. We are observing and learning. We do not need the ego's help to do this.

Letting go of limiting beliefs and installing new and more positive beliefs can take place at any point in our lives. It is never too late to disconnect from limiting beliefs and take up ones that are more encompassing and flexible. It is always interesting to investigate the things that we blindly accept as truth. And as Socrates said, "The unexamined life is not worth living."

Who Says So ?

The Healing Time

Finally on my way to yes
I bump into
all the places
where I said no
to my life
all the untended wounds
the red and purple scars
those hieroglyphs of pain
carved into my skin, my bones,
those coded messages
that send me down
the wrong street
again and again
where I find them
the old wounds
the old misdirections
and I lift them
one by one
close to my heart
and I say
Holy Holy.

Persha Gertler[31]

---

[31] Marilyn Sewell, *Claiming the Spirit Within: a sourcebook of women's poetry,* Beacon Press, 1996

The Wound

You and all beings are equal in wanting to be happy;
You and all beings are equal in wanting not to suffer.

Shchen Gyaltsap

My friend Peter has a great interest in helping people help themselves, and his work as an expert in human potential knows no bounds. He is very outgoing and proactive man, and, naturally, he meets all sorts of interesting people. Many years ago, Peter asked Babbie and me if we wanted to go out to dinner with him and his wife, Carol, at the Grafton Inn in Grafton, Vermont.

This dinner happened in the "New Age" era of channeling and, because we were interested in such phenomena, we were invited to have dinner with a rising star of the New Age, Meredith Young, who channeled a being named Agartha and worked with plant divas. It promised to be an interesting dinner. Meredith brought a friend along with her, a short haired, bright-eyed woman who combined a love of laughter and fun with a piercingly serious nature. Her name was Caroline Myss and Babbie and I enjoyed meeting her a great deal. The dinner was filled with laughter. I don't think we even spoke about channeling. Subsequently, we attended Caroline's early workshops, which were held in the Hanover, New Hampshire area, and we got to know her. Caroline was not always popular with attendees. She can be very frank, which is a quality I admire, but which others sometimes feel is intimidating. I remember that her workshop attitude at the time was, "But you asked for this!"

When Babbie and I were working at the Omega Institute, complete strangers would often come up to us and say "I know I have met you or seen you somewhere, but I can't place it. I can't remember when we met or where." We were mystified. After a while we solved the mystery. Peter and Carol and Babbie and I were the audience and inquisitors in Caroline's first video. These people had seen us in the video. Omega is the kind of place where many people had seen the video.

The video explained the function of what Caroline then called "energy centers" in our bodies and the effect they have on our outer condition. Caroline decided to use the term "energy center" rather than "chakras," the ancient eastern term for these centers, because she didn't want to scare away the mainstream audience of those days. Over time her work has evolved and she has investigated the psychological, physical and spiritual dimensions of these centers in many bestselling books.

Caroline first became famous for her work with Dr. Norman Shealy. They worked together as a team. She studied the anatomy of the human body and, with his help and encouragement used her gift of "seeing" for what is called "intuitive diagnosis." After a while, with just the name and age of a person (who was often sitting hundreds of miles away in Dr. Shealy's office) she could diagnose their condition over the telephone with 80% accuracy, achieving a much higher success rate than conventional and often more invasive methods. She told me once that she was able see disease working or beginning in people before it even manifested.

Caroline's work is fascinating, and her book the *Anatomy of the Spirit* is one of the most interesting books ever written on the subject of how spirit manifests. But it is her book *Why People Don't Heal* that gives insight into the ways we avoid evolving into our best self; how we maintain our wounds. Carolyn began to study why, despite the best care, a positive attitude and with a good prognosis, many people don't heal. It is now accepted by many that real healing comes from within. Our body is the best healer we will ever encounter. We are not talking here about emergency medicine, although our mental outlook when we are seriously injured is important. What Carolyn investigated was the question of why, if the body is so powerful and therapy so helpful, people with chronic disorders don't heal. She could find the pathology and discover the psychological and spiritual dimensions and causes of disease but, even armed with this information and given good care, many people still were unable to heal physically. What she discovered is that sometimes people don't heal because in some way they don't want to heal. Even though our disease may be debilitating and uncomfortable, we choose it over healing because it is familiar. More, we even protect ourselves subconsciously from the possibility for change. She also discovered that getting physically well is not necessarily what healing is all about. We may heal ourselves; we may discover and work with and even transcend our wound but still die. According to Caroline, dying from a disease does not necessarily mean that we have not healed.

Our emotional wounds are similar to physical ailments, and the two are sometimes connected to each other. But often our emotional wounds do not manifest as physical illness. Many times these wounds are well hidden (especially from ourselves) and we have to use awareness, personal responsibility and inner work to make discovery. Other times these wounds are right in front of us.

My father was diagnosed with prostate cancer. As usual, the doctors had to operate right away. After the operation, his urologist pulled me aside and told me that Dad only had two or three months to live, there was nothing more they could do. They were against any aggressive therapies, which they felt would do more harm than good; so no chemo and no radiation. The fact that he did not go these routes may have saved his life in my humble opinion.

My father was lethargic and depressed and did not care what happened to him. I did not want to give up so easily and did much research into alternative therapies. I discovered a clinic operating in Louisiana, where a brave doctor was administering laetrile and doing diet work with his patients. This work was illegal, but he managed somehow to keep going. Despite the scorn of the medical establishment, people were having good results and others were dying without pain or heavy sedation. I witnessed this myself.

My mother and I took my father to Louisiana from Maine. He traveled down in a wheel chair. He was in rough shape when we checked him into the hospital there. Three weeks later he walked out of the hospital and came home on his own. He lived for two more years until his cancer came back and he died a slow, bad death. When his cancer returned, rather than going back to Louisiana where he had been healed, he submitted to the cut, poison and burn therapy offered by the more prestigious cancer doctors in Boston. He was always worried about doing the "correct" thing. By the time his cancer came back, he was alert and well enough to revert to pattern. He died in this way. Why did he choose it?

Stephen Levine has said that our feelings about death are twofold. One half of us welcomes death, like a big peaceful sleep, while the other half wants life and joy. I remember watching my father in the last two years of his life, when he was in remission and thinking, "He doesn't really care; he doesn't really want to live." Perhaps without the drinking and self-indulgent behavior that had given him pleasure before his illness, his life seemed dull or meaningless, or, perhaps, he was simply more reflective. When his cancer manifested a second time he made a choice that was the antithesis of what had been successful for him the first time. My mother and I had made the first choice for him. The second choice was his. There are deep forces moving in our lives. If, deep inside, we would rather die than live, we might die sooner than later. We might even arrange it.

There have been studies done to see what qualities people who live long lives exhibit and one such study observed a group of centenarians to find a clue to their longevity. The one quality that an overwhelming number of people in the study shared was "delight". They loved life, new things, and small things. In my hospice work with the many very old people for whom I have cared, I have noticed this as well. Those who still found delight in things, despite their illness, fared better. My father's mother lived until she was in her nineties. Fragile and thin, with some difficulty walking, she still took great delight in life, in little things like the birds and her flower gardens and the amazing characters in Charles Dickens. I can remember when she was in her late eighties reading me a passage aloud from Pickwick Papers with tears of laughter pouring down her wrinkled cheeks. Her body gave her a hard time, but she still found delight in life. Once, I took care of a 99 year-old woman who loved hymns. She would have me sing hymns to her a cappella, and then she could not stop herself from joining me in her old voice. She took enormous delight in the doings of her big Vermont family. She clearly demonstrated the power of delight.

Sometimes one of the greatest enemies of personal and spiritual growth is the glorious mind. Remember that line of Rajneesh's, "the mind can only doubt and the heart can only believe." The ego, and its servant the mind, are interested in maintaining the status quo, the comfort zone. This is true whether we are living in emotional or physical pain or in bliss. Although we believe we want to move beyond the pain, often our wounds become our emotional and physical home or a big room there. People are said to "marry their wounds" because their wounds give them a sense of purpose, a reason for being, because wounds can be a good excuse for stasis, not taking action, because we can use our wounds to stay in what the mind and subconscious perceive as a safe zone.

How does this work? Let's say we had a miserable childhood. As a result of this childhood we have dysfunctional behaviors. For an example, let's say we have a great deal of anger and we drink too much alcohol. The anger is justified by the treatment we received as a child and the drinking is to assuage the emotional pain we still suffer. We can justify our behavior based on our horrible childhood. This seems completely logical, and sympathetic friends may even say our behavior is understandable. They are not doing us any favors, however, because this kind of logical thinking is a big trap. Although we seem to have every reason for acting the way we do, and "everyone" (remember "Who says so?") even agrees that our response to our horrible childhood is reasonable, we will never progress as long as we use our past as an excuse for our current behavior. We will dwell in our wound instead. We eschew personal responsibility. We become stuck in an unpleasant state.

Probably everyone has emotional wounds. If this were not so, we would live in a completely different world. It is because the world acts out of its wounds that so many of us live in pain and poverty and that the ultimate disassociation of war exists. But if the world is going to change, we have to individually tackle our wounds. We all need to heal, and the more of us who heal our wounds, the greater our chance for a better world. We call this work, "healing the wound," because in a spiritual sense all wounds are "the wound." Because, in one form or another, we all share the wound, we can also share in this important healing work.

195

Most, but not all, of our wounds occur due to the emotional pain we have experienced in our life and much of that pain came in our childhood. Even people who believe they had an idyllic childhood will recognize, upon investigation that their childhood was not all roses. If our parents were kind, we may have inherited an inability to admit the dark side of things. Later this becomes problematic as we continue to live in denial of our unpleasant feelings. We may have encountered others who were not kind, like mean teachers or bullies. We may have been wounded in a relationship later in life and have set up defenses to prevent our being hurt again, but that simultaneously guarantee we will not experience deep intimacy.

Wounds are passed down from generation to generation. For instance, if a father's method of discipline is hitting, then his child might very well become a hitter when angry at his own children. Hitting is abusive behavior, even if condoned by parts of society, because it is a direct assault on a human being's safety and dignity. It is harmful and unnecessary. The young person who is disciplined in this way can develop a storehouse of resentment and anger which they will often carry into their adult life. Sometimes abuse will create a passion to help others who have suffered the same wound. This is a much better outcome, but, because our compassion is often fear based, our wound remains unhealed. We are still acting out of the wound. It is difficult to be an effective healer when you have not healed yourself.

The wound may take a completely different form as it evolves, adapting itself to each new host, if you will. A typical case is the wound of scarcity, resulting in the so-called "spoiled child." A parent who had a childhood of scarcity may be over indulgent with her own children. She finds it nearly impossible to say "no" to their requests because she remembers her own unhappiness as a child in a household of scarcity. So she sets no sensible boundaries. At some point the children grow up and have to make it on their own. Suddenly, when things are not simply given to them, they become frustrated and angry. They discover the world is not a toy store. Their vision of abundance is converted into a world of "not enough" as they struggle for more things. They may take up hoarding and embrace scarcity just as their grandparent did! The wound is passed down.

Like the ego, the wound is universal; it doesn't just happen to us, it is a part of everyone. The generation that ends "the wound" will be the one that finally changes the world. We each need to ask for help if necessary.

When we clearly see the wound of any person who we believe is a source of our pain, for instance a sibling, parent, or spouse, and we understand how their wound has affected us, we have a choice. We can continue to blame them for our condition, or we can forget our story for a moment and endeavor to feel how it must be to be them, to suffer so much that they feel compelled to hurt others. They may be completely unconscious of their unskillful or mean behavior. By envisioning what it would be like to be them, by entering their world, we can discover the power of compassion to free us from our own wound. When we stay stuck in the story of how they hurt us, this freedom is impossible to achieve. Ironically, if we are honest with ourselves we can discover compassion for them through our own experience of the same wound. This is the secret of true forgiveness. We can only truly forgive from the opened heart.

When people tell us how powerful forgiveness is, and then tell us that we should forgive someone who we feel has abused us in some way, we may find it very difficult, if not impossible, to truly do so. If we feel we have been abused, that our dignity has been assaulted, or we feel betrayed or that someone has taken advantage of us, forgiveness can end up being no more than a fine idea. Attempting forgiveness in difficult circumstances can result in frustration, because we know that, deep inside, we have not really released the wound. Forgiveness is powerful medicine, but how do we forgive the deep wounds that bind us and hold us back, that keep recreating themselves? Again, we use compassion.

My own experience of this came in an interesting way. When my father died I thought our business was over. He said "I love you" to me for the first time in my life just before he died, and I accepted that as a great move forward for him. Years later, I was working with Julia Cameron's book, *The Artist's Way*. While doing an exercise around creativity I got into some heavy anger. The exercise revealed to me how my father had always tried to repress my creative side.

When I wanted to write or do something creative, he would scoff at me and say "no one makes any money doing that" and other less skillful remarks. Making money was my parent's highest criteria for the successful human being. The exercise in Julia Cameron's book brought up the many times this suppression had happened. I was angry for days as I relived his repression of my creativity. This anger ignited all my other anger towards him, which I thought was long past. All the indignity I had suffered as a child seemed to rise to the surface. This anger lasted quite a while. Every time I thought of him it arose. There was *no way* I was going to forgive him. At first the anger felt good, but, over time, I grew weary of it, and I began to feel frustrated with my own inability to truly forgive him in my heart.

One fall, on my guidance day during my personal retreat, I was sitting on a porch overlooking the islands of Penobscot Bay in Maine. I was reading the wonderful book called *Embracing the Beloved* by Stephen and Andrea Levine, and it was open in my lap. I had said a simple prayer asking for guidance and was simply sitting; waiting for any revelation. Quite suddenly a breeze came up. It blew the pages of the book to a chapter containing a guided meditation and stopped. Of course, I followed the guided meditation. It was a grieving meditation. I had not thought about my father in a long time, but suddenly in this meditation he arose, and I began to cry in grief and sorrow, I recognized this as the sorrow of a lost relationship that never was and never would be, the relationship a loving father can have with a son. I grieved our loss, our sad life together, and I *really* wept, and it felt right and good. During this release my father's wound was suddenly revealed to me. As a child he has been abandoned by his true family, put in an orphanage, adopted by a wealthy woman and, when very young, sent off to boarding school. He had never had a father himself. And, in seeing what his experience must have been like, I saw how his wounds had been passed on to me, and that we shared the wound. In this moment I was able to forgive him and my load was eased significantly. And it was exactly while this was all happening that I learned how compassion allows us to experience true forgiveness. I understood that sometimes it takes a great deal of personal work to reach this place of compassion. I had come some distance in my personal growth since he had died. I had learned to sit quietly. I had learned to take time for myself and to nurture myself. I had learned how to seek wisdom and revelation. I also saw, once again, very clearly, how we are given revelation when we can handle it and not before.

I came to understand that when we share the wound of those who have wounded us we can reach true forgiveness. There are different ways of doing this, all of which involve a measure of personal responsibility. When we let go of our expectations of others or our desire that things be different, we can enter this realm of true forgiveness. In this case, grief gave me a very deep and profound inner release that I can feel right now just writing this paragraph.

By the way, I kept right on weeping that day and it began to rain heavily. It rained all night and into the following day when I was to leave. I was still pretty tender in the morning as I loaded my car, and I actually was not that aware of the weather. I don't listen to the radio or watch TV when I am on retreat, so I had no idea what was going on. I took the ten o'clock boat to the mainland and it kept right on raining. I was a little concerned because the little Dodge Colt I was driving had bad tires, but I trusted I would be OK and continued on. I got onto the Maine Turnpike, had another short intense weeping session, and suddenly as I came over a hill there were state police beside the road waving cars through a huge puddle. I began to realize that this rainstorm was not the usual affair. When I got to Portland, I decided to get off the Turnpike because I could see a long line of cars stopped just beyond the exit. It was obvious that the traffic had come to a standstill. At the exit toll booth man told me that Route 1 (my alternate choice) was also closed due to flooding and the Turnpike was to be completely closed soon, so I headed inland, going west, up the watershed, finally making my way south again in the rain and, by then, dark. Taking detours around flooded areas, I made it down to my mother's place in southern Maine. It had rained 16 inches in a 24-hour period, a record I believe. I definitely found it interesting that, as I wept profusely, the rain washed down in a massive torrent. The deluge began exactly with my own downpour, with the washing out and healing of my wound. I asked for revelation and was answered powerfully. It seemed as if the gods had wept with me.

In order to heal our wounds we need to be aware they exist. Of course we have usually spent a bit of time papering them over, indulging them or burying them. The more we are aware of our reactive behaviors, the more we can follow them inside and find out how they are connected to our wounds. We never know when we will strike pay dirt, but, by staying aware, we will eventually encounter our wounds: the hurt places, the raw places, the unfinished places.

Subconscious wounds can arise out of nowhere and quite suddenly. Once I was going to go on a camping trip with some friends. I kept all my gear in one place so that whenever I wanted to go camping I would not have to forage throughout the house. When I went down in the basement I discovered most of my gear was gone, borrowed or lost. I was furious and very upset. I told Babbie I just wasn't going to go on the trip. My four sons seemed to think it was OK to borrow my stuff without asking. Tools went missing frequently, and it seemed like, whenever I wanted to make or fix something, I had to spend an hour just finding my tools. I asked the boys to put things back, but this didn't always happen. I took the attitude that "boys will be boys," yet I still felt upset when I couldn't find a tool or something I needed. For some reason this time became the last straw. I had been looking forward to the trip, and I had been happy in the knowledge that all my camping stuff was in one place, ready to go. I was really angry and upset.

Babbie is a wise and conscious person, and we sat down and talked about my heavy reaction. She reminded me that the lost gear was just a story, but my reaction was so strong that there must be something deeper, and if I could focus my awareness perhaps it would be revealed. At first I was resistant. I wanted to stay in my ego, and in my justified anger, but with coaxing, we worked on it right there, standing in the kitchen together and in short order I discovered a wound. I started by paying more attention to the emotion I was feeling and I realized that, not only was I feeling frustrated and angry, I was also feeling some kind of grief. When I followed the grief inside I came in touch with the wound that was generating my over-reaction every time things were borrowed and not returned.

This is what I discovered. When I was growing up my father kept us moving around. He moved from job to job or simply to a new location every two years. Every time we moved, my mother took the opportunity to give away or throw away my things. She often disposed of the things she knew that I liked. She did this deliberately to make me feel upset. When I was sent away to school, she repeated this pattern giving away or throwing away almost everything I owned. When I came home, I felt more like a guest than a family member. I never felt really at home. The camping things I had carefully collected and put in one place represented the whole idea of finally having things that belonged to me that would not disappear. Finally, I could own and control something of my own. So, when the boys used my gear without asking, and I could not find any of it, I went ballistic. It triggered the old childhood wound of no place or thing of my own. Here was the cause of my anger and over reaction. This revelation calmed me right down. I took the focus off the boys. I got some gear together and took the camping trip. I grew more patient.

By paying attention to overreaction (using awareness), we can make this kind of discovery. Also, this kind of revelation automatically invokes personal responsibility. I could see that my reaction was way over the top. I owned my story and with that ownership I stopped putting my burden onto my kids and I stopped the wound from continuing.

Understanding that over-reaction can be a sign that a wound is present is a helpful tool. If we notice that some things seem to cause us undue pain or anger every time we encounter them, then we may be in the presence of a great opportunity for healing, an opportunity to own and let go of our wound. By now, we understand that we do this by letting go of the story, sitting with our strong emotion and focusing on our inner reaction. This will often reveal the true source of the emotional upset which has been triggered by a story. In this way, we may experience direct contact with our wound. When this happens we can own it. With ownership, we come to understand that it is our wound that is causing so much difficulty and not the stories we are experiencing. This knowledge alone is usually powerful enough to stop our acting out, and laying our wound onto others.

Once we discover a wound and own it, we can begin the work of healing it in ourselves. Asking for help in this regard is very powerful, through prayer or through others. Like my grief that caused the gods to weep, we do not know what form our healing will take. Neither do we know when it will take place. We can relax in the knowledge that it will take place when we are ready, but not sooner. No need to push the river, we make the request and we will be provided for, and that is a certainty in my experience. We are not given more revelation than we can handle, and the timing is usually perfect. Each time the wound arises is an opportunity for embracing mercy for oneself and others and for letting go.

Like warriors for consciousness, when we make contact with our wounds and take personal responsibility for them, when we heal ourselves, we are on the forefront of healing everyone's wound, "the wound." Stopping the wound is a noble act of personal responsibility. As we heal our own wounds, we develop deeper compassion; we heal not just ourselves but the hurt in the world.

What's Time To A Pig?

"I'm late! For a very important date!
No time to say hello, goodbye!
And when I wave I lose the time I save!
I'm late! I'm Late I'm Late!"

White Rabbit

Before we can do our inner work we have to make it a priority. As soon as we do this, we come face to face with the idea of limited time, a handy doorway out of our inner world and back into the stressful outer world. If we believe that there is not enough time to do our inner work, how we will make progress? Central to our journey into consciousness is learning how to turn time into an ally.

The Sakyong, Mipam Rinpoche told me this story when we were enjoying a summer picnic under an apple tree.

A man was walking down a country road, when he saw a farmer out in a field, standing under an apple tree with a pig under his arm. Curious, the man entered the field and approached the farmer. "Excuse me, what are you doing?" "We're waiting for an apple to fall," replied the farmer. "You mean you are waiting for an apple to fall into the pig's mouth?" the man said in amazement. "That's right," said the farmer. "Isn't that going to take a long time?" asked the man. To which the farmer replied, "What's time to a pig?"

This story, though simple and amusing, is filled with implications and interesting views about the way in which we hold time. Our relationship to time is a very important ingredient in the quality of our life, but, generally, we don't give it much thought. When Albert Einstein was finished studying and theorizing about time and space it was a sense of God and the sacred that filled his understanding. How did this happen? He entered his inquiry through the door of science and exited with respect and awe for the divine; for the "elegant patterning". His understanding of time had shifted his appreciation of the universe. Although we may not experience such profound results, our understanding of time also needs to shift when we take up our inner work. It is useful to embrace the belief that there is plenty of time, rather than not enough, so that we can relax into our inner work and give it space while simultaneously, and paradoxically, remembering that life is finite, so we do not become spiritually lazy. Holding this distinction, walking this edge, living in this paradox, we are able turn time into an ally.

Leaving science out of it, there are two simple and fundamental ways we can view every day linear time. Like the man who questioned the farmer, we can take the view that time is contractive. In this view, time is like a fast evaporating puddle; there is not enough of it. Or, we can be like the farmer (and the pig for that matter); we can take the view that time is expansive, like a large, beautiful, and bottomless lake. Which view we choose has a great deal to do with determining the fundamental quality of our life. Our view of linear time creates a context in which we hold much of the content of our life. When we choose to do inner work, it is most helpful to embrace the expansive view.

Unfortunately, in the modern world, the prevailing view of time is the contractive view. This is the ocean we swim in; life is often described as a "rat race." Most of us view time as limited and finite, and therefore we try to fit as many activities as we can into it. With newer and ever more powerful technology, we can now get more tasks done in less time. We even have created a word, for performing more than one task simultaneously, "multitasking." We seem to have forgotten that one of the big promises of technology was that it would allow us to enjoy more personal time and less work time. Most people now work more hours and have less family and personal time than ever. Technology's early promise was more leisure, and more time to enjoy life. Instead we have used the time provided by technology to do more, to fit in more tasks. We have electronic devices and workbooks for keeping careful track of time. We try to squeeze the most out of every moment by carefully compiling complex schedules. No one discourages this attitude; in fact, employers don't mind it a bit. They call the amount of work we can achieve in a given period of time "productivity." More productivity is considered better. The *quality* of the time we spend is not a concern. Technology didn't break the promise of more personal time, we did. Our view that there is never enough time has remained constant, so that, even with all our labor saving technology, we still think and act as if we don't have enough time.

Because we try to fit as many tasks as possible into our allotted time, and technology is making the accomplishment of more and more tasks possible, the volume of tasks is increasing. Our lives are literally filling up with more and more to do, and becoming more and more task oriented. There is even an exponential factor. Many tasks rely on other tasks being accomplished and in this way our tasks become a giant spider's web in which we seem to be permanently snared. We begin to believe that the accomplishment of tasks is what life is all about. The present becomes non-existent as we lean into the future, into the next task or engagement on the never-ending list. We become driven by the list in an unconscious quest for something we have forgotten and left far behind. What was the original intention of living this way, anyway? In the end, many of us lie on our deathbed, dazed and wondering where life went. Often at this point we feel robbed; the culprit? There wasn't enough time to do what we wanted or, sometimes, even to discover what that was. But actually there was plenty of time, it was our view that was misaligned, and that is the good news. We can change the view.

The idea of limited time causes stress. It makes us uptight and nervous, anxious and agitated. We feel a constant sense of urgency. This is not a good condition for doing our inner work. It is not a good condition in which to live our daily life either. We organize ourselves to death to take advantage of the limited number of minutes and hours allotted. We forget that it is our view of time that has created this situation, a view that has become a self-fulfilling vision. Since everyone around us is moving at the same frantic and busy pace, like lemmings we fail to question the entire equation and the result is our own stressed existence in a busy and frantic society. We are like ants gone wild.

Our personal view of time is so much a part of our inner landscape that we often don't recognize that there is an alternative view. In my inner work, I used to practice with a talented rebirther. Rebirthing is the practice of conscious connected breathing. It is called rebirthing because, sometimes, practitioners re-experience their birth during a session. This is not the point of conscious connected breathing, however. The purpose is to let the body release old trauma and stress that has been stored at the cellular level. The facilitator helps with the breath, reminding the breather of what breath to use, and keeping them from hyperventilating or getting into other unhelpful patterns. Sometimes a rebirther will review the experience with a client after a session, but this is not necessary.

When energy is released, it sometimes appears in the form of images of past experiences, while at other times it manifests as an emotional release, such as crying and yelling. The releasing is not always a pretty picture, but it is a gift. By reliving parts of our life we have repressed, we are able to see the teaching those parts have for us. In rebirthing, whether we can label a past experience is not as important as releasing the energy that we have been holding. With rebirthing we don't need to know the source of emotional release. We don't need to review the stories. The release is the gift, not the story we may encounter. As rebirthers say, "you don't go through your garbage when you throw it out; why review released negative energy?"

Conscious connected breathing is an excellent inner work practice because it does not discriminate. This practice takes one right to whatever stored energy is ready to be released in the moment and facilitates very deep release. You cannot plan what you are going to encounter, or what you want to investigate. It is a practice that takes us beyond psychological review. On a few occasions, I have experienced what is called "suspended breath." In this state I stopped breathing for five minutes. This sounds impossible, but it happens often. Suspended breath is a very strange experience, because you are not really present when it occurs. You do not know it is going to happen and you do not realize when it is happening. It is a state of complete shutdown, no senses at all, no consciousness. All I could remember, when coming out of this state, was the return of light and consciousness and the breath starting again. One day, after having this experience, I suddenly saw from a place of deep contentment and peace, the underlying urgency that infused my life. Amazingly, I had never really been conscious of the existence of this undercurrent of urgency before. With the rebirthing experience as a foil, I suddenly saw and felt its energy very clearly. There was a tension in me that was so constant; so old, I never knew it existed. Inner work sometimes calls forth wonderful surprises. In this case, I discovered that my urgency was the result of the belief that there was not enough time. I imagine many of us live our days with the unacknowledged, undiscovered tension of urgency humming along just beneath the surface.

The breath, of course, is very powerful for healing, for helping us through hard times, dealing with stress, for relieving anxiety, and for moving through difficult physical stretches. It can be an indicator of our state of mind, as well as a catalyst for changing that state. In this respect, it can also help when we are learning that there is plenty of time. By slowing our breath and making it steady we can change the physical states that are caused by stress and mental tension. Because worry (including worry about time) causes increased heart rate, we can use the breath to slow the rate and induce relaxation. My kids used to tell me to "take a deepie Dad!" when they wanted me to relax. Simply taking a deep breath (or several) while focusing on relaxing the body is a simple, but effective, way to relieve stress and pressure. We just forget to do it sometimes.

As accomplishment becomes more important than being, quality of life plummets. Lost in doing, we forget about inner work. In fact we ask, "Who has the time?" We have also forgotten how to be in our doing. Leaning into the future we often miss the full experience of what is occurring in the moment.

The idea that there isn't enough time is simply a belief and, like all of our other beliefs, it shapes our reality. In fact, this particular belief is one of the most perfect examples of this truth. Again, when we believe there is not enough time, we stuff as much as we can into what we believe is always a limited time span.

What happens when we take up the belief that there is plenty of time? Urgency diminishes and, what is most extraordinary, we create a reality in which there is plenty of time. Rather than filling our schedules and making everything run to the second we leave plenty of time for both events and the spaces between. Our belief creates plenty of time.

Babbie and I now live in Panama. The contrast between the way Panamanians view time and the way we North Americans do is marked. At first, we were frustrated with how long things took to get done. After a while we began to notice how relaxed most people were in their dealings. Our urgency had no effect on their response. We had no choice but to go with the flow. Imagine this scene. We worked with an attorney to get title to some property and close a land deal. We made appointments with the lawyer but whenever we went to his office we would always have to wait at least half an hour. When we finally got into his office we would have a pleasant conversation about things before getting down to business. When we were through with the business, we would have another friendly conversation. He quite literally "gave us the time of day," a practice that seems forgotten in our "time and billing" crazy world. The cost was always the same, no matter how long the meeting. It was very civil. Over time, we noticed that while we were waiting other people dropped by who had not made appointments and often he could fit them in for a few minutes. All this happened at a very leisurely pace with no urgency at all. One day, we dropped by his office without an appointment. We waited the customary amount of time and then visited with the lawyer for a while over a small issue. We still began and ended with a chat about things. How different from a professional visit in the United Sates in which a lawyer gives you an exact block of time, and then charges for increments of the hour. Forget talking ten minutes to talk about life, and what you have been doing since the last time you met. It might cost you a half hour of billable time! Eventually, we grew accustomed to the Panamanian way, their ease with time, and we came to see how much less stressful their lives are. We could feel the change in us. It is amazing how busy we all seem to be with the big lists of chores we create, and all the urgency we put into them.

We do not want to stuff our inner time into a tight schedule. At first, when we have yet to experience the value of inner time, and because it can be a little bit scary, we will chop it off the schedule before anything else. Time for inner work is often the first thing we drop because it is not regarded by our culture or ourselves as being important, and yet our inner life is the central core from which all of the rest of our life evolves. I know very few people who consider making conscious time by and for themselves a major priority.

Bringing the belief that there is plenty of time into our lives is not difficult. It is a conscious act and choice to view time in this way, and the rewards are extraordinary. When we find ourselves overwhelmed by events and things that "have to" get done we simply tell ourselves, "There is plenty of time." Another way of doing this is by asking ourselves "what would I do right now if there was plenty of time and why am I not doing it?" We are the bosses of ourselves, right? We can put down or take up what we want. If the schedule we are creating has too many items in it we can remove them. We can learn to say "no." We are responsible for the way we embrace time.

There is a spiritual paradox in all this. While there is plenty of time, we won't always be here to enjoy it. We want to live our lives as if there were plenty of time in order to be more present, while at the same time staying aware that our life span is finite, and therefore that we need to take advantage of the plenty of time or experience we have. This is the big picture. We enter daily experience with the view that there is plenty of time for each task while also keeping the view that our time is finite. The long view, that our time is limited by the death of the body, keeps a steady flame glowing under our lives that propels us, while in our daily experience we keep the view that there is plenty of time in order to stay aware and to experience equanimity rather than frustration.

Adding another layer onto the paradox that there is plenty of time, but it is limited, is that eternity is said to be found in the moment; right now. This is a metaphysical reason that it is important to take the view that there is plenty of time. With plenty of time we can relax into the present and experience it more deeply. The more we experience being present, the deeper becomes our understanding of things we cannot rationally explain. Our wisdom grows. Rajneesh said, in talking about the name "Mojud" and its two meanings, one who is conscious and one who is present to the present: "If you are present inside, if you have a presence of consciousness, the second thing will automatically happen – you will be present to the present.

You will not have any past, you will not have any future – you will have only this moment. And this moment is vast, this moment is enormous, this moment has eternity in it. Only those who live in the present, only those who are present to the present, know what eternity is, know what deathless life is, know the mystery, in the inexplicable mystery."

The farmer with the pig under his arm is our guru. His question is loaded. It sets us thinking. What's time to a pig? We laugh. The pig is not a human being; time is nothing to it. But don't we treat our own lifetime this way? We differ from the pig because we can conceptualize time. Concepts become beliefs. We create our reality through belief. Since time responds perfectly to our beliefs about it, we can actually alter time. The belief that there is plenty of time is expansive. It removes stress from our lives and allows us to walk on the earth with less urgency and more peace. The understanding that we have a certain span to walk in this manner is the big container that keeps us moving forward. Time becomes our ally, our safe nest. Suddenly there is time to do our inner work alongside the understanding of why we need to get on with it.

Just Sit

"The purpose of meditation is to awaken in us the skylike nature of mind, and to introduce us to that which we really are, our unchanging pure awareness that underlies the whole of life and death.
In the stillness and silence of meditation, we glimpse and return to that deep inner nature that we so long ago lost sight of amid the busyness and distraction of our minds."

Sogyal Rinpoche

When I was in college, I was accepted into a poetry class taught by Helen Chasin, a Breadloaf Scholar and serious poet. She was the writer-in-residence at the college. Many students wanted to be writers, or thought they already were, so that each semester the list of applicants for her course was long. You had to submit a work to apply, she only took a few students, and, every semester, you had to try out again. I was very excited to be accepted into her class. I remember our first assignment very well. She told us to write a poem about a flower. There was heavy groaning from the class. After all, we were serious about writing, and we had important things to say; new ways of expressing our feelings and emotions. "A flower? Flowers are so ordinary; they have been described ad nauseam, we complained." "Exactly" she said, "very challenging."

Meditation or "sitting" poses the same challenge. It is so described. There are thousands of articles, books and teachers concerning this subject, but to write about inner work without some mention of this vital practice would be to ignore a principal tool in

211

learning what our life is trying to teach us. When we sit, we come face to face with the nature of the mind; how it pulls us away from awareness; from the moment; from now. In meditation we learn to release ourselves from that insistent pull, and, in so doing, we experience equanimity, a peace and calm that is comfortable with all things. At the very least, in any sitting, we will discover our current condition. We will see clearly the anxiety, tension, or fearfulness that often lie just beneath the surface of our daily thoughts and actions, usually working away invisibly.

When we sit, we not only observe the ever-busy mind, but through intelligent practice, we experience real peace by releasing ourselves from its control. This peace is the foundation for a more centered and focused outer life. Once we experience inner calm in this manner we gain the certainty that this tranquility exists. The knowledge that we can access this place is a great boon. How often have we wanted to feel peaceful and at ease? How often have we desired to be calm and less stressed? Meditation is the doorway to inner peace; the place of true calmness that we can access as necessary. So, by sitting, we can fill our being with peace. And this peace is cumulative. The more you sit, the more accessible it is when you are not sitting.

Meditation has physiological as well as psycho-spiritual benefits. Dr. Dean Ornish has helped many people prevent and actually reverse heart disease with a combination of meditation and diet with no surgery. I have read that men who meditate experience eighty percent less heart trouble. At the Omega Center in Rhinebeck, New York, Dr. Jon Kabat-Zinn taught health care professionals meditation and mindfulness to help them cope with the high stress of their profession. His course was one of the most popular at the center, year after year. It was always full. As for our spiritual growth, most, if not all, spiritual teachers sit daily. With meditation the question is not "is this good for me" but "what is holding me back from this vital practice?"

Despite the well-documented benefits of meditation, there are many misconceptions and many reasons why people do not take advantage of this practice. "It is complicated. It is exotic and weird. It is religious somehow and much different from my religion. We don't do that in my peer group. I would need a teacher to do it. It is hard. I can't sit still. Special clothing is required. Special equipment is needed. There are too many different kinds of meditation. How do I know I am choosing the right one? People will think I am strange. It is painful; you have to sit on a cushion on the floor. I don't have time." Ed Quinn, a Vipasana meditator who works in the corporate field uses the term "inner focus" rather than meditation when he teaches meditation, in order not to scare away his participants. He told me that often people would come up to him after an inner focus session and say, "that was meditation wasn't it?" as if they had done something naughty, or he had tricked them into something they would have never done otherwise.

People talk about meditation as if it was something complicated and difficult to learn, but meditation is really quite simple. The mind sometimes tries to hold us back from trying meditation by making a big deal out of it. At its core meditation is simply sitting quietly and not letting our thoughts run away with us. That's it! We can forget all the special requirements and judgments and simply make time and sit down for a minute. Using a chair is fine. Since meditation is an inner practice we can take it with us wherever we go. Although some conditions are more favorable than others, we can meditate at any time and in almost any condition. Out on the porch is fine. Riding in a car (not driving) is fine. In the waiting room is fine. Thich Nach Hann teaches a walking meditation. Consider what Sogyal Rinpoche has to say on the subject:

> *"Sometimes when I meditate, I don't use any particular method. I just allow my mind to rest, and I find, especially when I am inspired, that I can bring my mind home and relax very quickly. I sit quietly and rest in the nature of mind; I don't question or doubt whether I am in the 'correct state.' There is no effort, only a rich understanding, wakefulness and uncertainty.*
>
> *When I am in the nature of mind, the ordinary mind is no longer there. There is no need to sustain or confirm a sense of being. I simply am. A fundamental trust is present. There is nothing particular to do."*[32]

---

[32] Sogyal Rinpoche, Glimpse after Glimpse, HarperSanFransisco, 1995

Here we will focus on developing a daily meditation to take place in your home or workspace.

Even though meditation is basically sitting quietly and not letting our thoughts run away with us, there are some things that help the process and others that make it more difficult. A nice quiet room is preferable; so find a quiet place to sit. I prefer silence to background music or chanting, but this is a personal choice. It is a good practice to learn to be comfortable with silence and stillness. Good posture is very helpful. If you are sitting in a chair, make sure it has no arms and that it feels right. It should fit you in a way that allows you to keep your back straight and your feet firmly on the ground. The seat should not be too soft. The reason for good posture is that we need good energy flow for the best benefit and we want to stay awake. If we sit on a cushion and cross our legs, we also want to keep the back straight. We do not have to strain to keep the back straight. We can envision a string going up from the head and holding us in a straight posture. Often we straighten out more as we move deeper into meditation.

In Tibetan meditation, practitioners keep the eyes slightly open, while in many other styles practitioners close the eyes. Open eyes are soft eyes, not viewing eyes. What works for you? Closing the eyes is easy. Some focus on the third eye between the eyebrows. Some people have a mantra they say over and over as they sit, often internally; others are silent. Many follow the breath in and out. If you don't have a mantra, following the breath is an excellent way to practice. I like to close the forefinger and thumb of each hand into a circle and place them palms up on my knees. Some sit with their hands folded in their lap. Do what is comfortable for you. Contrary to some people's ideas, there is no need for pain. If you feel pain, shift your body to release it and find a more comfortable position. You can also play with pain using the breath. Breathe into the pain; stay with it without making it wrong and see what happens. But dealing with pain is not the focus of meditation, and it is just as well to be comfortable. It is not necessary to sit on a cushion or zafu. If you find that sitting cross-legged, tailor fashion in this way is uncomfortable, then don't do it. Sitting in a straight chair with your feet on the ground is fine. All this getting arranged is important, as Mipam Rinpoche says like "mounting a horse;"t aking our seat. We are demonstrating our intention. This only takes a moment but it is important.

From meditation sessions with a Theravada Buddhist monk I learned to begin my meditation with nice even breaths. On exhale, I release the tension at the top of my head. I work my way down the forehead to the nose area and face, then the jaw, exhaling and relaxing. I relax the shoulders. I hold the body straight but easy. I can repeat this pattern for a while and then enter into meditation.

At this point, both beginner and old pro encounter the same phenomena. What happens? We start thinking. Often, when we begin our meditation the mind is like a wild animal; untamed and used to having its own way, it does not like being confined or channeled. It takes us on little voyages. This is precisely what we don't want to happen, but when we resist we energize the resistance and become lost in the resistance itself. Because of this undesirable phenomenon, many believe that it is necessary to rid ourselves of thought, but this is a futile idea. The Tibetan teachers say "it is a tall order to ask for meat without bones and tea without leaves." And Sogyal Rinpoche Says: "As long as you have a mind, you will have thoughts and emotions." So what we want to do is not rid ourselves of thoughts but to change our relationship to thoughts. We want to tame and train ourselves to let them pass on rather than try to vanquish them.

The Indian teacher, H.W.L. Poonja gave very good advice in this area. He taught his students to envision a room without doors or windows and without ceiling and floor. Thoughts simply pass through the room. He used a wonderful phrase when talking of thoughts that interrupt meditation. "They will arise, don't try to stop them, but don't let them land," he would say.

Our meditation is focused on our breath or our mantra; then a thought enters. This is normal; when it tries to land we go back to our meditation, our focus on breathing or our mantra. In the early moments of our meditation the thoughts usually have more success in landing. We find ourselves swept away into a story or fantasy. Suddenly, we realize that we are not meditating. Often, because we have taken a dedicated quiet moment, important thoughts and observations arise, perhaps about our day or our life, but thinking about these things, no matter how important they seem, is not the purpose of our meditation. This is another way the mind carries us away. I like to remind myself that "right now I am meditating not ruminating." In our house we have an expression. We say, "I am not in that compartment right now." This reminds us that we have dedicated certain times for certain things. The things I am not doing right now will have their time. When we are meditating, and distractions come up, we remind ourselves, "Right now I am meditating. This is the compartment I am in." The distraction has its own compartment and time for reflection.

The mind is infinitely clever. When we notice that we are wandering, daydreaming or reflecting, it can trap us again by carrying us into self-criticism such as, "I am not doing this right" or "this is so frustrating". We might compare ourselves to some standard or person. We must also let these distractions pass through the room with no walls, doors, windows, floor or ceiling. No matter what our thoughts, whether about important issues in our life, or the quality of the meditation itself, we simply resume concentration on mantra or breath. Each time we consciously return to our practice we lessen the power of the tales that arise. We get better at catching ourselves when we go astray and bringing our attention back to the meditation. Each time we become conscious of the mind's action, of an arising story, and let it go, the stories lose power. The wild horse settles down. We have not frightened it by trying to dominate it nor are we riding it every which way it desires.

As stated earlier, when we sit we see the state of our mind clearly in a way that we usually do not. We are watching the bumper cars and ourselves in them. I sit in the morning and am sometimes amazed that at such an early hour, after a nights' rest, that I have so much tension both in body and mind. I have learned that I have days when my meditation is wonderful, and days when it is bumpy. Both are fine. That's the way it is. Some days it is hard to stay focused and on others the meditation flows very smoothly. Expecting a great deal from our meditation, every time we sit, sets up an ongoing expectation that can rob our focus and carry us away into judgment.

How long should one sit? Kirpal Singh taught that to make a practice of sitting everyday for even five minutes was more important than skipping a meditation. The act is more important than the length of the sitting. Keeping the practice is the important thing. Often, I find that when I think I am going to just have a short sit, I end up falling into the meditation and forgetting about the time. It is true that the longer you sit the deeper the benefit. For instance, I have found that there is a point at around forty five minutes into my meditation (I checked this) at which my body of its own accord, in one big wave, sheds an entire layer of tension that, even in my relaxed state, was not noticeable before. At this point, without effort, my posture straightens even further. It is as if some cosmic puppeteer has pulled a string that seems to align me perfectly. This only happens when I am not intending it, expecting it or thinking about it. As we meditate longer the body often becomes taller and the back more strong and straight. We seem to inhabit our body more deeply.

To meditate is to learn the nature of the mind. Mipam Rinpoche tells us that, "true liberation is life without the illusion of 'me' or 'you'" and that "meditation is the practice that reveals our non existence." [33] Our mind works hard to assemble the illusion of our self, our ego. Meditation helps to undo this work. On a more mundane level, it increases our ability to focus on things more fully in our daily life. It is very powerful tool for centering and calming when we feel upset. I have even used it when I had an asthma attack and was far from help and had no medicine. Just sitting in a clean air environment and breathing calmly for a long time I was able to dispel the attack, rather than feed the fear of not enough breath. When I have trouble sleeping at night I will often get up and sit for a while. When I go back to bed I usually enter a very deep and peaceful sleep.

There are many meditation teachers to help us learn. As usual, we need to use our discernment to find what works best for us. From the austerity of Zen practice to the chanting and sound that sometimes occurs in other practices the same benefits apply.

Without meditation we can still learn, make discovery and grow, but to gain the serenity we seek, the calm center, we can find no greater ally than the still and focused mind that sitting in meditation engenders. Meditation is the proven and ancient counter

---

[33] Sakyong Mipam, Turning the Mind into an Ally, Riverhead Books 2003

to the urgency and stress of our daily lives. As things go faster and faster, it becomes an even more important practice.

The Magnificent Gesture

ALI IN BATTLE
Jelaluddin Bakhi - Rumi - early 1200's

Learn from Ali how to fight
without your ego participating.

God's Lion did nothing
that didn't originate
from his deep center.

Once in battle he got the best of a certain knight
and quickly drew his sword. The man,
helpless on the ground, spat
in Ali's face. Ali dropped his sword,
relaxed, and helped the man to his feet.

"Why have you spared me?
How has lightening contracted back
into its cloud? Speak, my prince,
so that my soul can begin to stir
in me like an embryo."

Ali was quiet and then finally answered,
"I am God's Lion, not the lion of passion.
The sun is my lord. I have no longing
except for the one.

When a wind of personal reaction comes,
I do not go along with it.

There are many winds full of anger,
and lust and greed. They move the rubbish
around, but the solid mountain of our true nature
stays where it's always been.

There's nothing now
except the divine qualities.
Come through the opening into me.

Your impudence was better than any reverence,
because in this moment I am you and you are me.

I give you this opened heart as God gives gifts:
the poison of your spirit has become
the honey of friendship.[34]

The ego is undoubtedly the source of most of the world's troubles, as well as our personal problems. Many do not even know it exists, blindly obeying its demands without question. If we do know, we might be unfamiliar with how it functions. We have become so accustomed to the ego's voice, so deceived by its subtle and clever disguises, that, when we are faced with the choice between the ego and love, we find it extremely difficult to choose love, even though it is love we truly desire. The gesture of letting go of the ego, choosing love and opening the heart, is the quintessential spiritual gesture, the epicenter of all spiritual practice and growth. Until we learn to make this difficult and profound inner gesture, our spirituality will be nothing more than a highly evocative and fascinating intellectual experiment. The opening of the heart is the great treasure on the spiritual path. Only the voice of the ego would argue otherwise. Opening our heart when it wants to stay closed, ignoring the ego, is a profound inner gesture and is often accompanied by a difficult struggle. Working with the ego is included in the Inner Work section of this book, rather than the

---

[34] Barks, Coleman with Moyne, John, *The Essential Rumi*. Castle Books 1997, page 223

Action section, because it is more an inner challenge than an outer action.

When Babbie and I used to produce the Noble Adventure relationship workshop with our friends Don and Martha, a great deal of the work we did focused on the ego; understanding how it operates and learning tools to deal with it. Intimate relationship is one area in which we can be sure we will encounter the ego in all its glory. If we want to learn how to let go of the ego, there is no better practice field than intimate relationship and no better ally than our partner. Remember the theory that it is much easier being a guru if you don't have a partner, and isn't it interesting that so many gurus are single! For those of us fortunate enough to be in relationship, there will be no end to egocentric issues. Consciously dealing with these issues is central to creating a vibrant, alive and healthy relationship. With practice, we can develop the skills necessary for working with our constantly arising egos. Our issues can become fewer as the wisdom developed over time influences the way we respond to the ego.

Whether we are in an intimate relationship or not, the ego is, more often than not, the root cause of our all difficulties in the world. What is the ego? Here we can describe it as the voice of fear; the voice that tells us to attack others, withdraw or defend ourselves. The ego teaches us that we are always in danger; danger from others who are trying to take advantage of us. It reminds us that there is danger everywhere. Everywhere there are things to fear: in our family, in our job, in our environment and in all our relationships. The ego disguises itself as our best friend. It is always watching out for our safety because it believes we are always unsafe. As long as we take the ego's view we will feel unsafe, no matter what actions we take. We will try to control the world and hold onto it tightly, thinking safety resides in control and manipulation in one form or another. The ego has us spend time reviewing the past and planning the future so that we can feel safe. The irony is that the more we deny the ego and its plans, the safer we discover we truly are. But to discover this we have to take the sometime difficult action of letting go of the ego. Often this has all the appeal of jumping off a cliff. Nevertheless, we now understand that sometimes we have to jump off the cliff in order to experience new levels of consciousness and

221

understanding. We have to let go of the branch when the ego wants us to hold on more and more tightly.

Identifying the ego and letting it go is a daily practice of inner being. As we let go of past fears, false beliefs, coping mechanisms and unskillful behavior we will find ourselves walking the world with less and less fear. We have to stay humble, however, because, at any time, the ego can leap up and create trouble. The ego is very powerful, and it is used to having its way, especially since it has been able to disguise itself for years as our best friend. Indeed, we are quite adapted to its counsel and its logic. We need to be vigilant and aware, watching as it arises and then doing the extraordinary; performing the great gesture of spirituality, denying its counsel when there is an opportunity to choose love. Christ was certainly the great teacher and example of this gesture, and is an invaluable inspiration for a world still locked in the embrace of the ego.

Awareness helps us to see when we are in the grip of the ego; it is often a terrible and fierce grip. Denying the ego is the most difficult inner battle we will ever encounter. This is where saints part ways with lesser mortals. The ability to truly let go of the ego is the mark of extraordinary spiritual progress. This is "turning the other cheek" or, in Ali's case, dropping the sword. As long as we stay under the sway of the ego, and do not work to thwart its influence over us, there will be situations in which we find ourselves reacting blindly with passion, rather than responding with wisdom and compassion. Denying the ego is in itself an act of wisdom. Each time we achieve this we make a great step forward. The challenge is constant.

It helps to understand how the ego operates in order to be aware of its presence. The ego is very active in our interpersonal dealings. This is an excellent place to begin inner work with the ego because any progress here will be reflected in our relationship to the larger world.

When a person makes a remark that hurts our feelings or somehow denies our dignity, we often go directly into reaction. We will usually attack them, defend ourselves or shutdown and withdraw from the conflict. These classical reactions of the ego often happen so quickly and compulsively that we are unaware that we are in the grip of the ego. The ego has taught us that we are not safe in various situations, and we have developed escapes so that, rather than taking personal responsibility for our reaction, as Ali did in battle; we automatically choose an old reaction. If we are fearful and take no action, but instead, either consciously or subconsciously, chose a strategy of later revenge, or deny and bury our reaction, we are letting the poison of the ego into our system. This happens when we use passive aggressive strategies to cope with perceived attacks. Many of us feel emotional pain the moment we perceive an attack, while some of us deny the pain and our subconscious deals with the matter. It is important to get in touch with our feelings and to be aware when we feel offended or hurt. How do we react? What method do we usually choose? Some people blow up in instant anger, others stuff it down. Some will laugh to cover their anger. When we see ourselves using our personal coping mechanisms we can be sure the ego is at work. We all have our own ways of honoring the ego.

Staying aware, we can quickly see the moments in which this happens. Taking personal responsibility for our reactions immediately takes us out of the dangerous loop of judgment and blame which carry us right along with the ego's plans. Using judgment and blame, the ego can justify taking unloving action. It can justify separation, revenge, anger and then rage. Taking personal responsibility as soon as possible for our ego based reactions also helps us to avoid one of the big allies of the ego, the voice of reason and logic that says things like "of course you should be mad, look what they said," or "you have every reason to withdraw your love." As stated earlier, these statements are always so logical, and yet, because they keep us under the sway of the ego, they are useless for relieving the situation. They do not contribute to our personal and spiritual growth. Denying the ego and replacing it with love is the major practice we must undertake if we want to grow spiritually and it is, without doubt, the most difficult. The entire world, the collective consciousness, is in the throes of the ego. It is hard to leave this mighty river. The current is strong. Few even try. Our progress, however, does not require everyone, or even a single person to change. If we wait for that, we will never change ourselves. We can leave that idea behind. Most of us are simply ignorant of the workings of the ego, and, even when we become aware of its control over our lives, we often shy away from making change, from letting go of this old friend. It is that logical voice of reason that keeps us coming back. But as we recognize it for what it is, a trick to keep us from change, which the ego sees as dangerous, and we stop applying its counsel, something remarkable begins to occur. We develop a new faith that sustains us; we begin to realize that we are intrinsically safe. Perceived assaults on our dignity, someone's rudeness, or being dismissed or demeaned begin to lose their power over us. We begin to recognize ignorant and unskillful behavior and become more able to separate it from the idea of personal attack. In fact, the more we practice letting go of the ego, the more we come to understand what *true* safety is all about. Feeling truly safe is a spiritual condition, the reward we receive when we let go of the ego. Rather than letting fear maintain and run our lives, we choose love. Love is spacious and easy rather that constricting and tight. The difference we feel is profound. Over time, as we begin to see our ego pulling us into a situation, we are able to question its authority. We can remind ourselves that we are safe regardless of what someone is saying or doing. It is our choice.

Sometimes, when I mention the ego, people remind me that the ego is important, that it has vital functions. They are upset that I question the ego's council. My response is that the ego doesn't need their support. It can manage on its own very well. The real work is understanding the ego and how it functions, and then learning how to ignore it when it is going to invite pain, trouble and suffering.

The gesture of choosing love, of letting go of the ego is an inner gesture. Often we make it unbeknownst to anyone but ourselves. Sometimes it is a real struggle, but over time, in certain common situations, it becomes easier. The two practices, "And I'm OK" and "Say it later" are very helpful in dealing with the ego when it suddenly arises.

The Rumi poem, *Ali in Battle* is perfectly descriptive of the workings of the ego. Rumi invites to us "learn how to fight without the ego participating." Ali is in a battle, a place where maximum passion is unleashed, where anger is always justified. The ego rules the battlefield. But what happens? A man spits on him, and Ali becomes aware that he is in the throes of passion. He becomes aware

224

that he has been swept away by his ego, and, right in the middle of the battle, he lets go of the ego. The man he was about to kill is awed by Ali's ability to ignore his ego and to maintain "his deep center." He says, "How has lightening contracted back into its cloud?" This is what happens when we find ourselves under the power of our ego, lightening strikes. We have the choice, right in the heart of the moment, a choice that can be extremely difficult; to deny the ego, withdraw the lightening. The man is stupefied. "Speak my prince so that my soul can begin to stir in me like an embryo." Through his action; through his choice Ali has demonstrated the "field of possibility" and inspiration is dawning in the man. Ali's response is truly interesting. Ali was quiet and then finally answered,

"I am God's Lion, not the lion of passion.
The sun is my lord. I have no longing
except for the one.
When a wind of personal reaction comes,
I do not go along with it.

There are many winds full of anger,
and lust and greed. They move the rubbish
around, but the solid mountain of our true nature
stays where it's always been.

There's nothing now
except the divine qualities.
Come through the opening into me."

To say "I am God's lion not the lion of passion" means that Ali has chosen to embrace love rather than the ego. To the mystics, God and love are one in the same. When he says, "I have no longing except for the one," he is denying separation and embracing union. The ego of course is all about separation, about me, about my feelings, about my position and my outcome versus other.

Ali is reminding us that the ego has many winds, and again, that out true nature is not ego. He names some of the manifestations, lust and greed. They "blow the rubbish about" means that they create no true value, only worthless distraction. Once the ego is banished there is nothing but the divine qualities, which are love, compassion, understanding, tolerance and union. To say "come through the opening to me" is to invite his former opponent into his heart where the divine qualities are residing. His heart has just opened. He invites his opponent to open his own heart, to share the joy. He then says:

"Your impudence was better than any reverence,
because in this moment I am you and you are me.

I give you this opened heart as God gives gifts:
the poison of your spirit has become
the honey of friendship."

The "impudence" of the man awoke Ali from the grasp of the ego. He became aware of the reflection of his own ego in the man's action. The ego is universal and shared by all. When we move beyond reaction, and see how the ego works in others as well as ourselves, how it separates us and denies us wholeness, we are better able to access compassion rather than ego behavior. Ali and his opponent became one as he acknowledged their mutual situation and the opportunity which allowed him to feel compassion. God's gifts are given freely with no strings attached. The ego likes strings. To say that, "The poison of your spirit has become the honey of friendship" is to acknowledge that the man's anger awakened Ali's open hearted nature and compassion. Seeing that he and his former enemy were both one and alike makes them friends. This is how great wisdom works, the wisdom found in our deep center.

Although often extremely difficult, this is the complete program for dealing with the ego. When we are in the throes of anger or any other ego manifestation we can choose to be aware of our situation. Are we attacking someone? Are we defending ourselves? Are we withdrawing, hurt and angry? At that moment we can make the choice to take personal responsibility for our reaction, drop the ego, and, when we do, we see the one, the universality of our condition, our heart fills with compassion rather than separation and love does the rest. What we thought was an enemy has awakened us from our passion and moved us to our own deep center, the place where wisdom rather than ego resides and guides. We find ourselves in a place of deep safety.

Doing open hearted listening can give us the same experience as Ali. Since inner work is about discovery, and since many of us are not really familiar with how powerful an influence the ego exerts, we can use the open hearted listening practice for identifying and working consciously with the ego in our own relationships. This exercise was one of the most powerful we shared at the Noble Adventure, and the participants practiced it several times during the retreat. Babbie and I use it in our relationship. Openhearted listening has been called other names such a conscious listening and compassionate listening. No matter what we call it, it is a powerful tool for making change. When we use it, we can gain quite an understanding of the workings of the ego, the struggle to let it go, and what happens when we do. We can adapt the fundamentals of this exercise into our communications with others, becoming more compassionate listeners. Here is how it works.

When you have a disagreement with someone, and you feel upset, you ask the person if they are willing to do open hearted listening with you. They do not have to do it right at that moment, but if they agree, it should be soon. If they do not want to sit and listen to your story and your truth then, to get things started, you can offer to listen to theirs. The ego likes to escape doing this kind of work. Whether you are the listener or the person telling the story does not actually matter, both positions bring great benefit. The listener learns to work directly with their ego as the desire to attack, defend or stonewall arises. The storyteller learns to speak the truth about their feelings, letting go of the ego's desire to judge and blame. Both involve awareness of the ego and an opportunity for letting it go.

We will call the person asking for openhearted listening "the speaker" and the person listening and responding "the validator."

The speaker, feeling hurt, unheard, angry or sad about something involving the validator asks for open hearted listening. "Would you be willing to do some open hearted listening?" they ask." Babbie and I have a rule that we will always answer "yes" to this question, however, we can also ask for some time to cool off and get centered before we listen. Here is the full form.

Open Hearted Listening

It is important to begin this process, from agreement.

The speaker or aggrieved person asks: "Would you be willing to do some openhearted listening?"

Validator – "Yes" or I would like to wait until a little later." (If the answer is "no", we try to agree to listen later. Saying "yes" when we want to say "no" can lead to the most challenging personal work we have ever attempted.

The process is divided into two parts:

Part One – Mirroring – The speaker tells their story and the validator mirrors the story back to them as well as they possibly can. Refinements and additions to the story are OK, but it is important, especially when starting out, to keep the process short. The story is best when fully understood, so being short and concise is very helpful. The validator controls the pace, asking for refinements, if necessary, and digesting the story by parts. If it is a long story, the validator can ask to mirror individual parts rather than the entire tale. They can also ask the speaker if they would be willing to pause if they need to mirror any complicated part. Both speaker and validator *work together* to get the story exactly right. The story must include the speaker's feelings. They need to remember, thoughts are not feelings. We often say things like "when you did this, I felt that you were X." A feeling is a direct emotion such as anger, hurt, or sadness. Remember, there are only a few emotions and we all share them. The emotional level is where we can transcend the ego in openhearted listening, where the opportunity for compassion exists.

When we are the speaker, we have to take responsibility for our feelings. Instead of saying, "When you did X, *it made me* feel (sad, angry, hurt)," we say, "When you did X, *I felt* sad or angry or hurt (the appropriate emotion). This removes blame for our condition from the story and away from the validator. It helps keep the story from triggering their ego. It is a statement of truth since we know that no one but ourselves can make us feel a certain way. The action of the validator has simply triggered our reaction. We own the reaction. Mirroring is the intellectual understanding of the situation.

After the mirroring, or during it if it occurs in pieces, the speaker decides whether the validator understands the story correctly, if the mirroring is accurate, and, if necessary, helps refine the story. Once the speaker has determined that validator has the story right, the process proceeds to part two, the validation. At this point, it is skillful for the speaker to thank the validator for their work in getting the story correct.

Part Two – Validation – The goal of the validation is for the validator to empathize with the speaker's emotional reality. The validator tells the speaker that he or she understands the feelings of the speaker, taking responsibility for their own part in the story. This is not assuming blame or guilt for the feelings of the speaker. The validator shaming themselves is not a part of the process. After the validation, the speaker determines if the validator *really* understands, or is truly validating the speaker's reality. The validation form is often some variation of, "I can understand how, when I did X, you felt X". *It is not re-mirroring.* It is best kept short.

Validating can be very difficult because the ego usually wants to interfere. It wants to tell its side of the story. It wants to slant the validation in a way that justifies our behavior. The ego might pretend it can't understand the story or is too tired to do the work. It might elicit nervous laughter. As the validator, it is often very difficult to set the ego aside and find the place where we can really feel what the speaker is feeling. It is hard to forget our own side of the story. It is hard not to defend our actions, those that precipitated the story to begin with. Really doing the validation well is the magnificent gesture at the core of all true spiritual growth, letting go of the ego and replacing it with compassion. This is what Ali achieved when he said "I am God's lion not the lion of passion."

The speaker is the judge of whether or not they feel validated. If they do not feel completely validated, they gently help the validator by telling them what isn't working, or what is missing, and the validator tries again. Sometimes this takes a while. Once the validation is accepted the speaker thanks the validator.

Sometimes, when a speaker cannot accept a validation, they are still subtly blaming or judging the validator. The speaker needs to focus their awareness on their own inner condition to see if this is so, especially if the validator seems to really be trying, but is not getting through. The speaker has to work through any lingering blame and take responsibility for their feelings. This does not mean denying an emotion. Emotions can be expressed in openhearted listening through tone and skillful expression rather than judgment and blame. If we are angry or sad, for instance, it would be inauthentic to pretend we weren't. We would not be able to be validated.

It the validator is feeling guilty about their part in the story, it detracts from the validation as the attention shifts to themselves and away from the speaker. This is yet another clever ruse of the ego's.

As I said, when it is our turn to be the validator, there is little doubt that we will come face to face with our ego. We may also discover the ways the ego has devised for being unable to validate the speaker. It is very important to remember that this exercise is not about who is right. Remember the expression, "being right isn't it!" Being right is a trick the ego uses to keep us thoroughly hooked.

Many of us can't help thinking that our validation is the same as a confession that we have been bad or are wrong. We will exhibit all kinds of behavior to exit this place. In our childhood many of us felt great shame when we did something wrong, shame that was exacerbated by pointing fingers and angry parents. When we are confronted with our own unskillful behavior, and its effect on others we squirm, we laugh nervously, or we can't think of the right words. When this happens we need to remember to have mercy on ourselves. I often use my kind voice saying things to myself like, "Babbie is really angry or upset about my behavior, and I'm OK. I am still a good person who simply acted in an unskillful manner. We all act unskillfully sometimes." I also remind myself that what I am hearing is her experience; it is not necessarily right or wrong if it is different from my experience. We have agreed to work with her experience, not mine. I can still have my experience of the event. I just can't go there when I agree to validate her experience.

Tips and reminders for Openhearted Listening:

Speaker and Validator - Try not to get into a conversation about the process while you are doing it. This is often the way the ego defeats the whole process. Talk about what worked and didn't work later.

Speaker - Keep blame out of the process including subtle blame. Own your feelings. Your validator triggered them but is not responsible for them.

Validator - Remember this story is not about you. It is usually about an action that you took which triggered a reaction in the speaker. Regardless of how they phrase the story, this is always true.

Validator - Remember, the validation is not a repetition of the mirroring. Keep it direct and short and focus on feeling the truth of the speaker's emotion. Especially unhelpful are phrases like, "I understand how you feel that way because I once had the same thing happen." Your story is not helpful, but, instead, detracts from the force of your empathy. The power is in the eyes and the voice. Crying or laughing, and long validations are signs that we are feeling uncomfortable and distract from a good validation.

Both speaker and validator - Stay with the story. Don't digress and analyze. Stick to the form. Keep it simple. Attempts to alter the basic form do not work.

If the validator cannot reach validation after several attempts, they can ask to try later (within 24 hours).

The twenty-four hours rule - Openhearted listening is not a back and forth practice in which one person goes after the other. After a validation it is best to not discuss the story for 24 hours at least. If the validator *has done a successful validation* and still has an issue about the story at that time, they should wait for a day to ask for openhearted listening. Otherwise, the emotional connection shared during the open hearted listening gets diluted into chatter and mental dissection or worse, justification and blame. Going back and forth can defeat the wonderful moment of compassion and the experience of the heart opening. It also distracts the validator as they contemplate what they are going to say in response to the speaker's story rather than staying in the present moment as is necessary.

Again, a person who is asked to do openhearted listening in the thick of an emotional exchange can ask for time to settle down before listening, however, the shorter the time period, the better.

The realization that we can understand and even empathize with how another person feels about a situation and still have our own feelings is powerful. There is no reason to attack or defend, and we have a great opportunity to take responsibility for our actions. We may learn that, sometimes, the way we act has a negative effect on others that we never knew about or expected. We can do some inner work to find out why this behavior occurs and find out how to let it go.

When we are asked to do open hearted listening, the strong resistance we often encounter in ourselves, whether through nervous laughter, anger, defensive behavior or stubborn refusal, is the direct experience of the ego. Using awareness we can see how powerful this force is. We can see how it binds us into a habitual reaction pattern that separates us from others.

The ego will always be waiting to take us over, despite our hard work. But, by recognizing its voice, becoming aware of its presence, and knowing how it functions, we can minimize its control significantly. Learning how to let go of the ego in challenging situations is vital to our quest to be loving and compassionate. The gesture of opening the heart in the face of the ego is the principal act that will bring the kind of change we all deeply desire into the world. It is the magnificent gesture of a spiritual warrior.

Action

What if your heart took over the creation of your reality?
What would the world be like then?

Action Overview

Through the practice of awareness we come into contact with the world in a conscious manner. By taking personal responsibility for our life we discover the obstacles to our own evolution into a more loving, courageous and compassionate being. Through inner work we discover the resources and develop the inner skills that can overcome these obstacles. Yet, until we take action, by manifesting a new response, or a new way of being in the world, we do not seal our learning in reality. It is still theoretical, and it has achieved no empirical value. We will never know if what we have discovered is true for us, or if the changes we have embraced in our inner work are effective or helpful in the outer world.

To make our inner work real we may be required to jump off the cliff, to take courageous and heroic action in a situation, often for the first time; to stand up to or contradict an authority figure; to act in a way that may offend others but represents our own truth, or to speak authentically for the first time. In taking action we test our new understandings. Then, we can use awareness to notice the feedback from our action and refine our approach. We can then take improved action. In acting on our realizations and honoring our inner work, we discover the rewards of all the work we have been doing. We meet the world with a new face. Over time, we experience change fully.

Make It So!

*"A prince is just a conceit until
he does something with generosity."*

J. Rumi, *The Far Mosque*

Awareness, personal responsibility and inner work focus on how we view and interpret the world, and how we react or respond internally. This work is reflective and introspective. The fourth component of learning what our life is trying to teach us, action, transforms our inner work into a new reality so it can become more than theories, ideas or feelings. Action gives birth to the new person that we are creating through our inner work. The Bagavad Gita tells us: *"Not even for a moment can a man be without action. Helplessly all are driven to action by the action born of nature."* Becoming conscious about the nature, power and use of action is a vital part of our journey.

With action, we focus on manifesting our inner world skillfully and powerfully. It is the point at which we test our new understandings and discoveries and also hone them. Spontaneous action, action we take without this cautious, preliminary consideration, also alters our inner world, creating change through discovery and experimentation. In either case, once integrated, new action can become a part of the natural fabric of our lives, a new way of being.

Our action is our contribution to the world, and it is how the world sees us. When our inner world is filled with fear, the actions we choose reflect this fear. We act in ways that are judgmental, scornful and intolerant. We are inflexible and opinionated. We feel discontent and agitated. The actions we take are often reflected back at us by others. Thus, when we are unloving, we find ourselves attracting unloving energy. This is why doing our inner work is so important, because it eventually manifests as action, and action changes our outer world by attracting its own reflection.

In the same fashion when our inner world is filled with compassion, love and understanding these will be made visible by the action we take. We will find ourselves going to mercy before judgment, kindness before scorn, and compassion before separation. Our action demonstrates the choice and power of love and, as a result the world becomes more open, forgiving and joyful.

The difference between these two ways of being becomes clear once we have embraced awareness. Awareness quickly puts us in touch with suffering, first our own and then that of others. We become aware of our fear, and we see the same fear in others. We discover how alike we are. From this awareness of similarity compassion arises and judgment diminishes. We discover that, when we work with our fear and bring love and mercy into our own lives, we free ourselves bit by bit from our suffering. We realize that by being compassionate towards others we ease their suffering in the same way. We keep paying attention, and we awaken to what is real. We discover the unified nature of life, and separation and fear begin to lose their terrible, lonely hold. As we progress, the choice for the holy, for love, for compassion becomes more compelling.

This choice is deeply reinforced by taking action that manifests these states. It is an act of compassion that teaches us the beauty and power of compassion. It is an act of love that draws us to become the lover. We experience the profound effect of such action in ourselves and witness the harmony it creates in our immediate world. These changes are not intellectual ideas, but powerful forces we learn to work with through action. The action we aspire to, as the fourth vehicle of our quest to learn what life is trying to teach us, is action that is rooted in love and compassion. We practice to create action that is intentional, purposeful and skillful. Like Ali in battle we aspire to do nothing that does not come from the deep core of our being.

There is more to this than our personal evolution. Discovering and taking action with the power of love and kindness are vital to creating a world that is kind and loving; the world most of us deeply desire. By doing our own inner work, working with fear and learning compassion for ourselves, we automatically bring change to the world around us as we encounter it in a kinder and more skillful manner. Thus changing the world is a very personal endeavor. If we really want to change the world and make it more peaceful, we are required to experience peace within ourselves. To end war, we have to end the inner wars. If we want peace, we have to begin with ourselves. For most of us, there is plenty of work to do. We will know we are nearing inner peace when our vision of the world softens and becomes more flexible, when our judgment is less active.

Most of us spend our lives vacillating between ignorance and compassion, between action that is selfish and unkind, and action that is loving; between consciousness and unconsciousness. This is nothing new. Kabir, the 15th century poet-mystic, said of our condition:

> "Between the conscious and the unconscious,
> the mind has put up a swing:
> all earth's creatures, even the supernovas,
> sway between these two trees.
> and it never winds down."[35]

Because we swing back and forth between the conscious and the unconscious, change is slower than we would like. However, one interesting way that we can speed up our evolution is by forcing change through action. We do this by taking skillful action, regardless of our inner condition, in the moment a skilful action is required. For instance, we can deliberately ignore the ego when we notice it wants to react to events unskillfully, and instead we can choose to respond carefully or withhold action until it's possible to respond truthfully without judgment or blame.

One of the interesting things we learn from NLP (neuro-linguistic programming) is that, by taking a new and different action, we actually create new neural paths in the brain. By creating new neural paths we alter habitual, reactive behaviors. Thus, action can be both a reflection of our inner state and a force that changes that

---

[35] Bly, Robert. The Kabir Book, Becon Press, 1977 page 11

state. In other words, creation moves in both directions, changes in our inner world creates new action and taking action creates inner change. Thus, through action, we bring about new states of being. This is good news. It means that we do not have to wait for our inner being to achieve perfection before we begin taking conscious and powerful action. We can eliminate the requirement of inner perfection as an excuse for not taking action or as a prerequisite for taking action. We can simply jump off the cliff.

Whether action manifests from our inner being or we impose it, having an action practice, is very helpful. As we now know, each of us contains "basic goodness." A primary task of spiritual growth is accessing and manifesting this goodness and appreciating it in others. We are taught general rules for this process such as "to love our neighbor" and to "practice forgiveness," but often no specific means or forms for doing these things. For instance, with absolutely no training, and parents and friends as our usual models, we are expected to know how to deal with the difficult emotional situations we experience in our relationships. The same is true with the basic action of bringing love into the world around us. We have no real training. We know we are supposed to act kindly, even when we feel under attack. We've been told to turn the other cheek. But how exactly do we do this and reconcile such action with anger and feelings of being diminished? When we practice specific, compassion-based actions we can learn to access and manifest our own basic goodness more easily, thereby altering our habitual, conditioned responses.

This section of this book is composed of specific action practices that we can use to exercise compassion, become more skillful at communication and enhance all of our relationships. Because they all involve ways of choosing love in the face of fear, in moments when we might rather keep our hearts closed, these are very spiritual practices. But they are very subtle. For one thing, they do not require the cooperation or knowledge of others. Often no one else will be directly aware that they are occurring. However, these practices can dramatically change our world view, create personal equanimity, and diminish our fear. They contribute to an evolving sense of physical and emotional safety in addition to being a boon to others we encounter daily.

With the action practices in this section we will be applying more consciousness to everyday action. Rather than learning anything entirely new, we will be refining and enhancing familiar daily actions, like communicating and listening, and becoming more conscious of their effects. In many ways, these action practices are a form of "seva" or service, and life offers many, many opportunities for their application. Using these practices helps to keep us conscious and aware.

If we need recognition for our service, then these action practices are not what we are seeking. I call the kind of action we will be practicing "love as a subversive activity." We are learning and refining action that brings love into the world, but we do it without seeking acknowledgement, without fanfare. This lack of self-congratulation and pride gives compassionate action authenticity. We are not being tested, we are not seeking a good grade, and we do not need anyone's opinion or approbation. The wonderful well-known description of love, from First Corinthians in the Bible, defines what we are working to achieve as we use these practices:

> *"Love is patient and kind;*
> *Love is not jealous or boastful;*
> *It is not envious, arrogant or rude.*
> *It does not rejoice in wrong.*
> *Love does not insist on its own way.*
> *It is not irritable or resentful;*
> *It does not rejoice at wrong, but rejoices in the right.*
> *Love bears all things, believes all things, hopes all things, endures all things.*
> *Love never ends."*

The Bhagavad Gita tells us: "The world is in the bonds of action, unless the action is consecration." Consecrated action is holy action, action that brings wholeness. Love is the energy and the force that brings and creates wholeness. Therefore it is to loving and compassionate action that we devote ourselves. And it is this action that increases our consciousness and frees us from the bonds of suffering.

Many like to believe that if we go to church on Sunday and say our prayers daily, we have done our spiritual requirement, and then we can beat our slaves on Monday. Again, it is easy to see that religious fundamentalism can become an excuse for limiting love and enjoying the fellowship of judgment. Behind the walls of our religion, supported by fear, we allow ourselves to judge who we believe is deserving of love and who is undeserving. When it comes to judgment, it is usually easy to find companions and consensus. We join other like-minded people for this purpose. The reality is that love is unequivocal. We are either manifesting it through our inner world and outer action, or we are not, and we instinctively know the difference as we tune in with awareness. By compromising with our judging self, the mind has created the notion of conditional love, but this is not love. There is no half-love, no middle place. Love is all or it is nothing. Through action we can make this discovery over and over. Unconditional love is the province of saints. It can be difficult to manifest, but we have to practice if we want a lick of the ice cream cone.

All of our awareness, personal responsibility and inner work do nothing really until we bring them into reality through action. As the British commanders used to say when presented with a good idea from a subordinate, we need to, "make it so." With scholarly work we can all become great pundits but, in order to learn what life is really about, and in order for the changes we want in our lives to take place, we are definitely required to take action. This seems obvious, and yet, because we habitually avoid change, we avoid new action as well, diminishing our own potential and possibility. Because we do not know what responses new action will engender, and because it can be difficult to stretch into a new way of being, taking new action is very often an act of courage. There is rich reward here. Repetitious acts of courage, the willingness to try new things, create a field of courage and we become encouraged, or filled with courage. Our courage, our ability to voyage into the unknown, to try new things, to challenge ourselves, and to maintain our integrity in the face of personal attack are all enhanced; our self esteem is strengthened. We become more of who we really are.

Taking action enhances our personal integrity because action is the way in which we unite our inner world with the outer world. Action breaks down the barriers fear has created between these two worlds; so that our world becomes less fragmented, more whole and congruent. Without action it is difficult to create firm boundaries or clarity about who we are and what we believe. The more comfortable we become with our response to the world through skillful action, the safer we feel. The difference between action and inaction is the difference between coming forth and hiding, between being a participant in life, the one alive and engaged, and the numb observer seeking safety in disengagement. There is much truth to the old phrase, "actions speak louder than words." Oliver Wendell Homes said, "A life is action and passion. It is required of a man that he should share the passion and action of his time, at peril of being judged not to have lived."

It helps to understand some of the difficulties we encounter when taking action. Often when we take a certain action for the first time, the action doesn't work out the way we had envisioned or hoped. For instance, when we try to use authentic communication, speaking our truth without judgment or blame about something that we have formerly repressed or denied, we may fumble our words and feel awkward. The person with whom we are sharing our truth might react negatively, so that we suddenly feel uncomfortable and emotionally unbalanced by their reaction. We can have mercy on ourselves when this happens. It is not unusual, when taking a new and more conscious action, to encounter obstacles both from within and without. Learning how to act more consciously takes practice. It is exactly like the tired but apt simile of learning to ride a bicycle. When we first try to ride we fall and it is very frustrating. Then we go a few feet without falling and experience the joy of movement and balance, a wonderful but brief experience. Though our experience was brief, we have gotten the taste of balancing and we keep on trying until one day we ride joyfully and naturally. An awkward attempt or a rebuff, as we try new ways of being, is not an excuse for quitting; we can use this feedback to develop our skill. Using awareness, personal responsibility and inner work to review our unskillful or frightened reactions, we become more adept at turning habitual reactions to fearful and unpleasant conditions into balanced responses. While new action does not always come forth perfectly, there are also wonderful occasions when our new action works very well. These moments are very exciting and gratifying.

Becoming aware of some of the ways we avoid action can help keep us in action. One of the classical ways we avoid action is by studying about it. We read books, attend workshops, join church groups, or take up psychological studies or philosophy. Great scholars learn scriptures by heart. We talk of love, or study inspirational stories and scripture without translating these teaching stories into personal action. But again, until we express new understandings through action they simply remain ideas, no matter how glamorous or appealing; no matter how many people agree with us. Until we bring what we are learning into our own life through action, no important change in our lives or personal contributions will result. This is what the Bhagavad Gita refers to when it states: "He who withdraws from actions, but ponders on their pleasures in his heart, he is under a delusion and is a false follower of the Path."

Why are those of us who withdraw from action under a delusion? Why are we "false followers of the path?" Because we are not speaking the truth as we know it in our hearts; we are not entering the world fully with its pain and difficulties. We must take action in order for our truth to be real, in order to brand it into our hearts and minds through experience. When we do this there is often less need for us to explain and discourse, rather we can exemplify and demonstrate possibility.

As the Gita makes clear, we can't really avoid action even if we try ("the world is in the bonds of action"). Total renunciation, withdrawing from the world, is not the answer it tells us, if we wish to attain supreme perfection or enlightenment. Even if we are not interested in seeking these lofty ends, without action we will be unable to achieve the psychological and spiritual growth that makes our lives more meaningful, more peaceful and spiritually rich. We are encouraged to use the life before us, taking action with what is being presented moment-by-moment, but often we fool ourselves into not taking action. We become very withdrawn, renouncing the world, thinking, "no action is perhaps the spiritual way," we drop out or numb ourselves to life. But, when we withdraw from action, we actually slow or stop our spiritual growth and limit our spiritual experience. Of course, there are times to withdraw and practice one or more forms of renunciation, but a life dedicated to renunciation becomes dry and brittle. Action, entering life fully, is necessary for living the ordinary life extraordinarily. We are encouraged to engage with the situations of our everyday life. The mundane world offers us the greatest spiritual treasures. The world right around us is filled with opportunities for skillful and loving action.

We are all acquainted with those who are experts in things spiritual and yet sometimes act in less than a spiritual fashion. The Samaritans were the biblical representatives of this condition. In the spiritual literature of India the term "pundit," or a person of deep knowledge, is sometimes used less as an honorific than as a pejorative term. Unless action is included in our spiritual path we run the danger of becoming hypocritical, like pundits, able to easily proclaim what is correct, while ignoring how difficult it is to achieve it for ourselves. Action makes it possible for us to speak from experience rather than conjecture or knowledge. It keeps us honest, vulnerable and humble.

In our western culture another popular way we avoid spiritual action is through diversion. In a materialistic world we are often too busy to do the personal work that facilitates conscious change. We have created our schedules so there is no room for our personal work. Our lives are filled with things that require upkeep and maintenance. We have little or no time for contemplation, much less action based on that contemplation. We are busy, but when we are not really going anywhere in our inner life, nothing is fundamentally changing. When we feel the inner discomfort and dissatisfaction that sometimes arises in a quiet moment, we quickly find something to do like go shopping or watch TV. We turn up the music. For this reason, as Christ said, "It is easier for a camel to pass through the eye of the needle than for a rich man to enter the gates heaven." Our attachments and diversions weigh us down. They are the invisible cage we have built to provide some kind of meaning to our lives. Wealth is highly prized, not just for survival, but also because with it we can buy or cultivate distractions from the hard practices of awareness, inner work, personal responsibility, and action. Often we invest our distractions with great meaning, actually identifying ourselves as the distraction. We become "horse people" or "car people" or "boat people," for instance. A hobby sometimes becomes an obsession, a *raison d'etre*. But, when we worship the golden calf, we throw away the golden path. Our culture's fascination with acquisition and goods is in part an attempt to run away and hide from our true condition. We can gain more by running toward that condition. The experiment in materialism as the path to happiness is a complete failure. In a 2006 survey of the over 180 nations, the United States ranked 150th in happiness.

In addition to avoiding action, we often limit the action we are willing to take by putting it in distinct compartments. We might say to ourselves, "I do volunteer service and that is my contribution," or "I go to church every Sunday so I am a spiritual person. This is how I do my part." These are good things, but the action we speak of here, and that will become our practice, is more often a daily, moment-to-moment endeavor. It is a part of every moment, not placed in a special compartment or time slot. In every conscious moment, we have the opportunity to choose action that is beneficial and loving (especially when we include ourselves as a recipient). We do not have to be a devout religious person; we do not have to take special classes or live in a cave for ten years. Bringing love into this world requires no special training; a degree means nothing. The beauty of this path is that it is available to all, everyday, all day. It is what Krishnamurti described as "the pathless path." There is no "one way." This is what Rumi meant when he said, "There are a thousand ways to kneel and kiss the earth." And there are thousands of moments when we can choose love rather than fear, when we can make others feel better by holding their unskillful action in a safe container, when we can take action that is nurturing. Sometimes we don't succeed, but we know the way, and we have our four strategies to help us get there.

Even though we must engage with the world, action is always solitary. We are the only person who can take the action that will result in our personal and spiritual growth. Since we are fully responsible for our evolution, we are the one who creates our new self. Our practice of personal responsibility makes this easier to understand. We have free will. We determine what is right and wrong for us. No one can take serious action on our behalf. Prayer and vision are helpful in creating change, however, the old expression, "the Lord helps those who help themselves" speaks to the necessity of outer action. Like unconditional love, the solitary nature of action is unequivocal. The prophets travel into the wilderness alone. The choices they make there are made in solitude, away from distractions. Our path is uniquely ours. We are responsible for our life, a continual work in progress, a becoming, continually defined and redefined by our actions.

It is not long before taking conscious action reveals a remarkable and wonderful truth: that the equanimity and joy we are seeking in life are directly related to the amount of love and compassion we can generate for others and ourselves. The foundation for effective action is compassion. Whatever our practice, whether it be deep listening, darshan, or authentic communication, to be effective it will always be rooted in love and compassion for ourselves and for others. Taking compassionate action soon makes it clear that there is no other way, no other path to equanimity and lasting and deep inner peace. Compassionate action lies at the heart of all positive change for the world and our selves. Taking action is the engine that moves us forward. The speed of our forward movement is determined by the frequency of our action. The more action we take, the more progress we make, and yet there is no hurry, no urgency, because the river is always flowing towards us.

There is a wonderful mystery associated with compassionate action. When we choose selfless acts of love and compassion, we get back far more than we invest. This kind of compassionate action is synergistic, that is the whole is greater than the sum of its parts. Both the giver and the receiver enter the stream the giver initiates; both gain more than they could have alone. This is a secret known by many caretakers and saints. By letting go of attachment to the self in the face of the suffering of others, they experience an amazing peace and grace that one cannot seek. Action taken for reward, for pride, for recognition or out of fear won't gain this deep grace. We are encouraged by their example to be selfless in our action. This selflessness comes from our inner work, as we learn to recognize the voice of fear, the voice of the ego, but choose to open the heart in instead. When we do this, we experience what they experience. Theirs is not an exclusive club, all are welcome. Selfless action is a major work of life; perhaps the most important contribution we can make in our short span.

Babbie's mother was a wonderful and generous person, and she loved children. Her family had supported the Children's Memorial Hospital in Chicago for many years and she became a volunteer there. She worked in the children's cancer ward. She was a wise person in the ways of compassion, and she believed in and demonstrated the instructions about love in Corinthians very well. Her volunteer shift began at around six in the morning, but she would usually arrive at five o'clock. It wasn't because she was eager to be of service to the kids that she arrived early. It was because she also wanted to make the life of the nurses easier. When she arrived, she would do many of the mundane chores that would otherwise take up their valuable time, so that when they came on shift they could go right to work helping the children. She spent a great deal of time with the dying children. She gave the same love and attention to them that she gave to her own children and grandchildren, and, no doubt, they adored her playful nature. She could slip into child's play in a heartbeat. Her spirit was uplifting. This was all before Babbie and I began our own hospice work, and even before there was a hospice movement in the United States. I was amazed that she could surround herself with what I perceived to be such misery and sadness, and I asked her why she did it. Her response was, "Because I love it." It was a long while before I understood just what she meant, but it is very clear to me now. Doing the kind of deep service that takes us beyond our own comfort level, we are rewarded with undeniable and extraordinary love. During the time we are doing this work, we often find ourselves surrounded and supported by this love. While all of us want to be in this space, ironically it is often the same space occupied by sorrow or tragedy. Angels, however, hang out in the rooms of the dying.

After Babbie's Mom died, a new children's cancer care center was built. A plaque was installed in her honor describing her as "a beloved angel to children, parents and nursing staff on 2 West for many years." We all have this same kind of opportunity.

In Andrew Harvey's book, *A Journey to Ladakh,*, he describes the seminal event of his voyage into this ancient kingdom as a meeting with a venerated holy man, Thursky Rinpoche, at the Shey monastery. The treasure he was seeking on his voyage is contained in a few simple sentences given to him by Rinpoche.

> *"As long as there is Samsara, there will be an evasion of the inner perfection that is man's essence. This is perhaps the saddest of all the tragedies of Samsara, and the most painful. A man is starving in one dark room, while in another just across the corridor from him there is enough food for many lives, for eternity. But he has to walk to that room. And before he can walk to it, he has to believe that it is there. No one else can believe for him. No one can even bring the food from that room to him. Even if they could, he would not believe in the food or be able to eat it."*[36]

Here is a message for all of us. It is a message filled with truth and great hope. The starving man personifies the spiritual condition of many, many human beings. Like the feast across the hall, love is all around us, our spiritual inheritance is nearby, spirit fills every moment, and yet we are starving for it. We are living in paradise and are blind to it. The story begs the question, why doesn't the man get up and cross the hall to the feast room? Why don't we embrace a spiritual view? Why is it we spend our lives starving for spiritual nourishment when it is just across the hall?

Nothing is going to change for the starving man until he is aware that he is starving. So it is for us. Sometimes, when we stop doing for a moment, we become aware of a fundamental discontent. This is what the Buddhists call our "dukha" or suffering, our existential condition, which can also be described as our yearning for "the one" or wholeness. We might wake up in the quiet of the night and not be able to go to sleep, and we notice we are actually unhappy; that we always seem to want something that we can't or won't describe. If we look further, we find that our lives are an attempt to satiate this discontent, and that the system we are using is not doing the job. We are sitting in the wrong room. We are looking in the wrong place for the feast. We can be glad, because awareness of our condition alerts us to the possibility for change.

What if the starving man sits in his foodless room blaming the weather and others for his condition? He'll spend a great deal of time judging and blaming rather than getting up and going across

---

[36] Harvey, Andrew, *Journey In Ladak*. Houghton Mifflin, 1983, page 207

the hall. You can see where this is going. Once he accepts responsibility for his condition he can begin to dissolve the beliefs that prevent him from joining the feast. He can stand up. He replaces the beliefs that are not working with beliefs that do work.

The most important thing he can do, once he recognizes that he is starving; that he is the only one who can change this, and that his beliefs have held him captive, is to actually get up and cross the hall to the feast. That is where we are now, in the four strategies for learning what life is trying to teach us. We are at the action point, the place where, as the old tire ad has it, "The rubber meets the road." It is time to move into the feast room.

The most wonderful truth of Rinpoche's story is that the feast is right in the next room. We do not have to make a long journey. Many of us think we need special training or that we must meditate for years, or that we must have a great teacher, or that we must travel to a special site, that we must have special knowledge, achieve a certain position or adopt a particular lifestyle, in order to make it to the feast. We believe we are unworthy. Not so. The feast is right now, right in front of us. It is laid for all. If we want to feel spirit, if we want to know love, if we want to journey into consciousness we do it right here, right now, right in our own lives, exactly as they are right now. The wisdom we need is within us; the necessary experiences forever flow towards us. The feast is right in the next room.

Without action, without getting up and walking into the feast room, *nothing* changes. The moment we take action *everything* changes. But what kind of action is necessary? For best results, for results that are uncommon, we will need to take "consecrated" action as taught in the Bhagavad Gita. Webster's defines "consecrate" as "to devote to a purpose with deep solemnity or dedication." We can also consecrate ourselves to the Divine or to love. We can take as our deep purpose what Rumi calls, "being the lover." When our understanding is mature, we can see that these purposes are all the same. We may name love different things but its nature is always the same.

The action component of our work is about consecrating everyday actions. Which everyday actions can we use to become more skillful, more aware, more compassionate? Well, each day we are listening, seeing, speaking, and being. When we consecrate these simple actions they become powerful forces that affect our lives and the lives of friends, acquaintances and strangers. With consciousness, they become an unending source of remarkable personal experiences, profound and perfect. When we consecrate these actions (and all action) we receive the perfect teaching, even as we offer the perfect gift.

The journey into consciousness, and learning what our life is trying to teach us, brings us naturally to moments in which we have the opportunity to choose consecrated action. As we peel away our fearful beliefs, we see love shining out at us, and we know that it has been there all along. As we grow more and more familiar with this love, we begin to want to express it. We can do this through consecrating everyday action.

Loving and compassionate action joins us to all who are currently, or ever have been, dedicated to expanding the field of love and compassion. Expanding this field benefits all beings. We too are immensely benefited, because it is through the exercise of this action that we finally encounter bliss and joy, that which we deeply seek, the nectar of life. Again, this is a great secret that can only be discovered and experienced through selfless, consecrated acts of kindness and compassion.

251

Say It Later

Learning to Speak the Truth

Angeles Arrien is a cultural anthropologist, author and educator and a master of symbol and psychology. A descendant of Basque Shamans, she is an intriguing storyteller, and in her workshops she often presents wonderful teaching tales, many of which she created. Arrien has a wonderful way of connecting the wisdom teachings of indigenous people with modern dilemmas, bringing the relevance of these teachings into synch with the challenges of our modern world, and showing how these teachings apply just as perfectly today as they have in the past. Years ago I attended a talk in which she spoke on the seventh initiation of indigenous people, learning to speak the truth, or authentic communication. In our relationship work Babbie and I have worked a great deal with the power and necessity of authentic communication, so we were excited to discover that reverence for this important action is ancient.

Unlike older more wisdom-based cultures, "consumer cultures" have few if any defined initiations, no uniform and empirical system of passing down wisdom from one generation to the next. There are religious exceptions but, in our mostly secular society, cultural initiations are the exception rather than the rule. The initiations of indigenous people forced the initiate to understand, not just theoretically, but through powerful experience, the value of harmony with the world around him/her and how to maintain it. Because most of us seldom experience such profound and direct teachings, we have no vision or a very cloudy vision of our own evolution, our own becoming or our deeper purpose and place in the world. This disassociation with our fundamental meaning, our disconnection with both the natural world and our deep self is a cause of much suffering. It is one reason we sometimes feel lost and out of touch with what we suspect might be a deeper meaning to life and our personal existence. It is why we sometimes strike out and attack that which is unfamiliar to us. Knowing little of our place in life's scheme, and having no way to make discovery, we feel fear. Many of us have become disconnected from the natural world and our own spiritual nature. We keep driving around in our bumper cars, hoping that everything will be explained someday, and sooner, rather than later, would be preferable. But this is not how it works. To truly know our inner nature we are required to express ourselves.

The expression of our truth is an ancient action through which we actually discover our place in the world; the true shape of our being and our individuality. It is how we create firm boundaries, and allow others to know who we are and what we value. Because we are beings of discourse, of speech, and because we live in a world of constant communication, the ability to speak our truth without judgment or blame is as important today as it always has been. When we take up the journey into consciousness, when we determine to discover what our life is trying to teach us, we necessarily arrive at the seventh initiation. The action of speaking the truth without expectation, or the anguished imperative for change, is a great adventure in itself. It is one way we discover the nature of our personal truth as well as our self-deception.

Learning to speak our truth, using awareness, is a way we create the mirror, our reflection; how we are seen. The reflection of what we say, the reactions and responses of others, reveal to us our deeper nature, and creative spirit. With authentic communication, we discover who we are as we simultaneously become that person. We take our place in the world. Our vision manifests. Arrien tells us *"the principal guiding the visionary is telling the truth without blame or judgment."*[37] As we learn to speak authentically in this way, we begin to fulfill our personal vision of who we are. The congruency of our speech and our action defines us. When asked what his message was

---

[37] Arrien, Angles, Ph.D., *The Four Fold Way, Walking the path of the Warrior, Teacher, Healer and Visionary* Angels Arrien, 1993, page 79

Gandhi replied, famously, "my life is my message." His life was consistent with what he spoke and taught.

Arrien tells us, "Many times we are forced at an early age to hide our true selves in order to survive. At some point this hiding becomes unnecessary, yet we find it hard to break the habit."[38] We have become clever at dissembling, being quiet when we really need or want to speak, shading our truth, and hiding it behind judgment and blame. In order to get to the center of ourselves, we have to forgo these patterns and learn how to be authentic. But long established habits, and our fear, can make this very difficult.

Wouldn't it be nice if, whenever we are feeling attacked, ridiculed, or criticized, or when our views and beliefs are discounted, belittled or ignored, we could respond skillfully, articulating our position clearly and expressing our feelings without blame or confusion; without slipping into emotional chaos? Like a great tree in a strong wind, we would bend while staying firmly rooted, combining the flexibility of an open heart with the power of our truth.

Unfortunately, when we are not in touch with our truth, our roots are sometimes shallow. Yet, it is a fundamental reality that before we can speak from our center we must know and understand what our heart and our mind contain; we must know our truth. Often the reason we become so befuddled when we feel verbally attacked or criticized, or we feel "put on the spot" is that, in the moment of confrontation, we have no idea what this truth is; the perceived attack is striking at places we have avoided, ignored or failed to explore. Sometimes, a part of us actually secretly agrees with our perceived antagonist. Naturally, we become confused and off-centered. Like the tree with shallow roots we are easily blown over. When this happens we often grasp for an old familiar reaction such as shutting down, escaping, angrily attacking back or defending ourselves. Unfortunately, every time we choose to react rather than respond we continue the cycle of ignorance that prevents us from learning the truth about ourselves as revealed in the unpleasant encounter we are experiencing. Our reaction becomes our final statement, and, we hope, the end of the experience. We try

---

[38] Ibid. page 80

to "put things behind us." We shut down our ability to learn. Our teacher appears and we quickly go into reaction. Often we believe our reactions are the truth, and we begin bouncing off each other's reactions doing the old bumper car routine, like actors in a soap opera we get lost again in the never ending stories.

In a similar fashion, the natural desire to stay emotionally comfortable and move away from confrontation, discomfort and pain is another obstacle to discovering our truth. As discussed earlier, when we successfully avoid confrontation, we also rob ourselves of the rich discoveries about ourselves that are often found in painful situations, in disquieting and disturbing encounters. For instance, when we deny or ignore an unpleasant situation that has not been consciously resolved. We might go through an unpleasant encounter with our partner or boss, or even a complete stranger and simply "let it go" because we prefer not to revisit the encounter. Of course, often, we are not really "letting it go," actually, we are "holding it in." The unresolved energy is added to an internal storehouse of resentment and unresolved anger. Eventually, this suppressed energy can cause emotional damage though a sudden unconscious explosion over some unrelated, even minuscule event or detail. Sometimes this anger leaks out daily, in little unpleasant interactions and passive aggressive behaviors that make us unpleasant to be with and generate a continuum of unhealthy encounters. Denying this energy exists, unfortunately, does not diffuse it.

Besides missing the lesson, another drawback to the seemingly natural and completely reasonable approach of "letting it go" or avoiding confrontation, is that it is by the engagement in these confrontations that we learn how to respond skillfully to such situations. Without these experiences we may never learn the methods needed to respond to them. Speaking the truth skillfully can only be learned by actually doing it. Avoiding, denying or ignoring these experiences insures that we will continue to handle confrontation with, what could be called, "our outdated personal software," our well-honed, almost mindless, reactions.

It seems we are in a vicious cycle, an apparently inescapable situation. When we feel attacked and engage in confrontation, we often end up in old and ineffective reactive patterns. When we avoid a confrontation or deny our feelings, we store unresolved energy, build resentment and miss an opportunity for learning about ourselves and developing better communication skills. On top of all this, in both cases, there is little or no resolution.

How can we break out of this cycle and learn to speak our truth without fear? Where can we acquire this seemingly rare ability and the wonderful freedom and personal power that accompany it? The action practice *Say It Later* provides an interesting route to this extraordinary place of personal power. Very simply, "say it later" means that, when we find ourselves overwhelmed by an interpersonal confrontation or a situation, rather than react in our traditional patterns, rather than shutting down or running away, we choose to respond at a later time, we literally speak our truth later.

Say It Later is also an action through which we can experience the power of personal responsibility, using the time we set aside to prepare our response for initiating, sometimes intense, personal explorations (doing our "inner work"). These explorations are the growing roots of our tree. Our truth lies in what is true for us, what we feel, what we are experiencing. It is personal, not necessarily universal. Through taking personal responsibility and keeping our investigations personal, we discover and accumulate more truth about ourselves and about our part in the difficult situations in which we sometimes find ourselves. We come to understand our own repetitive, dysfunctional patterns of behavior. As we discover what is deeply true for us, we are able to speak it clearly rather than being sucked into the stories. Again, as we find our deep truth, we see it has nothing to do with judgment or blame. We are also reminded that no one can "make us" feel a certain way. We are responsible for our own feelings, and our reactions, no matter how awful or difficult the situation.

The *Say It Later* action practice helps us to stay in integrity with our feelings. It gives us the space to make discovery before speaking, before going into old ego based reactions. Rather than blindly engaging, we learn how to center first and how to develop the art of skillful response. And, with *Say It Later*, when our habit is to "let it go" or to avoid confrontation, we can do this, but only if we make the commitment to ourselves to "say it later;" to confront the situation later.

When we commit to the *Say It Later* action practice, we make a personal vow to come back to the subject and deal with it once we have removed ourselves from the intensity of an uncomfortable encounter. Reflection gives us time to marshal our forces, to get in touch with our truth, to learn from our fear, and to speak out when we would have blown up or suppressed our feelings. *Say It Later* breaks the cowardly cycle of avoidance, repression and resentment. The more it is applied, the more it restores or enhances our self-esteem and personal integrity. Speaking our truth is a powerful way we can release energy that would otherwise get pushed down and stored. It is an excellent way to release emotional pain, by giving it voice and letting it go through the truth. It is an ancient method of releasing the energy of fear. It is also the province of true leaders and visionaries.

Ironically, one of the biggest obstacles to speaking our truth clearly in a confrontational moment is the tremendous cultural pressure to counter perceived attacks instantly with just the right phrase; to be "on top of the situation" and "in control" like characters in a movie. That's fine for scripted movie characters; however, to actually do this in real life, we have to be able to make responses that are firmly grounded in our own deep truth. Until we are familiar with our truth, and know it more intimately, how can it arise when we are under fire? This is like looking for a file that has not been filed or is lost, while your boss is yelling at you to find the file. Trying to meet the expectation of the culture to make the instant perfect response, we fail time after time. Since we have not been given a script, we need the time to create our responses from our own unique emotional configuration.

Just to make things more difficult, we tend to judge ourselves when we fail to respond quickly and skillfully. Once again, the self-judge guides us further away from the truth of our situation. Listening to self-judgment we become lost in the story of our deficiencies. We might vow to ourselves that next time we will make the perfect response! We will try harder with what we have, rather than expanding on our current experience. We might develop a strategy for avoiding certain encounters. But, we completely miss the reason that we don't have a reliable and truthful response. We have never fully investigated or become familiar with our truth. We have not opened our hearts to ourselves.

The cultural expectation that we make an immediate and perfect response when we feel upset or attacked, as well as the self judgment that arises when we don't, can be relieved by using the *Who Says So?* practice. Who says we must respond to perceived attacks instantly? What if we don't feel comfortable and centered, don't know what to say or are completely stunned? When we become aware of an old ineffectual reaction coming up, like frustration, withdrawal, or irrational anger, why can't we choose to say what we are really feeling later, when we know more about what it really is? We can.

In addition to giving us a method of discovering what is true for us, the *Say It Later* action practice also provides us with the opportunity to learn how to speak our truth with clarity and power, often for the first time.

Here is an overview of the action practice *Say It Later*. Because this practice follows the four strategies for learning what life is trying to teach us, it can be easily remembered.

When we become aware that we are experiencing a heavy emotional reaction to something we are being told, or we are upset by the way someone is behaving, we stop adding energy to the encounter and recognize we have an opportunity to "say it later." Signs that we need to disconnect with the situation at hand are confusion, over reactive anger, rage (expressed or not), an inability to articulate, feeling stunned, deeply hurt or an urge to withdraw and escape. Sometimes we experience irrational humor, laughing inappropriately at something serious, sometimes without control. Using dismissive words or phrases like "whatever," "oh sure," or "yeah… right" are another indicator that we are experiencing emotional confusion. Resorting to these protective or attacking phrases actually only creates bad feelings, they are insulting and dismissive. We also might become aware that we are judging and blaming, or find that we have become lost in the story. As soon as we become aware that we are in reaction, we give ourselves complete permission to withdraw from the situation in as orderly and dignified manner as is possible. Taking a deep breath or two can be helpful. Withdrawing can be challenging if our ego has us under its command. As soon as we are aware that this is occurring, we let go of our need to be right or to be heard; we step out of the story. This can be very challenging but great rewards lie just ahead.

When we realize we are not in touch with our truth and are reacting from emotional confusion it is not just perfectly OK to withdraw, it is wise. We really do not know what to say or how to deal with things in the moment and need time for reflection. It is OK to withdraw because we know with *Say It Later* we will be speaking our truth later. This is not cowardice or avoidance. It is a highly skillful response in itself. Remember, there is no law that says we must respond in the present.

The *Say It Later* practice can also be used when we realize later that we wish we had said something in a past situation. We might become aware that we are feeling uncomfortable about something. There is no reason we cannot open a past situation up for review. We might have agreed to something without thinking or accepted an insult without responding. To rectify the situation we can use the practice of *Say It Later*.

It helps to understand that our perceived antagonist's sense of urgency or their desire for immediate resolution is not important. They may want to talk, "right now!" because they feel they have the upper hand or they are dissatisfied and want to say more. Their ego may have run away with them, they may have to be "right." They may be using the situation as a ventilator for anger, anger that may not even be about the current story. We need to realize that, sometimes, because the other person (or the group) is reacting from their ego and are beyond emotional control, they will not be able to absorb anything but the most patient, loving and open hearted message, and even this may not be possible. If we can't give this kind of response, it would be much more useful to "say it later." We acknowledge that the situation at this point will probably not yield any healthy resolution, and we make the promise to ourselves to "say it later." We have two choices at this point. We tell the other party that we need some time to reflect or think about what has happened. We need to be the judge of whether this reasonable approach will work. Our second choice is to keep the *Say It Later* strategy to ourselves.

Sometimes, informing the other party of our plan to withdraw and talk later just adds fuel to the ego dance that is taking place. I have had many clients for whom this choice is simply not an option. The other party is too volatile, too "in their ego" and won't hear of a pause. In this situation, it works best to keep the strategy to ourselves; withdrawing without comment is the best strategy.

Withdrawing from a difficult encounter skillfully is important. During the situation we listen to what the other party has to say, their story. This can be a work out for our own ego. We go to awareness. In addition to our awareness of our own reaction, we try to stay aware of their behavior and listen to what they are saying. If possible, we acknowledge their position. We can say something like "I hear what you are saying," or "I understand your point." These acknowledgements help us to withdraw from the story more easily. They can help calm things down. Often when we stop fully engaging in the story, it will end fairly soon, in other words, when we stop talking. Again if the other party demands an immediate response, as the ego often does, or they keep attacking us, we tell them firmly we will talk about things later when we are more centered and resourceful. "I can't respond right now, I need time to consider what you are saying," or "I need some time to consider what is happening" are usually totally honest statements! "I'll get back to you very soon," lets them know you are not blowing them off. Obviously, it is very important to keep such an agreement, otherwise saying these things will just be seen as an escape mechanism and will have no future value. Again, if this solution seems unworkable we have to withdraw.

If we have a tendency to avoid encounters, we need to be aware of the moments in which we feel uncomfortable, or feel the need to escape or are reacting with an avoidance strategy. Focusing our awareness on what we are feeling in the moment, we make a vow to ourselves that, once we have done our inner work, we will "say it later." As above, we withdraw from the current conflict. We keep our vow.

When we are feeling emotionally disturbed by the confrontation, we can exercise compassion and mercy for ourselves by reminding ourselves once again that, regardless of what has happened, we are not a bad person and have a good heart. Like everyone, we possess basic goodness. When we think back on the confrontation and feel tightness or anger, we can just breathe and let things settle; we work to open the heart. Over time, just letting things be for a while becomes easier as a result of our rising self-esteem and continued practice. As we develop trust, we simultaneously discover that things usually work out, as Rumi says, in an "elegant pattern" that we cannot always immediately see or understand.

The intensity of a difficult encounter will usually determine how long the ego will reign before we can settle down, take personal responsibility and comfortably begin our inner work. As we know, anger causes the release of "flight or fight" chemicals that keep our angry energy close to the surface. It is a good idea to take a break for a while from an encounter, rather than to rush into the next part of the process, which is, you can guess, taking personal responsibility. This can be hard to do when the ego has us wired into a story and strong chemicals are flowing in the body. Sitting in meditation for a while or simply following the breath are very effective ways to calm the mind and release tension. Getting to center can take several hours or even a day.

As soon as we feel settled, we move to personal responsibility. The truth about our self gained from a difficult situation or encounter comes from two sources. The first is our reaction to these situations, and the second is the possible truth of the other party's complaint or observation, no matter how unskillfully presented. Personal responsibility is about owning our reactions as well reviewing the other party's accusations objectively. Awareness of the difference between the story and our personal reactions (the feelings aroused) is important. If we drop back into the story, and the need to be right, to have our part of the story accepted and acknowledged, we will simply find ourselves right back arguing the details of the story; who did what to who, when and how did they do it, and why they are wrong. So the focus is on our feelings, the emotions that we experienced or are experiencing as a result of an encounter.

Personal responsibility is honoring these feelings and owning them, while consciously avoiding blame and judgment. As we know by now, no one ever "makes" us feel the way we do. To make any progress at all, we always have to own and take responsibility for our feelings. This can be difficult to understand and even more difficult to accept. The neural pathway that blames others for how we feel is usually well developed. Again, we often need to remind ourselves of the truth that our feelings are not caused by someone else. A perceived "attack" on our dignity simply stirs up our fear and insecurities. It is obvious that these belong to us. It is important to recognize that the other party's part in the affair, no matter how volatile or malicious seeming, is actually calling forth areas in which we feel volatile or are not whole. It is hard to accept the cliché that our antagonists are very often our teachers, but it is so often the truth.

Once we commit to personal responsibility we turn inward, away from the story, and objectively review the feelings that have been exposed by our reactions. We also test the truth of any accusations we have experienced. When reviewing feelings, one of my favorite questions is: where and when have I experienced this type of reaction before? What does this situation remind me of? If we simply ask this question without trying to force the answer, it is amazing how often and how quickly an answer arises. Often, we find that we have an unrecognized pattern of behavior, which the current story has touched off or highlighted. I have been amazed at the self-discoveries my clients and I have made by letting go of blame and judgment, staying with our emotions and following them to their source, while trusting that a revelation can occur when and if we are ready for it. In this way we often discover things about ourselves about which we have been totally unconscious (sometimes for years). We have uncovered behavior patterns that were not constructive or helpful in our lives and yet were so hidden that we were completely unaware of their presence. When this happens we are encountering our truth, that which is absolutely real for us. We are able to see how our beliefs form our reality, sometimes negatively. We are often able to get to the source of our beliefs and question their validity. The encounter we have just experienced suddenly has depth and meaning. Sometimes we feel tremendous freedom when this happens while, at other times, the truth is not pretty or comfortable and reveals the work to be done. Both responses are a gift. This is the real material for our personal and spiritual growth, and it has arisen out of conflict, out of an area in which we now see we are not whole because we are unable to accept its existence without fear.

Objectively reviewing accusations made about us during an encounter is another path for self-discovery. Gaining the neutrality and objectivity needed to review these accusations is definitely an exercise in letting go of the ego. Sometimes the accusations are way off the mark, but surprisingly often there is a grain of truth to be found, and sometimes the accusations are totally true and our ego simply doesn't want to let go of its defensive stance.

We may not like the truth we discover about ourselves. When this happens we have yet another opportunity for exercising compassion. Everyone acts unskillfully from time to time. All of us have some unpleasant corners in our psyche. That nobody behaves perfectly all the time seems pretty obvious, but it is amazing how much we demand and expect ourselves to do just this! Mercy, or compassion in action, has magic qualities. As we vaporize our own self- judgment, down come the walls of judgment that keep us from having compassion for others. I mention this again because even subtle judgment of others and their behavior is a major impediment to our being heard. Judgment is easily sensed. The second it arises, people stop listening or start letting the ego drift in the door. If we want to be heard we have to deal with our judgment and blame before asking others to listen to our truth.

Coming from our truth can be especially challenging because so often it requires confessing our culpability, our fear, our errors, our misunderstanding or our anger and confusion. When we own up to these by speaking our truth, we discover the freedom that can only be gained through the willingness to be vulnerable. Because we spend so much time trying to protect ourselves from real and imagined judgments, few of us actually experience the extraordinary freedom gained through vulnerability. This powerful force erases fear from areas of our lives that we have been spending time and energy guarding. As we speak our fear, we discover what it is like to feel safe about who we really are. Because all of us have the same fears, our vulnerability often creates empathy and understanding, where trying to be right or uphold a façade only offends and separates us from others. To speak the truth, we need to be willing to practice vulnerability.

Once we have discovered our truth, it is time to create our response. Our truth consists of what we felt during the confrontation or situation and sometimes what we may have learned. *It is not our judgments about the confrontation or the other person or our thoughts and observations about the story.* Preparing our response is not like preparing a legal case. Again, it is not an attempt to justify our behavior, make the other person wrong, or demonstrate our righteousness. Because we are going to be speaking authentically we have to speak carefully and skillfully; we have to be sure that judgment and blame will be truly absent from our statements. To sense whether this is true we need to ask ourselves if our heart is fully opened. If judgment and blame are still present in our response, it indicates a lack of self-understanding, which means we are unable at this time to come from our deepest truth. Although we have tried hard to make discovery, it is this lack of understanding *that is our truth at the moment.* We can relate this without judgment or blame. We might say, "When X happened I felt confused and angry, and I still am trying to sort things out." When we are open to sharing our difficulty in this way, we may be surprised at the response that occurs. People often interpret our statement of a lack of understanding as a request for help. Suddenly our antagonist is offering useful and appreciated suggestions!

In speaking our truth, we use the basic form of open hearted communication, a simple and specific form rather than a long story. We are not interested in detail. It is not helpful to tell the story of how we arrived at our truth, and it distracts from our intent. Whether we are in the midst of a confrontation or are practicing *Say It Later* we can use the powerful word pattern we learned in open hearted listening. We state the simple truth that "when 'x' happens or happened, I feel or felt 'y'." That's it. When you said or did 'x,' I felt angry and upset (whatever emotion was present). This is the undeniable truth. It does not accuse our antagonist of bad behavior. It simply references the behavior and informs them of its result. Again, we want to avoid the phrases "make me feel" or "made me feel" if we can. For instance, we don't say "when you said or did 'x,' it 'made' me angry." This subtly blames others for our state, puts them at cause for our condition, and makes us into a victim. If possible, if we have discovered some culpability on our own part, some truth in the other party's complaint, we can acknowledge this. Acknowledgement of this kind is a very powerful way to initiate an atmosphere of understanding, and it often helps the other party to listen more openly. It demonstrates openness and vulnerability on our part.

This is very simple format, but it is harder to do than it first appears! In order to learn how to speak in this way, we have to practice, especially at first! This means we say out loud the words we intend to say later. Saying the phrase in our head when practicing is not nearly as effective as speaking it out loud. I am often surprised that, in my practice sessions, unintended phrases and words join my message like "you never" or "you always" or "you made me feel." From verbal practice we learn how much more powerful our truth is when we keep it simple and direct. Practicing in this way makes it clear that embellishing the truth is not necessary, especially if we want to be heard.

It is important to be aware of eye contact. When practicing, imagine that the person to whom you wish to relate the truth is right in front of you. Will we look away or is our eye contact steady and even? Are we gazing, looking out but hanging on the fringe of real eye contact, or are we looking deeply and feeling comfortable? The extent to which we connect our eyes to our truth affects the power of our communication. We can use awareness about the intensity of this connection as feedback about the depth of our truth.

When I first began to use this form and then to help others to speak their truth, I would work through the four strategies. This involved staying aware of the moments when judgment and blame came up, making discovery about what was *really* happening and staying out of the story. The idea was that, knowing the truth and how to speak it, anyone could go forth and say it. But in many cases this didn't work. Everything seemed fine, we did our inner work, we knew exactly what we wanted to say, we knew the pattern for saying it, but when we actually arrived at the moment of truth something entirely different would come out of our mouths or we might find ourselves actually unable to speak.

I came to see that our old habits, our fears, our well-ingrained ways of thinking and speaking simply took over in the critical moment of encounter. With clients, I saw this happen all the time, even though they knew exactly what they wanted to say. So, I introduced rehearsals. I would act as the person to whom they needed to speak their truth and they would practice on me. Amazingly they still had trouble speaking the truth in its simple form, even though I was just a stand in. As the stand in, I was able to help them refine and simplify their message.

This demonstrates how deep the fear of speaking the truth can be. Sadly, we just are not accustomed to communicating in this fashion and have developed countless strategies to get the ego's point across, rather than our truth. When push comes to shove, we revert, often taking up the voice of the ego rather than speaking the truth. So practicing out loud is very important, actually saying the words, until we feel comfortable with them. We also stay aware of what is happening when we feel uncomfortable with our truth. There is even more discovery to be made.

When we are ready, we re-engage with the person with whom we had a conflict, and tell them our truth, taking full responsibility for our feelings. The great caveat of the *Say It Later* practice is that we must honor our promise to ourselves to "say it later" if we want to learn to speak our truth effectively. Creating a time frame helps us keep our commitment. As in open hearted listening, the time frame of our vow to "say it later" ideally should be no longer than 24 hours. At first this may be hard, and there always may be circumstances that do not allow this time frame. 24 hours is a goal not an absolute. However, we don't want the ego to use the 24-hour rule to slip out of our commitment: "Hey great, its past 24 hours so I don't have to do it!" It is better to "say it later" at anytime rather than not at all. Sometimes, our self-discovery process takes longer. However, in many cases, the longer we wait, the less effective the process will be, and the more likely we are to just let things go.

Many times we miss the opportunity to speak the truth later because we say to ourselves, "things are going along so smoothly now, I don't want to spoil it by bringing up my old upset." When we do this, we throw away an opportunity for significant personal growth. We are also avoiding the truth; often continuing a dysfunctional myth.

A client of mine recently decided he needed to speak the truth to his son regarding his concern about the son's drinking. Unfortunately, his timing was not great. His son had been drinking more than usual when my client brought up this worry. Immediately the son closed down and became inaccessible. I asked my client if he had used the *Say It Later* practice the next day, when things were more normal. His response was classic, "things were going along well by then and I didn't want to say anything." We are all tempted by this withdrawal strategy and yet, the best time to speak the truth is usually when all is calm, when things are going well.

In order for us to really gain the benefits of the *Say It Later* practice, we must honor the promise to ourselves that we will "say it later." The *Say It Later* practice is an act of personal responsibility. It takes courage. Avoiding the practice, copping out, robs us of or personal integrity, self esteem and the self confidence that we achieve when we know that we can always respond on our own behalf, eyeball to eyeball, person to person regardless of our fears.

When taking up this practice, we will be encountering some of our deepest fears. The good news is the bigger the dragon, the greater the treasure; the greater the challenge the more rewarding speaking our truth will be. Thus someone who scares us, or a topic that is difficult for us to discuss, often offers the greatest reward from this practice.

We like to think that speaking our truth (perhaps because we have put so much effort and time into it and it's so clear to us) will automatically result in understanding on the recipient's part or, better yet, induce a behavior change. We need to forgo this expectation. While it may be our desire and hope that others will come to their own useful conclusion about their behavior without feeling guilty or upset, this does not always happen. Having the expectation for someone else to change means that we are measuring the effectiveness of our truth by the response of that person (the listener). This measure ignores the difficulties others have with hearing uncomfortable truths, as well as the fact that they may be unwilling to do the inner work required to deal with uncomfortable realities. What we hope for by communicating authentically is simply to state our truth in a way we know is real for us.

Once our truth is clearly expressed, the process is basically completed. Our truth will then take care of itself. It may cause upset, or we may be pleasantly surprised at how well received it is. Again, the benefits we receive through this practice are not other people suddenly understanding us and making personal change, although this can certainly happen. What we gain from communicating authentically is a boost to our self-esteem and an encounter with our personal power. This is the real gift of *Say It Later*. The measure of our success is the equanimity we begin to feel as we begin to relate our truth to others. We are the only person who can measure this.

If we find ourselves still in our ego, if fear is still present, then we have probably not reached the core of our truth. Have mercy and access the four strategies to engender deeper understanding.

Obviously, speaking our truth is not an attempt to make others wrong for how we feel. We do not demand any behavior changes in this process. There is a place and time for asking for behavior change as well. We will be more successful in making these requests once we are more comfortable with the process of speaking our truth. Right now, using *Say It Later*, we are focusing on holding up the perfect and non-judgmental reflection of another's behavior and its results as it applies to us. This is far more effective in raising consciousness than suggesting how others should act or be, and much more effective than wagging the finger. There is no unnecessary and unfruitful concern about who was right or who was wrong.

What we often discover when we "say it later" is that many people are willing to listen because, like us, they desire resolution and understanding. The fact that we are not blaming them for our feelings and responses makes it much easier for them to hear us, and the fact that we are saying things later rather than in the thick of an incident also helps keep the focus on mutual understanding and investigation rather than blame. Sometimes, people will take our truth as blame because this is a habit many of us have. We feel we are a bad person at what can be interpreted as the slightest criticism.

When this happens it is helpful to emphasize that our story is not intended to blame them. It is about our reaction to their behavior.

I discovered this practice when a client needed to be able to respond to a difficult and overbearing boss. On many occasions she felt powerless to respond to his anger and vitriol in the moment. She found his condescending and arrogant tone both intimidating and infuriating. When he was angry with her, she felt fear and a sense of helplessness. I persuaded her that she had done enough personal work to realize that she could not continue to rationalize and accept his attacks without a real diminishing of her self-esteem. One day she got into a big argument with him, and he demanded that she do things she felt were personally demeaning. She felt overwhelmed and was too disoriented, angry and confused to say anything in the moment. Soon after that, we determined that it was a perfect opportunity to use the *Say It Later* practice and she agreed that she would speak to him when she was more centered.

In the past she had promised herself to speak up later but often found a good reason not to do so. She would let things slide, or she would rationalize her way out of a response. This time, she made a total commitment to speak her truth. The commitment made, she tried to relax around the whole process. When she thought back on the incident, and felt herself tighten up, she breathed deeply and came back into the present. Rather than thinking about the situation all the time and trying to force the answers (worrying), she trusted that answers to her confusion would appear. Every now and then she would check to see if anything had come up. This is like checking a pot to see if the soup is ready. Over a two-day period she had several realizations about the situation. Naturally, there was more to it than just the current event. New insights about her job manifested clearly. It is often like this. When we demonstrate our true and firm intention to move forward and grow, we are given answers and help effortlessly, often in unexpected forms. Remembering that she was responsible for her reaction allowed her to focus her attention on her frustrated and confused state rather than get lost in the story of her boss's lack of sensitivity. This allowed her to see that her frustrated and confused reaction to her boss's anger was an old pattern. The feelings she was encountering were exactly the same reaction that her long dead mother's insults and belittling comments had aroused: confusion, anger and the despair of feeling powerless. She realized that she was encountering an old wolf in new clothing. Here was a situation that had never really been resolved, and for which she had created various lifetime strategies of withdrawal and self-demeaning compromise. We discussed the fact that telling her boss how she felt would be the beginning of healing the old wound; an opportunity she had not anticipated.

To confuse things more she saw that she was afraid to speak her truth because she thought she might lose her job. But, by not speaking her truth she was out of integrity with herself, and this was creating shame and resentment. She was angry at herself for selling out to fear and not speaking her truth, and she was focusing all that anger on the insensitive boss. However, she took his abuse because of her own fear. Coming to grips with this truth, she began to consider, for the first time, what it would be like not to work in his company. This turned out to be the beginning of a very important step in her life.

We realized that, by dealing with the situation with her boss, she was being offered a unique opportunity to confront some old dragons and to fully stand up for herself in a way that she never could as a child. *Say It Later* became an opportunity to develop a centered rebuttal of the boss's tone and style and to, perhaps, create an awareness opportunity for him. The content of his outburst was unpleasant, but the context, the basic lack of respect, manifested by his tone of voice and his angry and rigid management style also required a response. The ability to "say it later" was an opportunity for her to discover how to hold her shape in the presence of these old demons by staying connected with her truth.

It took her a couple of days to achieve the necessary realizations for proceeding and to practice what she was going to say. But she kept her promise to herself and made an appointment with him on the third day after the incident. She told him how the encounter had affected her, but she kept her private discoveries about her mother to herself, not providing a great deal of detail or a distracting story. She was surprised at the result. She had expected him to get defensive, but, because he was in a more resourceful state than the day of the incident, he was willing to listen to what she had to say. He did not take her truth as an attack or blame. He understood that his behavior was not achieving the result he had expected. For her part, she stood in a new place, facing the representation of her mother and speaking her truth. This was deeply healing for her. In typical spiritual irony, her boss's momentary lack of skill, his attack, became the source of her healing, a blessed opportunity.

There's more. The commitment to "say it later" forced her to make an unanticipated and very important choice. In choosing to speak her truth she took the risk of losing her job. Thus, to speak her truth she had to also be willing to let this happen. The idea of losing her job triggered quite an investigation into her beliefs about survival and her trust in the world. She saw clearly that fear about money and survival were what was keeping her working for a disrespectful boss. Rather than doing work she loved, she was working for the belief that her survival depended on her job. She realized that she could live without the job, but not without her personal integrity, and from that point forth, she determined to speak her truth whenever possible rather than taking the hand of fear. She had gained new power. She could no longer be easily manipulated by her subconscious fear or someone's use of that fear. A fundamental shift in her relationship with her boss took place as she became more honest with herself and therefore with him. It is amazing how much can be discovered through small, intense incidents.

The big secret about *Say It Later* is that it is the practice field for *Say It Now*! Practicing *Say It Later*, we become more comfortable speaking our truth, until we are able to speak our truth skillfully, not just *later*, but right in the thick of confrontation as well. The power of speaking our truth we learn in *Say It Later* gives us the self-confidence and skill to speak our truth with compassion and strength in personally challenging situations as they are happening. The ability to do this (of course without blame or advice or judgment) allows others to really hear us in difficult moments when they normally would have closed down completely. We find we are much more in control of our emotions and our part in the situation. Of course, any time we feel confused and overwhelmed we can still choose to "say it later."

One of the greatest manifestations of personal power is the ability to speak one's truth clearly without fear. Thus, through the action of authentic communication, we experience for a moment true personal power, often for the very first time. As we practice, our roots grow deeper, our voice stronger. *Say It Later* is standing up for ourselves in a deliberate and conscious manner. As I have said, it is an act of courage. The results of the practice are cumulative. Each time we make the commitment to and execute the action of speaking our truth authentically we gain the release from our inner judge. Our self-esteem grows in a healthy, grounded manner. We feel the change in our being. We begin to sense the inner peace that comes for those who are willing to accept themselves as they are, without excuse and with compassion. The iron clad agreement to speak our truth, to "say it later" if necessary, drives us to discover what that truth really is, forces us to new levels of inner comprehension and compassion for ourselves and others. We move into previously threatening situations with new peace, the peace that comes from the knowledge that, whatever comes our way, we have a method of dealing with it honestly. No more running away, no more hiding, no more arm waving. We find we can "say it now" more and more often, and that we can stand in the winds of others' anger, upsets and personal attacks with more inner calm.

There is one caveat about speaking our truth. The Buddha advised that wise speech should be "helpful." We need to use our discretion. Wise speech, takes all aspects of a communication into account. There are times when wisdom dictates that speaking our truth will simply not be helpful. But it is important not to use this fact as an escape from speaking our truth when it is difficult. More often than not, speaking authentically is very helpful.

Speaking the truth clearly, with compassion that cannot coexist with blame or judgment, creates a powerful and undeniable clarity. Again, this does not mean that we do not feel or express the energy of anger. Sometimes our truth rides on passion.

When we honor our own truth by speaking it with deep intention, we are calling on the listener's highest good. By honoring them with our truth we invite them to speak in the same manner. We give them the opportunity to join us in the field of truth, to jointly embrace the compassionate view. Authentic communication is an action that regularly creates deeply spiritual and healing moments. Gandhi said, "There is no higher God than the truth." In the presence of the truth we often encounter unity, our oneness, our great similarity.

The Eyes Have It!

Connecting the Eyes to the Heart

*"My face in thine eye, thine in mine appears,
and true plain hearts doe in faces rest."*

The Good Morrow, John Donne

*"I have noticed that if you look carefully at people's eyes the first five
seconds they look at you, the truth of their feelings will shine
through for just an instant before it flickers away."*

The Secret Life of Bees, Sue Monk Kidd

It is said that more can be told in a glance than in a thousand words. The glance is one of the most amazing mysteries because, despite its brevity, it can reveal more truth than a tedious monologue, an angry exchange or a list of endearing platitudes. Often we watch someone's eyes for clues about what they are really feeling, and to sense the truth. Often, looking away can be a signal that the truth is being evaded. When we act unconscious, our eyes betray us, often revealing our inner beliefs and feelings without our knowledge.

From Neuro-Linguistic Programming (NLP) we learn that the direction our eyes travel when answering a question demonstrates where we are going for the answer. For instance, when we look up and to the left we are making a visual recall, remembering something we've seen. When our eyes are horizontal and move left we are using auditory recall, remembering something we've heard. There are six points of view plus looking straight out, which indicates we are imagining. NLP demonstrates how connected our eyes are to our thinking.

Our eyes often starkly reveal our internal emotional condition. Not only do the eyes reveal, they can also help in changing our behavior. Sometimes, just by taking new action with our eyes, we can affect internal change, creating confidence where there was little or none. Glancing, looking, and seeing, the eyes are an important component of conscious action.

Years ago, when I first started working with groups, a friend asked me to help him with a workshop he was presenting at a hospital. The group was much bigger in size than any I had worked with before that time. When it was my turn to speak, I was aware that my eyes were doing funny things, rolling up and almost disappearing as I spoke. The talk was fine, but the eye behavior was disconcerting, both to the participants and myself. My co-presenter spoke with me about it later.

That night I did some inner work, and I put myself back in the moment when my eyes acted strangely during the day's workshop. I realized that, although I was comfortable with my information, I was afraid for some reason. It did not take me long to go back to my childhood, a time in which speaking up was dangerous and scary. In my house a favorite phrase was "children are to be seen and not heard." My father would laugh when his friends came around and say things like, "Why don't you kids go out and play in the heavy traffic?" We were not encouraged to ask questions or to talk at all. Dinner conversation followed a nasty pattern in which my parents took out their own discontent by creating arguments with the children. A conversation with one of us would begin with a no win, loaded question that evolved into a downward spiral ending in shame or reprimand. No matter what we said, it was usually picked apart, contradicted, or something was found wrong with our behavior. Sometimes there were dire consequences, like being hit. I realized that my eyes were still cowering, awaiting the blow or the reprimand, when I spoke and felt afraid. The larger workshop called forth the deeper forces beneath my need for approval, as well as my unresolved fear.

The good part of this story is what I learned the next day. I determined that I would take conscious action keeping my eyes wide open and deliberately looking individuals in the eye as I spoke. When I did this, I was not only able to make a much stronger and better presentation, but I simultaneously vanquished my old childhood fear of speaking up and my fear of being in front of large groups, forever. By changing the way I used my eyes, I actually moved beyond my fear of speaking my truth in more difficult circumstances. In this respect, my eyes not only demonstrated I had a problem, but also became an important part of an action that resulted in significant inner change.

Noticing what our eyes are doing is an interesting awareness exercise that gives us immediate feedback about our current inner condition. Are we frightened? Are we angry? Are we sad? Are we totally confused? The eyes can tell us. When we are connected to our truth the eyes express this connection. When we are in doubt the eyes relay our doubt. When we suddenly find our eyes are being evasive what are they telling us? When our eyes glaze over it means we have left the present; perhaps we are daydreaming? Why? Why have we left the present? Are we internalizing? Are we preoccupied and worried? We can use our eyes to bring us back into the moment by focusing on objects or people that are right before us; by staying with another's story rather than running away into our own. Using the eyes, we can change our internal state from unconscious to conscious, from remote to present. We arrive right where we are meant to be, in the now. We can do this when we are driving down the road, or when we are with a group or an individual. We turn on our noticing and come right back into the moment. And others can easily tell whether we are present or not by watching our eyes. It is civil and respectful of others to pay attention to them.

The eyes measure our conviction, and demonstrate our presence. If we are telling a story, and we are unsure about what we are saying, we suddenly feel and show the uncertainty in our eyes. When we can't look someone in the eye, often it is because we feel ashamed, cautious or unsure about something, as in my experience at the workshop. When we take responsibility for the underlying inner condition, and we do some inner work, we are able reconnect with our eyes. We experience more personal integrity and personal power. This is highly visible to others.

As we make significant internal change through the four strategies we develop confidence. We understand how the truth works. We are able to be more genuinely ourselves. We are able to choose love and compassion more often. All this change is reflected in an alive quality in our eyes. Using our eyes well is one of the primary actions we can take to concretize the inner changes that are occurring as we journey into consciousness.

The eyes can be used for giving as well as for discovery. Visionaries, prophets and saints express their deep love and passion consciously through their eyes, which is why being with them is more powerful than reading their teachings. This brings us to one very amazing power of the eyes, the ability to transmit love and safety wordlessly. Because the eyes have the mysterious ability to transmit what we are feeling, they can be used for one of the most remarkable actions we can take to affect the emotional climate in the world around us. We can access the darshan.

Master and gurus are said to be able to gaze at us with divine love. Often the teacher will sit in front of the sangha and pour out his loving gaze. This gaze is called the darshan. The darshan is sometimes called, "Meeting the Master face to face." A true Master is believed to be a divine presence, and receiving his or her darshan is considered an experience of grace, actually seeing the Divine. Thousands of people went every week to receive this blessing from Sai Baba, the great Indian saint. Throughout India this is a common experience.

My first experience of the darshan occurred when Babbie and I were invited to experience Sant Ajaib Singh, a Sikh saint. He was passing through the United States on his way from Central America back to India. He held satsang in a former church on the upper west side of New York City. The church building was ideal for this because all of the pews had been permanently removed and the satsangis and initiates could sit on the floor. People brought their own blankets and cushions to sit on. Babbie and I traveled down from Vermont for the occasion but, since we were not satsangis, we had to wait outside the church until the preliminary meditation was over before we were allowed to enter. It was a huge church and it was completely packed. It looked like we might find space in one of the balconies, but, as luck would have it, Babbie spotted an empty spot on the floor up front. She was determined to get up near the front and overcame my fearful and non-deserving objections that the spot must belong to someone else. In fact it was the zone of the big cheeses of the American Sant Mat sangha who soon came back to a little less room. We had obviously, but unintentionally, challenged their supremacy and ruffled their egos, but the awkward moment passed, and they chose to be gracious. It was certainly not a time to act ungracious with Sant Ji sitting twenty feet away. So, we found ourselves sitting close to the front. In Sant Mat, as in many eastern paths, the guru is called the "Master." He was sitting up on the dais with his interpreter. After we all had settled in, things quieted down, and the Master started to give the darshan. Actually, he gives it all the time, but this was the conscious session in which he would give it to every single person in the building. There were hundreds of people. We sat and gazed up at him having no idea what to expect. He was dressed in white and he wore glasses, which I remember thinking would wreck the effect. His gaze traveled slowly over the crowd from the right side of the church across the center and the left. I remember feeling it come into our zone. It was like a spot light passing over the crowd. Amazingly, I could feel it approaching. When it fell on me I knew he was looking only at me. I felt the full power of the gaze, the absolute love behind it filling me, and I could feel this diminish slowly as it passed on. I came into the building skeptical, but willing to stay open, and I received something beautiful in return.

Once, after we were initiated, the Master came from India to the United Sates for a short stay, and we went to the big multi-day gathering and satsang. There were hundreds of people in a big tent during the meditation phase of the daily satsang. Babbie was feeling truculent and rebellious that day, not wanting to do the meditation at all. She sat at the very back edge of the crowd as far away from the front as she could get. She kept her eyes opened, watching above the sea of heads, to see what the master was doing. Suddenly the Master looked directly at her and pointed to the location of the third eye between his eyebrows, a very clear instruction for her to close her eyes and focus there. He saw every face in a thousand and gave the darshan to all.

Receiving the darshan is an unforgettable experience. After Ajaib passed away, I remembered the phrase "so above, so below." The teaching is that God made us in His image. We are all essentially divine. When we go beyond the idea of God as an anthropomorphic entity with a long white beard sitting on a throne, and understand the mystical teachings, we see that we are left with love. The spiritual texts tell us that love is what holds the universe together, the divine force field. God is often described very simply as pure love. We can choose to give our own level of darshan. We can all access love. Darshan happens when the eyes look at others with unconditional love. I experimented. What I discovered is an amazing and powerful practice and a very spiritual action.

In order for us to give darshan, it is necessary to remove all our judgments and fear and to connect our eyes directly with our heart. Because we are unconscious so much of the time, a state of unconditional love is not constant, but we can access this state in the moments we choose the darshan. Darshan is a practice of placing ourselves in this state. It is a practice of accessing this state. When we do this, we become (for a moment) ambassadors of love in the world, creating change silently wherever we go. When this happens we are actually "in" love, love is flowing through us, we are the agent of love, and since the world is a sea of fear, we become a point of relief. The effect of our darshan is profound and usually instantaneous, quite visible, if only for a moment.

What are some of the requirements of giving darshan? First, we need to feel love for ourselves and to shower mercy and kindness on ourselves. As we have seen this is a pre-requisite for manifesting true compassion for others. The biggest difficulty in giving darshan, the most common obstacle, is our ready judgment. Since this judgment so often stems from self-judgment, we have to deal with self-judgment using mercy.

Second, if we are unfamiliar with the power of our eyes, we will need to practice awareness in this area and begin to experience how our eyes work as messengers of truth and a source of personal insight. We can practice the action of learning from our own eyes as described above.

Like all action, the darshan is a culmination of other work we have done. It is a result and manifestation of our inner being work, the positive changes we have made, and the important revelations we have experienced. The more we have freed ourselves from our own self judgment and fear, the easier it will be to achieve the state necessary for giving the darshan.

The mechanics of giving darshan are simple. All we do is look at a person with complete love and acceptance of them. This can be anyone; someone making change for us for instance, or someone in line at the store; someone we are passing on the sidewalk. We remember that darshan is looking at someone with the eyes fully connected with the heart. Our eyes must be totally free of judgment, a reflection of our opened heart.

Because the eyes have so much power, judgment in a look is easily sensed. In fact, we are usually on the alert for it. Because we are going through the world ready for a judgment attack at any time, we have developed a system that scrutinizes all incoming looks and voice tones for the slightest hint of judgment. This is especially true when we are feeling insecure. Our alert system is on a hair trigger, but it is so much a part of us that we often don't recognize its existence. Because of almost everyone's heightened sensitivity to judgment, for our darshan to work, there cannot be the slightest trace of judgment.

Because the darshan is unusual, if given for too long it can seem intrusive rather than loving. It can cause discomfort. It can trigger the recipient's undeserving and suspicious nature. As a part of our program of love as a subversive activity it will be more effective if we make our darshan into a brief glance, a short burst. Our sensitivity to the recipient's level of comfort is an important part of this action. We do not want to frighten anyone. It is a sad commentary on our world, but nonetheless true, that love is often more frightening than judgment. Love is the more unusual energy.

When I first started this practice, I noticed that my first impressions of people were often judgmental. For instance, I would notice an overweight person at the checkout counter in the grocery store, and I would note that their cart was filled with beer and pasta and potato chips. I would immediately judge them for being fat and not caring for themselves. This all happens very quickly. I think many of us do this. We rush to judgment right at encounter. We judge clothing, physical appearance, speech, eating habits; the list is long.

How was I ever going to give darshan if my mind was traveling in this rut? Awareness allowed me to see myself judging others. If I wanted to give darshan this would not work. Then I noticed that, almost as soon as I judged someone else, I judged myself for my uncharitable behavior. I saw that, once I was into self-recrimination, my opportunity for darshan disappeared. I was caught in my own inner musings. To do darshan I realized I would have to stop this trend too. So, when I saw I was judging someone and then myself for judging, I stopped judging myself, shutting down the entire inner dialogue that was distracting me from the task at hand. What was left was my judgment of the other person, which I found was easier to undo and control. One method I used was to find something nice about the person and replace my judgment with kind thoughts that focused on the positive. I began to practice looking for the good and attractive in people rather than the negative. As Yogananda taught, I worked to "replace bad habits with good habits." This was more pleasant for everybody, and it was a step toward the final giving of darshan, but not the real thing. It dismantled the major blocks to doing the practice. In the final version there is no internal dialogue just the instant connection, the instant look of love as we let the love in our heart out into the world for a brief moment. We can get good at this.

With awareness we can use judgment as an ally that warns us that it is time to open the heart. We can let go of the judgment when it arises and in its place choose love. If we can't choose love, we can start by choosing non-judgment, we can ignore our judging. The more attention we give to judgment, the more energy it garners. The fact that we are not always in a loving state is perfectly normal. For most of us, how we deal with judgment, not whether it is present or not, is the more important consideration.

In this action practice, we use judgment as a cue. Rather than getting hung up on it, rather than turning it on ourselves, we turn it into the starting point for our darshan practice. We replace judgment by choosing to focus on opening the heart. Eventually this becomes our habit and darshan springs naturally from the loving heart.

The reality is that we all know how to do this practice. It is natural. If we are not used to it, that's normal, but, in fact, when I suggest to people that they "connect the eyes with the heart without any interference," they usually know what I mean. Most of us have received such a look, and may have given it ourselves.

It is totally possible for each of us to give darshan. The results are extraordinary. I have seen people suddenly smile, I have seen shoulders drop into relaxation, I have seen eyes smile back. I can tell, that in a brief second, the darshan has made a person's entire day better. I know that, when the glance is seen, the effect is instant and deep. Sometimes people are lost in their inner world and miss the glance. That's OK. There isn't a scoreboard.

Sometimes I receive the darshan from others, and I can feel their love relaxing me in some magical way. When we give the darshan we are sending love out into the world. We are doing that which is deeply gratifying, giving selflessly. This is the work we are here for. How grand that we can do it silently and unobtrusively, without fanfare or display. We are graced to be able to follow the saints' example. The darshan helps us to connect with our divine nature.

As more of us join in the action of darshan we will begin to understand what Rumi was referring to in *No Room for Form* when he asked:

> *Now, what shall we call this new sort of gazing-house*
> *that has opened in our town where people sit*
> *quietly and pour out their glancing like light, like answering?*

Deep Listening
"True Listening is Worship."

John O'Donohue

Many of us want to be of service in the world, and are inspired to make our lives and our work useful to others. The desire to help others is noble, however, our most effective and powerful service is offered from detachment rather than based in fear. The detachment we speak of here is defined by Angeles Arrien as "the capacity to care deeply or maintain compassion from an objective place."[39] To achieve this kind of detachment we have to let go of the need to fix things, and our anguished imperative to have things be different. We need to be willing to let others have their own experience and to honor their experience. When we do this, we are taking up the wonderful work of love as a subversive activity. This type of love is quiet and does not seek reward or recognition. Our goal is to be able to create loving space for whatever is happening in the moment, rather than trying to create a specific outcome dictated by our fear. We create a safe container for other's difficulties, rather than trying to force fear-based change onto them. This is very spiritual work for, while its effect is visible, its cause is often invisible. In the moments we achieve this, we are working with love at a very powerful level. How we help others is not forced but flows naturally.

---

[39] Arrien, Angles, Ph.D., *The Four Fold Way, Walking the path of the Warrior, Teacher, Healer and Visionary* Angels Arrien, 1993

Learning to listen deeply is an excellent action practice when our goal is compassionate detachment. Listening is distinct from hearing. As a counselor, I am blessed to have the wonderful opportunity to practice deep listening. In my opinion, being a good listener is more difficult to master than being an adroit advisor, in addition, the results can be extraordinary. In any case, before we can be a good advisor, we need to be a good listener. When I was younger, before I understood the power of deep listening, I used to drive friends crazy with unsolicited advice. They would tell me a story about their lives, and I would immediately provide a solution to their dilemma or advise them how to look at their issue in a different way. They told me the advice was good but they also told me they didn't really want it. Chances are pretty good that they already knew the solution. We all actually know the solutions to our own issues and, if a solution is obscure at first, we can usually find it, or coax it out, by using the four strategies. It turns out that most people do not tell their stories to get advice; they tell their stories to be heard. The less opinion and comment we share about their story, the more they feel heard. The deeper the level of listening, the greater the level of safety the storyteller feels. Sometimes people ask for advice, but actually, very often, they just want someone to listen fully and appreciate their condition. Often we find the solutions we seek by simply speaking our stories. Advice can get in the way of creating safety and compassion. To be a deep listener, one of the first things we have to do is give up the need and the desire to give advice.

When our kids were growing up, Babbie and I had an epiphany about giving them advice. As typical, fearful parents, we gave advice frequently and, of course, we felt confident this advice was both good and necessary. After all, it was born of our own experience. Weren't we doing what parents have done forever? Weren't we doing what a parent is supposed to do? However, we noticed that, the more advice we gave, the less the kids wanted to share their stories with us. One day we were listening to a radio talk show. A mother and her daughter were being interviewed. The daughter had just written a book about how wonderful her mother had been when she was growing up. When the interviewer asked the daughter what she felt was the salient quality of her relationship with her mother, the daughter replied that her mother had always given her good advice. The interviewer then asked the mother what she remembered about the relationship and the mother replied "I never gave her advice, if I could help it. I just listened. That way she always told me what was going on in her life."

Besides being some of the wisest advice we ever received for dealing with our own children, this recommendation to "just listen" opened up a new way of being with others, especially when they had something important they wanted to share. When we took this advice, our relationship with our children changed dramatically. They felt free to share their life and experiences with us and, because we did not offer advice all the time, they felt safe. Now our children are all adults. People are often surprised at how often the kids call us, just to talk. Of course, we still feel the urge to give advice, to try to fit them into a box that would make us comfortable, and sometimes we do offer advice. But advice can be taken as judgment, and we have noticed that there is a definite relationship between how much advice we give and how often we hear from our adult offspring. Too much advice definitely lowers the amount of true communication. By listening deeply we come to know when advice is really being sought, and we become more sensitive to the way it should be presented or if it should be presented at all. We learn the wisdom that knowing answers does not require stating them; that there are times when offering answers is not helpful, as when a person is in the middle of their own learning process.

A long time ago I read about a professor at the University of Chicago who added a new definition the word "duologue" to describe one of the ways we fail to listen. He defined a "duologue" as two running monologues. This is a very common phenomenon. It may even seem familiar. In a duologue, we can barely wait to have our turn to talk. As soon as we hear something in the other person's monologue to which we have a response, we stop listening, and focus instead on what we are going to say next. If both conversationalists choose this form, neither participant in the conversation hears what the other is saying. Each is trying to jump in and make their point, to continue their monologue. While we are waiting our turn, we cling to the point in our mind, lest we lose it, and we even begin to think about how to elaborate on it. The result is that we are not listening to the other person at all. I have a very knowledgeable friend who does this so often it is not much fun to talk to him. He doesn't interrupt (which he used to do before I brought duologues to his attention) but almost as soon as I begin to talk his eyes glaze over; and I know he is elsewhere or chomping at the bit to get in his response to something I have said. If I am talking on the phone, I can tell when he stops listening because he begins to say things like "right, right, right" or "yes, yes, yes", hoping to hurry me on to some conclusion. The definitive example of a duologue, according to the professor, is two television sets facing one another. Talking with my friend is sometimes like trying to have a conversation with a TV news show.

We have all experienced duologues. The main fear in a duologue is that we will lose a good response or idea that the conversation has given us. If we are ever going to be a deep listener we need to let go of this fear. In fact, we need to let go of the need to respond at all. If we want to practice deep listening, we may often lose our precious responses. Letting go of our need to respond takes some practice. It is fine to make note of an idea, but it is important to come back to listening as soon as possible. The decision to let go of our thoughts is the act of putting listening before our own commentary. Doing this we experience how powerful being a good listener really is, what a gift it is for the speaker. This internal gesture is also an exercise in trust, trust that the right response will be present when the other person stops speaking, whether it is our side of the story, advice or silence. Perhaps a completely different and better observation will appear in place of our first response. Perhaps no response will occur to us. This is fine. Silence is often the landing zone for deep revelation. Rumi wrote:

> "There is a way between voice and presence
> Where information flows
>
> In disciplined silence it opens
> In wandering talk it closes."

And John O'Donohue says, "There is a very important distinction between hearing and listening. Sometimes we listen to things but we never hear them. True listening brings us in touch with what is unsaid and unsayable. Sometimes, the most important thresholds of mystery are places of silence. To be genuinely spiritual is to have great respect for the possibilities and presence of silence."[40]

So, to be deep listeners we need to be comfortable with silence. This is an extremely rewarding project in itself. We can acquaint ourselves with the power of silence in our own homes. We can turn off all the noise and diversions, the TV, the radio, the stereo and notice the silence. When we are in the car we can leave the radio, iPod and the CD player off. We can seek time by ourselves dedicated to silence. By being with silence, eventually we come to understand its power, the power to reveal, the power to deeply calm, the power to heal. Silence allows us to fully experience our true inner condition.

For many of us, when we first choose to consciously experience silence we become aware of an inner discomfort, edginess, a subtle anxiety. We might notice that we want to reach for a switch and turn on some comforting noise. A foil to our busy-ness, silence alarmingly reveals the scale of our unconscious life, the urgency, the hurry, the lack of attention. Suddenly, the constant noise in our lives is revealed as yet another escape from what is real, especially noise that we choose to experience when there is an opportunity for silence.

Working with silence is a good practice for applying the four strategies for learning what our life is trying to teach us. We become aware of our discomfort with silence. We think it is the silence itself, or the lack of our diversions, but, with personal responsibility, we take ownership of the discomfort. It is not the outer condition that is causing it. Our discomfort is not caused by silence, rather, it is revealed by it. What is this discomfort? What are we running away from or toward? Why are we uncomfortable with things in the present, things the way they are right now? With inner work, we make discovery around ways to be comfortable with silence and ways to remove the obstacles to feeling safe in silence. We change our discomfort with silence into an ally. The action we can take is

---

[40] O'Donohue, John, *Anam Cara, A Book of Celtic Wisdom*. Harper Collins, 1991, page 71

creating moments of silence in our busy lives, moments for reflection and for acquainting ourselves with the beauty of silence, an extraordinary form of grace. These moments are miniature retreats from the daily hustle and bustle, islands of quiet sanity. We soon discover the world is a bit too loud. In all the noise, it is difficult to sense the deep river that is flowing under the surface of things. It is hard to understand our connection to nature when we have our iPod hooked to our ears. When I see people running down the beach with their ear buds in place while the breaking waves are making their beautiful and soothing sound and the sea gulls are crying above, I wonder that they are missing a great opportunity for connection with the natural world. This is not a judgment about enjoying music or podcasts. In our noisy world there are times when music can be more soothing than what is going on around us.

Leaning into the future we forgo quiet reflection in silence. We are seldom still. But, as we awaken, as we journey into consciousness, our equanimity expands, we grow more settled in our core. We become better and better listeners as we become more comfortable with ourselves and with being quiet.

Once we are comfortable with silence, we can share this comfort with others. In our deep listening, when moments of silence come up in conversation, we can sit calmly without the urgency to fill the space with the sound of our voice. In this way we make these silent interstices safe for those with whom we converse.

When someone wants to talk to us in a purposeful way, it is good to turn off the music and other noisemakers. At the mechanical level we remove possible diversions. We are also making our attention to them foremost and creating sacred space for our communication and communion. This allows our conversation to have its own resonance and, in the moments of silence that often fall in a conscious conversation, our mind won't travel to the distracting noise. Again, silence during our conversation is profoundly OK, if unusual. It is good to honor silence during a conversation. Sitting in silence with someone is a form of trust.

Another habit we obviously need to avoid, as a deep listener, is the pleasant diversion of day dreaming and following our imagination out of the present and away from the conversation we are having. We persuade ourselves that this mind wandering is OK because the story we are being told is boring, or too long. Yet, being able to listen to a story we judge as boring or too long is excellent practice both for listening and for patience, a key component of deep listening. This is because deep listening goes beyond the story. This is not to say that one must stay engaged forever with another's senseless ramblings or gossip. A respectful and skillful withdrawal can be a good thing. Or, perhaps we can turn the conversation into a deeper channel with a provocative question.

In deep listening, awareness is the shepherd that brings us back to the flow. With awareness we notice when we feel the impulse to stop listening, we notice the moment we have become absorbed and diverted by our own response; we see our own impatience clearly, or we see ourselves daydreaming about something completely different. Gently, and without self-reproach, we come back to the moment, to the listening. When our mind wanders in these ways, we simply bring it back; bring our eyes back to the other's eyes with full attention. Judging ourselves for having left the conversation is only another diversion. Coming back is the only path. Over time we find we are able to stay longer and go deeper in every encounter. We enter a state that encompasses more than the story to which we are listening. For the Masters, every moment, every conversation is spiritual, a revelation. By learning to stay fully present this can be our inheritance too.

Herein is the mystery and beauty of deep listening; that, by being completely present with the storyteller, we come to know what is true and what is not being said. We submerge ourselves in the essence of other and see in it our own life. We discover communion, the moment of full sharing, of empathy. By connecting with the essence of another person in this deep way, we become a real friend, perhaps for a moment only, perhaps for life. Without stating it, we are giving the other person our deepest respect.

There is a response to true acts of kindness. Spirit knows when the act is pure and from the heart. As we practice deep listening, keeping our hearts fully opened, it is not long before we encounter the face and its remarkable unspoken stories. Listening deeply while watching the face of the other person with soft eyes and an opened heart, we encounter the depth of others in a non-linear, spiritual fashion. In his book <u>Anam Cara</u>, John O'Donohue writes eloquently of the human face.

"The human face is the subtle yet visual autobiography of each person. Regardless of how concealed or hidden the inner story of your life is you can never successfully hide from the world when you have a face. If we knew how to read the faces of others, we would be able to decipher the mystery of their life stories. The face always reveals the soul; it is where the identity of the inner life finds an echo and image. When you behold someone's face; you are gazing deeply into that person's life."[41]

I believe that in deep listening we are given the opportunity to discover this gift, a privileged glimpse into another's life. This action gives us an unspeakable understanding of the profound spiritual truth of our oneness with others. When this revelation occurs we experience a holy moment.

The Rumi Poem, *The Night Air*, mentioned earlier in a slightly different context, is about a man who, before he dies, instructs the town judge to give his inheritance to the one of his three sons who the judge finds to be the laziest. "Laziest" here is used to identify the son who is the greatest mystic or lover of the three. Rumi says:

> *"Mystics are experts in laziness. They rely on it,*
> *Because they continually see God*
> *working all around them.*
> *The harvest keeps coming in, yet they*
> *never did the plowing."*[42]

To demonstrate his laziness (or spiritual understanding) each of the three sons talk about how they can know a man fully. After testing the oldest two sons the judge turns to the youngest and asks, "What if a man cannot be made to say anything? How do you learn his hidden nature?"

---

[41] Ibid., page 71

[42] Barks, Coleman with Moyne, John, *The Essential Rumi*. Castle Books 1997, page 30

"I sit in front of him in silence,
and set up a ladder made of patience,
and if in his presence a language from beyond joy
and beyond grief begins to pour out of my chest
I know that his soul is as deep and bright
As the star Canopus rising over Yemen.

And so when I start speaking a powerful right arm
of words sweeping down, I know him from what I say,
and how I say it because
there is a window open between us
mixing the night air of our beings.

The younger was obviously,
the laziest. He won."[43]

The window opens. The night air is sweet and cool. It is the breeze from the soul. The night air comes from the dark side of our being; the hidden places that we do not reveal. We experience deep intimacy when we share these places. When we mix "the night air of our beings" we find that words are not necessary and, if they come, they will come from a deeper place than our intellect.

Deep listening is a true voyage into the spiritual realm. It begins as an action in which we open ourselves more fully to others. We learn to avoid equivocation and escapes. We work to stay fully present, to be totally with another's story. In time we discover the truth that comes out of silences as well as from the voice, and then, when we see the true face, we experience deep communion. We experience grace and blessing as it flows over both the storyteller and ourselves. We mix "the night air of our beings" and we discover holiness.

---

[43] Ibid. Page 32

Peace at Home

"No one can bring you peace but yourself."
Ralph Waldo Emerson

When Babbie and I lived in Vermont we were extras in a movie that Jay Craven was making of Howard Frank Mosher's book, *Stranger In the Kingdom*. One of our fellow extras was David Dellinger, who also lived in Vermont. David had always been a pacifist; he refused to show up for the physical when drafted in World War II (a popular war) and was put in prison. He became most well known as one of the infamous Chicago Seven peace demonstrators that upset the carefully staged Democratic Convention in Chicago in 1968 during the horrible Vietnam conflict.

Each day at the movie site, we were made up like folks from the 50's, and we waited in a clapboarded town building for our scene to start in the cold, old, county courthouse. We extras played gin rummy and chatted, whiling the time away. Being with David was a blessing. He was unassuming, interested in all, and exuded the palpable peace of a person who has lived his convictions and is completely comfortable with them. He was very content with whatever transpired. He had a beautiful and caring wife too. Where Abbie Hoffman had intensity and anger, David had a peaceful demeanor and core. David abhorred violence; all his work; all his protests were non-violent. But he was strong and very courageous in the way that only a person with great inner conviction can be. He was someone who had always stood by his personal values. He had been put in jail numerous times. He took, anyone would acknowledge, tremendous personal risks. He seemed, in many ways, like an American Gandhi and, when you met him, you could actually feel the peace he exuded. It was very personal and universal, and he was entirely dedicated to a peaceful way of being. He had the power of peace. I felt privileged to have met him and to have spent a short time with him. We need many David Dellingers in order to survive the insanity of war and hatred.

The amount of creativity, energy, ingenuity and resources that go into making machines and systems whose sole purpose is to kill human beings is extraordinary and tragic. Arms manufacture is now the largest enterprise in the world, garnering more money than any other human endeavor. War is the sad evidence of how disassociated we remain from other human beings, the great majority of whom have the same fears, sorrows and joys as our selves. Disassociation, our denial of our fundamental sameness, allows us to vilify and negatively group other human beings and whole nations. It is a state about which we must develop awareness and take personal responsibility if we want to live a life of peace and be a person who can create peace around themselves. Becoming conscious of the forces that create disassociation and eliminating them from our own lives is an important step in developing the compassion necessary for the creation of a harmonious world. The work of peace begins with us.

I once took a tour of the nuclear missile submarine John Adams when it was in dry dock in Portsmouth, New Hampshire. A relative of mine was the boat's quartermaster. We went down to the shipyard one night, and he gave me a private tour. The John Adams was a huge vessel, 125 feet longer than a football field. Seeing it in the dry dock, flooded with light was an impressive sight. At sea, over a hundred men lived on board in two, six-month shifts. So, there were two complete crews. When I went aboard, the boat was torn up for refitting. The conning tower had a big hole in its side for moving gear and tools in and out while in dry dock, and below decks all the facing panels had been removed. Miles of cables, tubes and wiring were exposed. Looking at all the engineering and the equipment that was on board made it easy to see why the defense budget of the United States is so big. I was able to tour the entire ship, except the engine room, the most top-secret part of the boat. I saw "Sherwood Forest" (the two long rows of nuclear missile tubes), the captain's quarters, the crews' quarters, and the huge forward torpedo room in the bow with its own operator's booth off to one side. I toured the bridge. The only other sub I had ever been on was the WWII German U Boat at Chicago's Museum of Science and Industry. The John Adams was so impressive that I had to remind myself why it was created. My relative told me that when the sub put to sea again, it would be the most advanced weapon in the world, filled with new and better technology for killing than anything on earth.

The area I really wanted to see was the missile control room, the launch area. I wanted to know what is written on the button that, when pushed, kills millions of human beings and destroys our environment for hundreds of thousands of years, the button that represents the failure, and perhaps the end, of human civilization. We went down a ladder from the bridge and walked between two banks of old analog computers, (digital computers can be disrupted by outside magnetic and electrical forces). At the end of this short passage was the control area. There were two consoles, each with a seat and display panel, one seat for each row of missiles. Each panel contained a long row of colored, plastic, back-lit buttons. The panels were dead of course, but one could still read the print on the buttons. My cousin told me that the firing sequence for a missile went down the panel and that the bottom button was the one that was pressed for the actual launch. The button did not say "death and destruction" or feature a skull and crossbones, although these would have been more accurate than the military lingo it featured. Deep in the sea and far from the massive destruction just one missile would cause, the operator can push a lit, one inch square button that simply says "tactical."

The "tactical" button represents the ultimate moment of disassociation, the sum total of all our disassociation, and our failure to choose compassion, to choose love rather than fear as our guide. The idea that war is a "solution" to anything is insanity. Causing massive suffering is not a solution, but a horrible failure. We are all individually responsible for this abomination because, if we want the whole to change, each of us must take personal action. Individually, we are the source of the peace we all claim to desire. The micro (the individual) informs and creates the macro (the society). There is no reason to wait around for the macro to change, to wait for a political miracle, to wait for a new president, to wait for aliens to land and straighten things out, or to wait for Armageddon which is the current, crazy rage. Thinking that a new form of government or a new social order will do the job has created a long history of resounding failures and abusive, corrupt governments as we give away our power to those who lust for it. If we want a world more attuned to the spiritual nature of life, we have to become more attuned ourselves. If we want the world to change for the better, then we have to change in this moment, not later. One of the most important ways we can do this is to move from disassociation to connectedness, from preoccupation with our own lives to sharing life with others.

Again, in his wonderful poem of consciousness and love, *No Room For Form*, Rumi opens the poem at the moment of death, saying: "On the night when you cross the street from your shop and your house to the cemetery..."[44] In one line he gathers our major preoccupations in life, our "shop and our house," our work and our private or home life. The poem invites us to awaken from this preoccupation. Later he says "no need to wait until we die, there is more to want here than money and being famous and bits of roasted meat."[45] Here the cultural wish list of both ancient and modern man is neatly trumped by the conscious life. If we commit to take up consciousness before we die, to go for "more than riches," it is not long before we become aware that we have spent a great deal of time in self-concern, preoccupied with our personal situation, our relationships, our economic condition, our desires, our business or our pains. This seems natural, as everyone else appears to be doing pretty much the same thing, and these activities are sanctified by our material culture. This preoccupation, however, separates us from understanding about, and sympathy for, the concerns of others who are not in our immediate group, people sometimes as close as our very neighbors, as well as the vast world of people we don't know but with whom we interact each day. Sometimes, in isolation from others who we view as different, we gossip about how stupid this person was, or how unskillful they were, or how our religion makes

---

[44] Ibid. page 138
[45] Ibid. page 140

us better. We reinforce separation. But separation, as attractive and popular as it seems, keeps us afraid and unhappy.

As we know, every single person with whom we come into contact represents an opportunity for manifesting love and good will; for celebrating basic goodness. In this way, person-by-person, we have the opportunity to change the world into a more peaceful and compassionate place. The more of us that deeply comprehend that we are all connected; that we all share the same fears and longings, the more improved life on earth will be. One way that we can deepen this connection is to diminish the disassociation that occurs when we use modern electronic devices unconsciously. We can create some new disciplines. We can refuse to take calls on our cell phone, or other devices, when we are in a conversation with someone. We can pay complete attention to the person we are talking with, rather than talking while texting or looking over messages or surfing the internet. This focused attention was once considered civil behavior. It is respectful.

There are some conscious actions we can take to begin this process right in our own home. The primary perpetrators of disassociation in most homes are electronic: video games, television, radio and the computer. Besides creating disassociation through the shows and activities that are commonly accepted parts of our often violent culture, these devices can create disassociation right in the family! Both children and adults can get so lost in other worlds that they find the world around them, the real world, an annoying interruption. And, as David Frost said, "television enables you to be entertained in your home by people you wouldn't have in your home."

When our children were very young, we had a small black and white TV. When our kids began to argue over who could watch what and when, we got rid of the TV. It was never reintroduced. This had some very interesting effects. Quiet was the first blessing. The two children who were showing undoubted signs of video addiction lost their addiction and became avid readers. Without the distraction and noise of TV, we had more family time. We played games and read aloud, major boons to children's imagination and their ability to create syntax. Later, when our kids went to college, they were amazed at how much TV everyone was watching, and they thanked us for removing TV from their childhood. Many adults do much better without TV too. It is an interesting experiment to disconnect the TV and video games for a few weeks and see how much life changes. Some of us might also discover how addicted we are. Perhaps we have been using video and TV as an escape from discomfort. We can all enjoy the silence. We can expect a period of adjustment, but then we discover it is quite nice not to be hooked. Of course, some of us who are sports addicts will protest. Sports can be a huge escape from life, an escape from the frustrations of life and often from intimacy. For many, sports are sacred and resemble a religion, not to be questioned or tampered with. An occasional game is much different from hours of watching each week, or from virtual teams.

Anyone to whom you suggest the radical step of getting rid of their television will inevitably tell you "there are some good things on too." In fact, if I were given a dollar for every time someone said this to me, I would have quite a pile, but the amount of really negative and silly programs on TV generally outweighs the good. If I offered you a glass of poison and it contained a teaspoon of fresh orange juice would that be a good reason to drink it? We watch horrors on the news and over time become used to murder, death, and suffering in various forms, the main stuff of TV news and many shows and video games. All these programs reinforce disassociation, the idea that these things are happening to others, when, spiritually speaking, they affect us all. If we had never seen a TV or violent movie and we saw the evening news, or some of the increasingly violent videos that are produced by the thousands, we might go into shock. We are so inured to this kind of violence that, rather than being upset or angry about it, we no longer pay attention. I can remember the first graphically violent movie I ever saw, *The Godfather*. This movie represents for me the beginning of the era of violent entertainment that has continued ever since, unabated. I was so appalled by the raw violence that I left the movie. I felt physically sick. It literally shocked me, as it was no doubt intended to do. However, over time, I notice that I have grown more and more accustomed to violence and consequently more accepting. Watching violence is psychologically and spiritually toxic. Although there is a constant and huge stream of violence in our violence prone society, we tend to deny its influence, calling it simply "entertainment." One has to ask, why is it entertaining to watch other human beings being murdered, raped, violated, and abused? It may be accepted, but it is not uplifting. In any case, not viewing angry news and opinion, not listening to angry radio talk show hosts, not renting violent videos, can bring more peace into our lives and diminish the disassociation necessary to maintain violent behavior and an acceptance of violence. As we experience more inner peace, our barriers to violence increase in strength.

In many American homes the TV is an icon, often even called "the center of family life." This is a sad statement, because when we watch TV we are actually very close to cationic state. Yet, people talk about the whole family watching a show together as if this were important progress in creating a healthy family. A family that enters catatonia together stays together? Probably there is little or no correlation. About all that can be said is that the family is in the same room. That may be good, of course. Or maybe the family has a running dialogue about a show and this can be interpreted as a bonding experience.

Television commercials also subvert our spiritual values. The television is the electronic priest of the religion of materialism. Like the priests of ancient times who claimed to be the doorman for the heavenly realm that came after death, the TV, the electronic priest of the consumer society, promises that we can achieve happiness in life by simply buying more things. Watching TV can rob you of your life. The average person spends ten years of their life in front of TV. In reality intemperate TV viewing has the qualities of an addiction, but, like another legal drug, alcohol, because of its usefulness to commercial interests, we are encouraged to ignore its down side.

And, as if all this were not enough, Robert Bly has reported frightening phenomena associated with heavy video use. Young children who are not read to, and who watch a great deal of TV in their very early years, are unable to understand syntax. They cannot create clear sentences. This ability cannot be regained. Basically, these children will not be able to put thoughts together coherently. Schools are now experiencing a generation of children who have attention deficit disorders. Could there be any correlation? It seems clear that using TV for a babysitter can have lifetime consequences.

Removing, or limiting the use of electronic, or video, devices from one's life sounds radical, but it is easy, costs nothing, and creates amazing changes in our personal environment. It may be the most simple and least painful step in creating a more spiritual lifestyle. Like any addiction, the more painful the withdrawal from these devices, the more necessary it probably is. The benefits of disconnecting are numerous. We can discover them simply by unplugging for a day or two at a time. So many of us say we desire more simplicity and beauty in our lives and here is an easy way to create this. The peace that is created when the electronic world is silenced is palpable. And it creates time to take up other pursuits like music, art, or writing, or *really* doing things together. If it is impossible to turn off the TV for a while, we can monitor the kind of material we are watching, making sure to avoid violence and negativity.

When I was a young boy I lived in Texas, where I was born. In those days, there was no air conditioning, although some people had a "cooler," a big, vented box that hung out the window with a fan that blew air through dripping water. It wasn't cold air, just cooler air. In the evenings, in the cool of the day, people sat out on their porches and visited with each other. They visited while the kids played up and down the block. We knew who most of our neighbors were. Years later, after air conditioning and TV were introduced, I noticed that no one ever spent the evenings outdoors. There were many neighborhoods that had become just a row of houses, individual retreats from the world. In the evening everyone was inside, in the air conditioning, watching TV. In the winters in Vermont, driving through small towns in the dark of early evening, one can see the blue glow of TV light emanating from every house. It is interesting to see the difference in the small towns of the coastal plains of Panama. Few people can afford air conditioning or TV. Their favorite pastime is visiting relatives and neighbors, and having meals together. Panama is said to be one of the top five happiest nations in the world. In our sophisticated, electronic device saturated, air conditioned world we hear that there is worry about the loss of the family, of a lack of community. Perhaps, when we are feeling the isolation, we can unplug some electronics and walk the neighborhood in the evening, engaging with neighbors.

The computer is very useful on the one hand and very distracting on the other. I use a computer to write, to pay bills and keep track of things. I write emails and keep in touch with friends. It is very helpful. It is a superior device for long range communication with our family. It can be a wonderful aid for learning. But, I also am aware that I get distracted by it and use it to cruise the internet to read stories I like and to shop for things I don't actually buy. This can be time consuming if I am not careful.

It takes some discipline to use a computer wisely, the kind of discipline most kids have not yet developed, and many of us just don't have. For kids the computer often turns into a game machine, and the games are often the type that provide entertainment through simulated murder and killing. Parents are often proud when their children know how to use a computer. But this too begins an early pattern of disassociation; it separates young people from the natural world, as well as from a relationship with their immediate home environment. We can now enter "alternate realities" and "virtual realities," creating personas to replace our selves. Some of us are more comfortable in this world than the sometimes difficult real world, and we use it like a drug to escape the unpleasantness we experience in the "real" world. Some of us don't bother to learn the social skills necessary to function in society. Instead we hide in fantasy. This is dysfunctional behavior.

Senseless, gratuitous, murder and high school massacres are obviously a manifestation of dangerous disassociation. That people skilled in computer games are the new warriors, killing people with drones in far off lands from the safety of a base in the United States says a great deal about our culture of disassociation.

And let's not forget the cell phone, while we are at it. This device gets the award for being the most highly interruptive electronic detractor. Many of us will interrupt a personal conversation to take a call.

The TV, the radio and the computer, the iPod, and the cell phone are just a few of the addictions we share that are distractions from our path; that remove us from a more peaceful atmosphere. We may also have a hobby or a habit that is destructive and lacking in peace. When we unplug from these hobbies we make space for more calm and tranquil energy. It is surprisingly easy to simplify our lives in this way.

Experimenting with less of the electronic invaders is interesting, informative and healthy. It may create some difficulties as once again we awake to some uncomfortable feelings they have helped us to ignore. As we now know, when we cut off escapes from reality, we are forced to confront what is unpleasant and uncomfortable in our lives. It is up to us to honestly decide whether something is a bad habit or not. If we are honest and admit a few bad habits, we can replace them with good habits.

Real peace is an inner condition, and, while much of the work outlined in this book can bring us to this condition, the focus here is shutting down or limiting some outer distractions. In this way we can create more space for doing our inner work; the work that creates equanimity and peace. We long for the quiet simple life when it is right in front of us. We just need to push the "off" button sometimes.

Helping
Reconnecting with Others

"By giving to someone else, you touch that innate love that is the core of our being. Sometimes we become so self-centered and self-contained we stop feeling. People like to be reminded that the ultimate aim is love. If there's no heart in it, it's a very dull life."

Sharon Gannon, founder of Jivamukti Yoga Center.

Perhaps the best way to defeat disassociation is to connect with others; especially with those with whom we would normally not associate. Helping or service work, is the action that can take us from preoccupation with our own life directly into the experience of oneness, into the realization of commonality rather than difference, into union from separation and, depending on the type of service we choose, sometimes so far into love that we can even experience unity consciousness or bliss. The rewards of this action are numerous. It can create a container for all the other action work we are doing, the deep listening, the darshan, and learning when to speak and how to communicate authentically. Helping, or serving others, is the most powerful way out of our preoccupation with our own life. One of the most common ways to do this is through volunteer work.

The Canadian government decided that it would be interesting to move away from gross national product as a measure of cultural and societal success and instead use quality of life as the measurement. It ran a pilot program in Nova Scotia. The current, ubiquitous, gross national product model of the health of a nation measures the gross financial cost of everything purchased. This includes negative items, for instance: the cost of plane and car crashes, divorce, wars and sales generated from response to disasters. Canada decided instead to measure those things that improved the quality of life for citizens against those things that depleted the quality of life. Sustainability and improvement of the individual life of citizens were the core positive measures. Thus forestation and sustainable forestry practices would go in the positive column while deforestation would be a negative value. One of the most interesting things they discovered, which had not been measured before, was the economic value of volunteerism in Nova Scotia. In the quality of life measure, it was revealed that volunteerism was saving the government millions of dollars in social services annually. As a bonus, volunteerism spreads goodwill and is made up of thousands of acts of kindness. It contributed to the social well being of the community.

Some forms of volunteering are more rewarding than others. The determining factor is personal challenge. How personally challenging is the volunteer work we choose? Helping with a bake sale to raise money for the church is volunteering. It has several benefits. One is that it creates fellowship. Fellowship is an important way we can get to know others and begin to work with our differences. The bake sale often results in funds for a specific needy cause. Working with others, especially people we don't know well, is a step out of preoccupation with self. We can see that even something as easy as being a volunteer at the church supper takes us out of our self centered world for a short while. Helping with the bake sale however, for most of us, is not particularly challenging, and the deeper inner rewards that we receive when we move through personal challenges are sometimes absent. That being said, if we have never done any volunteer work before, helping out with community functions is a good place to begin our experience. It is, of course, not always true that we won't come across personal challenge in these situations either. Personality issues can arise in any setting, and learning to work with others can be challenging sometimes. And, as the Nova Scotia study indicated, all forms of volunteering contribute to better community.

Volunteer work that puts us in intimate contact with complete strangers, people from different social strata, or people who have a completely different set of problems than our own, can challenge us on a personal level. These are opportunities such as youth counseling, emergency medicine, or caring for the sick and elderly. For five years I volunteered and trained with the local rescue squad as an EMT and a driver, but the volunteer work that has been most challenging for me, and from which I have learned the most, has been hospice work, helping the dying and their families to experience death with dignity and without pain. I believe hospice is one of the most powerful volunteer organizations in existence. It matches all the criteria for personal challenge, it is volunteer work that is certain to make us more aware of our preoccupation with self, and it helps us to connect with others at deep level.

I became a hospice volunteer over 30 years ago, when my father died of cancer. The experience of the death of a loved one is how many are called to this form of volunteering. In my case, I was so upset with the indignities my father suffered in the hospital, and the useless operations that he underwent, that I wanted to help other people die at home, with their family nearby, if they so chose. When my father died, the hospice movement in the United States was just beginning. Many barriers had to be overcome. The idea of death outside the hospital was resisted by the medical community, which seemed extraordinary since people have died at home forever. Much of the work hospice did in the beginning included educating professionals about death with dignity at home. Nowadays, many volunteers join hospice because the volunteers who have cared for their dying family member inspired them to do so. I joined hospice to support the concepts of death with dignity, minimal pain and death at home, if so chosen. These goals are now well accepted in the United States, and it is the medical community that makes much of this possible, especially those most wonderful beings, the visiting nurses.

I joined the nascent hospice in my area and at first worked on the board of directors. I soon realized that this was not what I really wanted. I really wanted to be a volunteer and to work with the patients and their families, so I quit the board and took the volunteer training. I came into the work with a passion for change, but over time my focus became learning how to be with the dying and their families and how to create safety for people in distress without being overbearing, sentimental or a know-it-all. Hospice work is a great teacher of humility. Volunteers are frequently reminded of their own mortality, which reminds us to appreciate life more. Sitting with someone who is dying, or helping the family in other ways, means we have to leave our own life behind and stay fully present. As a volunteer we may do many jobs, mow the grass, take down the storm windows, go shopping, make a bed, and, when asked, help with dressings or moving a patient. Mostly, we sit quietly with the dying. Hospice work takes volunteers from millionaire's mansions to very poor people's trailer homes, from gated communities to slums. The idea that we are all alike becomes much more than a concept. As a volunteer, we can see how much separation has been created in our world. A volunteer is likely to lose many prejudices and fears as a result of this work. They will care for old people and young people, and people who die in many different ways. Each experience is different. Every experienced volunteer I have ever known agrees that the blessings received from hospice work are extraordinary and far outweigh the time and effort spent. Some say that to sit with the dying in a conscious manner is to sit with the angels who are waiting on the other side. Therese Schroeder-Sheker who plays harp music to the dying, and started a school in a Montana hospital for teaching others to do the same, has stated that she and her fellow harpists regularly see presences in the room of a dying person. The hospital in which she works is unique in that it has many harpists on staff. Whether one can actually see the presences or not, the room of a dying person can sometimes be a place of extraordinary peace and sometimes joy. I believe that the dying teach us to love fully and unconditionally. Being in that loving energy, we realize that that is where we want to be all the time. It is more than riches.

Hospice is just one example of volunteer work that is personally challenging and as a result, ultimately very rewarding. We can create our own volunteer work, helping a neighbor in need, taking a meal to the old person down the road, and sitting with a sick friend. There are many opportunities. If you want to take independent service action, just do it. Don't ask if someone needs help or tell them to call you if they do, go ahead and take action. Do what you know is needed.

Watching for these opportunities to help others is another way we can become more connected and less preoccupied with ourselves. To repeat, the helping work that garners the deep rewards and makes our lives more full will be the work that is the most personally challenging. At first that challenge might be the act of volunteering itself. The challenge varies from person to person, but whether we create our own form of helping, volunteer as an EMT or a fireman, a hospice volunteer, or a school coach, the action of helping brings us out of disassociation and into the world. It provides numerous opportunities to practice the other actions with which we are working. It makes the world a better place. It teaches us about the action of love in the world. It changes our lives profoundly.

Being Time
The Personal Retreat

"The indication here is that if we can develop this quality of inner peace , no matter what difficulties we meet with in life, our basic sense of well being will not be undermined. It also follows that, though there is no denying the importance of external factors in bringing this about, we are mistaken if we suppose that they can ever make us completely happy."

The Dalai Lama

As I mentioned earlier, for many years I have taken a week by myself. I used to travel to a friend's cottage on an island off the coast of Maine. I went in October, long after all the summer folks were gone. The island was quiet then, and the house had a wonderful view of islands, the pines and the approaches to Penobscot Bay. The setting for a personal retreat is important. A quiet place where nature abounds is most desirable. Camping far from human habitation and activity is an excellent way to spend time alone. I have solo backpacked in the Alaska wilderness and Wyoming's Wind River Range.

Time by one's self is a vital part of every year. Friends of mine go on silent meditation retreats. Wherever we go for self-time, the focus is taking time solely with ourselves, out of direct contact with others, to meditate, reflect, and intuit; to come into contact with the deep refreshment of silence and emptiness. It is not a substitute for daily practices but an important component of a spiritual life.

Consciously setting aside and spending a block of time by oneself is one of the most precious gifts we can give ourselves. We spend so much of our lives "doing" that most of us are not acquainted with the meaning and practice of "being." We are often frightened by the idea of being by ourselves, of being alone, and yet the treasure to be found in seclusion is as vast as the very emptiness and silence we fear. All the great saints and mystics found their connection with spirit, with oneness, in the wilderness or by sitting alone, in stillness and quiet. Besides being an important enhancement to our experience of the rest of our lives, time alone and time spent in silence and reflection is a great aid and boon before any major change or decision in one's life. The results are often revelatory.

Without the foil of "being" for all our "doing" it is hard to notice the frantic nature of our "doing." We become lost in our anxieties, our worries, our thoughts, and our story. We keep "looping," going back over the same stories, the same problems and the same solutions; knowing no other way, many of us live unconsciously, in a state of constant agitation. Yet, even if we have difficulty recognizing it, we all feel a deep need for peace and calm in our lives. We want to connect with our center, the place from which these vital qualities spring. We wonder how to bring it in, how to get back there. Spending time by oneself far from the normal conditions and surroundings of our modern life is a real adventure and an important path to our inner peace, the well where the deep and calming waters abide and the wellspring of equanimity.

Because this is such a powerful choice, once we have made the decision to spend time by our self, Gurdjieff's "second force" will usually appear to test our commitment (see *Keeping the Garden Watered*). Some possibilities: We set our retreat date; suddenly the phone rings, and an old friend calls to let us know they will only be in our area on the very weekend we chose to go away. Our partner tells us that there is an important dinner they expect us to attend right in the middle of our retreat. Our children suddenly announce a play in which they are performing right on the dates we have meticulously set up. Second force tests our conviction, commitment, and intention. "So you want to go spend time with yourself, eh?" the universe says,"let's see how committed you are." Many times we fail the test because the second force is so logical. Once again, the voice of reason becomes the guardian at the gate, keeping us out of the garden of expanding experience and, in this case, away from the novelty of time spent self-nurturing.

The choice to spend time alone takes more courage than we might expect. Many of us are not used to doing something solely for our own benefit. In addition, when the decision to take time to be by ourselves is new, it frightens our subconscious. Fearing change, fearing being alone, it keeps coming up with logical excuses not to follow through. It is interesting how uncomfortable many of us are with the idea of being alone and yet, it is only from being truly alone, even for a brief period, that we can learn that there is nothing to fear about this state and much to be gained.

It is helpful to understand the richness of the gift we give ourselves when we decide to nurture ourselves deeply through silence and being alone. In addition to gaining a deeper perspective of our own life, in addition to finding deep peace and calm, we benefit all those around us with these treasures. Sometimes, when others are confused and at loose ends, we are able to calmly hold our center because we know the center. We have experienced this place in retreat. It is real for us. When we reduce our own anxiety we help reverse the spread of anxious thinking in the field around us. This is especially beneficial to children as they are so easily conditioned by our behavior. However, even knowing the benefits of a personal retreat intellectually will not stop the second force. We will still be strongly called to other logically important activities. Until we have actually experienced the benefits of this practice, like Mojud, we will have to jump into the river with no guarantee. What we are given is the inspiration of the saints; the knowledge that this deep connection is fundamental to our ultimate well-being and our spiritual growth, as well as the well-being of all those we encounter in life. As a husband and father, I can attest to how useful it has been for me to leave the daily family life and return refreshed and better able to handle the seemingly constant calls for patience and quiet reason.

The purpose of our time by ourselves is to experience ourselves and our connection to life fully, to become comfortable with silence, to become grounded and centered, to discover and expand our inner peace, to be in the presence of our fear with no distraction, to ask for guidance and learn how to receive it, to experience the presence of the sacred in life, and to simply be. After a few days of a retreat, many people encounter themselves again, like a lost friend, left behind long ago. This can be a miraculous and joyful reunion!

Over time, and in talking with other personal retreat participants, I have discovered certain conditions that are very helpful for getting the most out of one's time alone.

Spend a week, if possible - A minimum of five days is best for this practice. This is because it usually takes around three days to fully unwind and disconnect from all the agitation and business of our normal lives. In comparing notes with others who spend time in retreat, three days is a very consistent benchmark. We often awaken on the fourth day to a noticeable shift in our level of tension and a lessening and letting go of the desire for planning and doing. It is amazing that this state can manifest so quickly when we reflect that we spend almost all of our time in the stress of thought and action.

It is hard to believe that we have created lives that are so busy 365 days per year that we cannot set aside five to seven consecutive days for ourselves. This may be an indication of how far out of balance our modern lifestyle has become. The Hopi even have a word for this, Koyannisqatsi, which actually means "life out of balance." For most of us, it is probably thousands of days since we have taken conscious and dedicated self time. It is not unusual to have never done any such thing. Even our vacations are usually packed with doing. It is amazing how little time we actually spend balancing our doing with being.

If you cannot set aside five to seven days or more for yourself, don't let the amount of time become a hold back. Any time alone in silence is always better than none! A day here and there throughout the year is a very helpful practice as well. However, for maximum benefit five days or more in one place is recommended. Travel time is separate.

Let go of Planning - In the first few days of a personal retreat I often find myself planning; planning what I am going *to do*: planning meals, scheduling bike rides, hikes and other activities. This is normal. We carry the scheduling of everyday life right into our solitary time. The idea that we must manage, control and schedule every event, so that we can fit in as much possible, is widely accepted in our western culture but is antithetical to the purposes of a personal retreat. The retreat is "downtime," and a part of our retreat is letting go of strict time schedules. Instead we try to get into a natural flow. We can take off our watch and let the sun be our guide. This is a great experience in itself. The attachment to time frames is very strong. We all know the phrases, "what will I do then? How much time should I set aside for that? When should I...?"

I have always experienced this scheduling agitation. It seems "hard wired" into my behavior circuits. Over time, I have found the planning desire amusing because I know it will dissolve after a few days of retreat and is therefore nothing to worry about. It helps to remind ourselves that detailed advanced planning is not a necessary part of our time alone, and that this pattern will resolve itself. It helps to be aware of this phenomenon in order to let it go, bit by bit. By the third or fourth day, the desire to plan all of the day's activities disappears; we become more responsive to the present and the desires and needs we find there. The freedom from a strict schedule is refreshing. It is a delight to let go of planning; to truly go with the flow. However, it is still helpful to include in one's overall plan a few disciplines such as yoga and meditation because they support the purpose of retreat. I sit in meditation before sunrise and then drink my tea and watch the sun come up, simple things.

Minimize Human Contact - Sometimes during my personal retreat, if I am not camping, I might go to the store to pick something up. This and a short conversation with someone or a "hello" when I ride my bike or take a walk is the extent of human contact. The purpose of the personal retreat is to spend time with *me*. Human contact can be distracting and interrupt an evolving seclusion and inner peace, pulling me back into the world. Even short conversations interfere with the secluded and solitary atmosphere we are creating. Sometimes we might want to call home, but I have found that this is not a good idea because we can very easily be swept back into everyday issues, regardless of our intentions. Those at home or at work are not sharing our process. For them life is still the business of "doing" and they reference our normal participation in this. When we are on retreat, they are literally "in another world." When going on retreat, it is much better to leave all of our home life, our business and other lives behind. There are easy ways to make sure we do not get pulled into our everyday life. If we are at a location where there is a phone we can simply unplug it or turn it off. Turn off the cell phone and other distracting devices too. We can determine that we are not going to make or take any calls. We can tie up as many loose ends at home as possible before leaving. In a personal retreat, we want to experience solitude. For this we need to be incommunicado.

Sometimes the mind likes to go to worst case. It says, "What if something bad happens that needs my attention?" If we are really worried about this, tell people to call only in case of a "real" emergency. If you are staying somewhere with a phone, don't give out the number except to someone close. It is important to never give your number to someone at work. Remember that bad news travels fast and can and will almost always reach you. Trust that everything will be fine. You will return home refreshed and better able to handle both the large and small crises of life.

One of the interesting discoveries about being by ourselves and away from our normal environment is that the world goes along fine without us; we are safe without being attached to the distractions and patterns of our lives. Letting go of our attachment to everyday worries is a part of the retreat gift and a part of our spiritual growth.

Find A Helping Environment - The environment we choose for our retreat is important. Our home is usually not a good place for a personal retreat. Spending a quiet day or two at home in silence with the phone and other devices disconnected is very beneficial, but a personal retreat is meant to remove us from things familiar that could distract us. It may be that even your own personal, isolated cabin in the woods may not be the best place to go for your retreat if when you are there you like to do chores. This is "being" time, "doing" can be a distraction.

It takes a few days of being alone to really reach the safe point, to drop into the space you have created. The best environment is one in which we are self-sufficient and do not have to rely on anyone for anything. A cabin in the woods where we can prepare simple meals for ourselves is ideal, but sometimes that takes some doing. An efficiency unit somewhere off the beaten track is also a good thing. Perhaps a friend has a house they are not using. In New England it is easy to find good, quiet places after the summer and the fall leaf peeper season have run their course and all the tourists and summer folk are gone. Going to an area after "the season" is a good way to secure a nice quiet habitation. There are cabins with kitchens available for the price of an average motel room and in beautiful hiking country or on a pond. Part of the experience is finding a good spot. It is not necessary to go to the same location each year, but sometimes it is easier to go back to a good spot because we don't have to take a chance on a new location.

Going out for meals is outside of the scope of our intention to be alone. It is too much of the world. We bring what we need to eat with us and try to keep it simple. Big menus and lots of food preparation can be a way of deflecting the discomfort of being alone, and over-eating is a way of dampening discontent and emotions, the forces with which we want to work. There are, after all, no rules, so, if preparing a good meal brings satisfaction and pleasure, we can do this from time to time. Many times I use the retreat for cleansing, dropping bad habits from my diet and fasting (more later).

As mentioned earlier, going into the woods and setting up a campsite is a great way to spend time by ourselves. It encourages simplicity, and it reconnects us with the natural world. This connection is, in itself, tremendously healing. The sound of the wind in the trees, the smell of the rain on the earth, the sunny days can deeply soothe us. Our rhythm becomes natural, up with the sunrise, down with the sunset. If just an hour spent in quiet woods can be deeply refreshing, a multi-day retreat is even more amazing. Days spent outdoors add a great deal of healing energy to a retreat. Again, human contact is discouraged, so a busy campground is not the best spot, although some campgrounds do provide some more private areas, particularly off season.

A wilderness retreat is an exceptional experience. Far from all humans and deep in the heart of the natural world, we sometimes come in contact with fears that we thought we had left far in the past, not to mention primitive fears. These fears can be great teachers. In the great sky and quiet of the wilderness, and the calming aid of the natural world, we are often able to go deeper into our spiritual condition than in any other place. Powerful revelations can occur in this extraordinary atmosphere. A wilderness retreat takes careful planning and usually additional travel but, if you are healthy enough and have spent some time in the outdoors, wilderness solo camping it is well worth the effort. The idea is to hike out to a remote spot and then stay there for a few days rather than moving around.

The vision quest is similar to the wilderness camping experience except that it is more focused and perhaps more intentional. On a vision quest a person will stay in a remote area usually within a relatively small circle they create for a few days. They do not usually eat but only drink water. At the end of the quest they often come back and share the story of their quest with guides who help them interpret what they have experienced. This was a traditional Native American practice. Nowadays, people pay guides to provide locations, gear, to outline the quest and interpret their stories. The vision quest is a very powerful and interesting retreat from the world. It is more intense than the personal retreat outlined here but shares the desire for an outcome of revelation and discovery. Many people have powerful experiences.

There are also traditional meditation retreats given by various centers around the country. There is often a focus on silence, simple (often silent) meals and a daily teaching. These retreats often happen over a weekend which is helpful to the usual work schedules of the participants. Because these are usually group events and strictly organized, they differ from the personal retreat, which focuses on being alone and is self guided. They provide a sometimes needed discipline. Like the personal retreat, organized retreats remove us from our daily patterns for a while and often useful skills are taught.

Go For Silence and Stillness – As earlier mentioned, we are so surrounded by noise all the time that we have lost contact with the extraordinary beauty of silence and natural sound. Our retreat is an opportunity to reconnect. Most of us listen to music, the radio, our iPod or have the TV on most of the time. Background noise is a comfort for an unsettled mind, a distraction from what is real and present, and it takes up space that peaceful energy could otherwise occupy. Many years ago I read that, in the United States, we burn a more than a super tanker of fuel oil every day just to provide electricity for television sets that are left on with no one watching. The noise of the television voices makes some of us feel safer. Noise is a constant in our lives. We sometimes feel lost without it. This is sad. Silence is a balm and profoundly spiritual.

Our house in Vermont was off the grid. We had a wind generator and a bank of batteries, as well as a gas refrigerator. A major benefit of the gas refrigerator was that it was totally silent. With all the other devices off, we could hear the wind against the building, the creaking, and the blessed quiet. Today, most homes have computers running and beeping, the refrigerator is always humming, a radio or TV is left on, or the washing machine is going. Once we become conscious of the lack of silence in the world it is startling. And, when we become truly acquainted with silence, we often find ourselves missing its blessings.

On retreat, silence can make us feel uncomfortable and nervous at first. Often this means the silence is acting as a foil to our normal agitation or nervousness. On retreat, we have committed to a brief time with less of both noise and busy-ness. Rather than turning on even a comforting noise like calm music, we can take a deep breath and rest and fall into the silence. We can explore our discomfort and our fear of silence. A few days into our retreat we will realize the beauty and peace that is found in this blessed condition.

TV is obviously not a part of the retreat equation. A personal retreat is not the same as a vacation for yourself, in which you simply do what you want and bring your home habits with you. We associate the word "drugs" with chemicals that are smoked, digested, or given by injection, but noise devices can be another form of drug. Obviously these are not in keeping with a retreat in which we are seeking inner peace. In retreat we can find a beautiful location and just sit for a while. We can take long walks discovering places that are empty of people and noise. In order to go deep we have to move through our discomfort with silence. Our goal is to remember who we are inside. We find ourselves in the silence.

Avoid Escapes - There are many escapes from the discomfort of being alone. Even reading can become a big escape, a way to wile away the time. Taking some inspirational books, or poetry, reading a few passages and contemplating them is a good idea, but, if we find ourselves reading and studying too much, we may have lost the inner track. Novels are not suggested because they carry us out of our present experience. Laptops should be left at home if we can't stay away from the computer when it is around. If we want to journal or write down thoughts and observations from our retreat we can use a laptop, but playing games, cruising the net or doing business are a part of our normal life. We are on retreat from this life. If we think we will be trapped and caught by the computer or any other device, we should leave them at home. As a rule, the fewer electrical devices we bring and the simpler we keep things, the better. Again, if we want to go biking, running or walking, it is good to enjoy the sounds of the natural world: the birds, the wind, the rattle of leaves, or the surf. Being out of doors in this way enhances our connection to nature. Our retreat is only a brief interlude from the usual, after all. We want to keep it sacred.

If we drink alcohol or have any kind of drug reliance, such as coffee or cigarettes a retreat is a good time to give them up. Be with and allow any discomfort that arises. This is a good time to look at perennial habits and review them for addictive qualities. Since health is part of the focus of the retreat, it is good to drop all unhealthy habits for at least a few days. It is interesting to experience life without our normal habits and addictions. However, during our retreat is not necessarily the best time to give up our addictions if the process becomes too distracting. Bringing a pet is not a good idea for a personal retreat. Pets can be highly distracting, and often serve just this purpose.

This is not a judgment of any of these escapes of course. Anything is fine in moderation, the love of a dog, a good meal, a glass of wine. However, on our personal retreat we are going for something extraordinary. To experience it we must make space by letting go of our daily habits and distractions. We know what these are. We need to be honest about our non-supportive habits, take personal responsibility, and leave them all at home.

Fast – Fasting during a retreat can bring significant results, physically, emotionally, and spiritually. It is a good way to spend the first three or four days of the retreat. It creates a unique alertness as well as purging toxins from the system, something that most of us seldom do.

Here is what Rumi says of fasting:

"There is a hidden secret in the stomach's emptiness.
We are lutes, no more, no less. If the soundbox
is stuffed full of anything, no music.
If the brain and the belly are burning clean
with fasting, every moment a new song comes out of the fire.
The fog clears, and new energy makes you
run up the steps in front of you.
Be emptier and cry like reed instruments cry.
Emptier, write secrets with the reed pen.
When you're full of food and drink, an ugly metal
statute sits where your spirit should. When you fast,
good habits gather like friends who want to help.
Fasting is Solomon's ring. Don't give it
to some illusion and lose your power,
but even if you have, if you've lost all will and control,
they come back when you fast, like soldiers appearing
out of the ground, pennants flying above them.
A table descends to your tents, Jesus' table.
Expect to see it, when you fast, this table
spread with other food, better than the broth of cabbages."[46]

Fasting closes the escape of planning and preparing meals and can deepen our discomfort, which accelerates our learning about ourselves. A good fast is cleansing. It clears the head and sharpens the mind. It is easier to fast when we are alone and not surrounded by temptation and others eating food we may desire. Fasting makes for a more challenging retreat while simultaneously creating a healthy physical aspect that is very beneficial to our self esteem.

There are many fasts to choose from, from fresh carrot juice to just plain rice to water. If we have not fasted before, we need to do some research and choose one that we feels right. Descriptions of different types of fasts can easily be found at your local bookstore or on line. Try to find a simple fast, and check to see what results are expected. During the fast it is often preferable to take walks rather

---

[46] Barks, Coleman & Green, Michael, *The Illustrated Rumi.* Coleman Barks and Michael Green, 1997, page 46.

than engage in more strenuous exercise. It is good to take it easy, but it is still necessary to move the body.

Exercise - If you have an exercise routine, you keep it up. Yoga, calisthenics, Tai Chi or some form of movement once or twice per day while on retreat heightens awareness and keeps us flexible. Whatever makes you feel well physically is good. Retreat is not lounging around and getting lazy with our practices!

Our walking and sitting can be meditative in quality, an opportunity to bring the mind into the present. To stay in the present, we can focus on what is right before us and leave thinking and problem solving behind. We can use our walks to practice the art of staying in the present.

Meditate - The time before dawn is often called the golden hour for its peace and serenity. In Spanish there is even a word for this time of day: *la madrugada*. Near or before sunrise is a good time to say a prayer, give thanks and then sit in meditation. I like to make a cup of tea first. If we have not developed a meditation practice, a personal retreat is a great time to start one. There are many fewer distractions than at home. Of course, the mind, the major distracter, is still active. A retreat presents a good chance to still the mind and to increase awareness about how the mind pulls us out of the present. A still mind adds depth and clarity to a retreat.

Remember, meditation is basically sitting still and letting the mind still. Some days our meditation is deep and very relaxing, other days it isn't. That's OK. It seems that judging and comparing the current meditation session to others is a way to distract oneself and circumvent the benefits of meditation; so, I say to myself, "don't compare." Some meditations are good, while some are not so good, but all are more beneficial than none. Let's review. A most simple and helpful explanation of dealing with the mind during meditation was offered by Poonjaji. The beauty and simplicity of his overall message is reflected in his response to an interviewer's question:

Interviewer: *So much emphasis is placed on getting rid of the thoughts, as though the mind without thoughts is tantamount to an awakened state.*

Poonjaji: *No, no, no. Let the thoughts come. If you reject them, they will invade forcibly through your door. Remove the door. Remove the wall itself. Who will come in now? .....Let the thoughts arise, but don't allow them landing space.*

Create An Intention – A retreat is more powerful when it has specific intention. It is a good time to ask for an answer to a perennial problem, or to seek vision. Intention is best fulfilled when we do not hold onto it tightly. Remember, this is an important component of visioning. We create our question or request, envision getting an answer and trust we will. Then we let that vision go. The personal retreat offers many rewards but perhaps the most precious of these are realizations and a measure of wisdom.

Usually on the fourth or fifth day of a retreat, often after fasting for three days, we can sit quietly and allow space for realization. Miraculously, it seems the very realization we need comes to us. From realization we gain some wisdom and insight into confusing and unresolved areas of our life. We can expect some very powerful and life shifting experiences in this way. In stillness and silence, in being alone, we discover our connection to that which has the deepest meaning in our life; we come into contact with the sacred context of our brief existence. (Please refer to my story in the earlier chapter *The Wound*)

In the Bhagavad Gita, Krishna teaches Arjuna, "He who has faith has wisdom, who lives in self-harmony, whose faith is his life; and he who finds wisdom, soon finds the peace supreme." Days into our personal retreat, after we have encountered and dealt with some of our demons, when we are relaxed and rested, when we are just "being," we sometimes get a glimpse of the perfect order of all things, Rumi's "elegant patterning." We can actually experience the Divine in the world around us. This glimpse and experience is more than an intellectual understanding. It is such a deep realization that even a brief encounter with it puts us in contact with the truth of our own absolute safety in the world and our connection to all things. We take this deeper knowledge back into our daily lives, and it sustains us.

Being Real

The Power of Disclosure and Vulnerability

I have friends and relatives who are on the Shaman path. Often they travel to South America to study with the shaman descendents of the Incas. Babbie's sister was in Ecuador a while back and asked the teacher Dona Maria, considered to be the patron saint of Cuzco, "What would your message to the world be?" She answered: "Expand the collective mesa, disclose each other, and grow old together." One interpretation of expanding the collective mesa is expanding our spiritual community and practicing inclusion. In order to do this we need to be able to practice disclosure. Disclosure is an important action and practice.

If we really want to help someone, and we feel we know something from our own experience that will be of real value to them in their current difficult situation, there is no more powerful action we can take than disclosure. Disclosure here means sharing our own experience regardless of how painful, embarrassing or depressing it has been. It means being vulnerable. When we allow ourselves to be vulnerable, we create the humility that allows us to touch others through the power of empathy, and create communication that is memorable, strong and deep. We align with others and, as Babbie's sister says, "We become aware of our inextricable connection with all. No secrets."

When we disclose ourselves, we offer another person our own experience in the hope that it will ease their suffering and may even be instructive. Disclosure is a demonstration of deep compassion for ourselves and trust. It is recognition and honoring of the human condition. Because of this, our disclosure validates

325

another person's experience and invites them to disclose themselves. Like our own disclosure, their disclosure honors their personal experience and makes manifest the source of their current condition. The masks are dropped, and we see who they really are as they see us. Again, as Rumi says, "there is a window open between us and we share the night air of our beings."[47]

Disclosure and vulnerability allow us to find gratitude for, and be comfortable with, experiences we consider embarrassing or painful. We see how these experiences fit into our lives, and we let them teach us. Disclosure leads us to the direct and real expression of empathy, the deep sharing of our human experience and, as such, it creates powerful and life affirming intimacy. Disclosure is not used or taken lightly. It is an action that requires social perception, sensitivity and skill.

If disclosure is such a powerful communicator, why don't we use it all the time? Pride and ego prevent us from sharing our painful experiences and our personal lessons with others; they tell us we have much to fear in being vulnerable. They say that the result of disclosure may be ridicule or shame or a negative shift in peer opinion, and that we should not chance these. Fear says things like: "What if the person with whom we are sharing our experience runs out and gossips about me? What if they ridicule me? What if they demean my experience?" For these reasons we keep our deep experiences safely hidden. This is a safe approach, but the treasure that can, at certain times, be of tremendous help and comfort to others and ourselves is forsaken. The risk we take in disclosure, when our disclosure is honored, is definitely worth the reward.

Nevertheless, it is true that when we take the risk of being vulnerable, there is the chance that our experience will be ridiculed, shamed or suffer negative opinions. Vulnerability, sometimes viewed as weakness is actually an act of trust and courage. It accepts life as it is. We will often be taking a chance, or jumping off the cliff, when we take this action, especially as we begin this practice and find our way. There will be a risk, but it is risk that can be

---

[47] Barks Coleman with Moyne, John, The Essential Rumi. Castle Books , 1997, page 32

minimized with certain understandings and skills. Disclosure takes courage but, when we disclose, we can still be cautious and skillful.

I first experienced true vulnerability when Babbie and I were producing retreats for couples with Don and Martha Rosenthal. Babbie and I had done much personal relationship work and, in the early retreats, I eagerly offered my opinions and what I had learned. Looking back at this time, I would say it was my pontificating period. As I mentioned earlier, I had many answers, and I was eager to share them. There was nothing wrong with my offering, the facts were true enough, but the goal of the retreat was to go deeply into the relationship experience, to look at how fear of intimacy manifests and creates difficulties. In order to facilitate this goal, it is very important to create emotional safety so that participants can feel free to voluntarily share their experiences without fear. My habit of simply stating various truths was not helpful in this respect. No one really wants to be told what to do. But people are very interested in the like experiences of others, particularly the presenters. Don pointed out that my offerings would be much more powerful and useful if I disclosed more of my own story.

This was really hard at first. Babbie and I had always dealt with our issues privately. What Don wanted us to do was confess to our own difficulties before a group, actually many groups. I was afraid to do this, but I saw its importance. I had watched Don and Martha share with the group. I decided to jump off the cliff. As soon as I began to share my process, my experience, I became aware of the more focused attention that participants paid to my offerings. Participants would approach me privately for more information. They obviously felt safer. It took time to get used to the process of being vulnerable. Fortunately, Don was there to remind me when I slipped back into my wise teacher, know-it-all roll. He was relentless, and I am forever grateful. By practicing disclosure, I learned its power.

Over time, I have come to see disclosure and vulnerability not only as a form of deep sharing, but also as a particular skill. The skill comes from learning certain criteria before making this offering. By making sure these criteria are met, we can diminish some of the personal risks we take when we decide, for the sake of healing, to disclose ourselves. While, ideally disclosure is speaking the truth regardless of outcome, I think it helps to move into this new arena carefully. At the outset, we can make our disclosure more useful and powerful by observing some simple parameters.

Timing is important. The power of disclosure might tempt us to use it too quickly, disclosing ourselves to someone who, with a little observation, we could see would be tempted to gossip and not respect our privacy. The best time for disclosure is when everyone is feeling emotionally safe. It is important to have created or to have experienced an atmosphere of safety before disclosure. This is true whether we are disclosing to a group or an individual. Generally, the rapport necessary for disclosure takes place after there has already been some communication; we would not just start telling a stranger our experience.

Come from trust and agreement. It is perfectly all right to tell someone that what you are going disclose is private and ask them to agree to keep it that way. Every time I work with an individual or a group I do this. Like me, many presenters ask everyone in a group to agree, at the outset, that everything that is spoken is said in trust and stays in the room. This action encourages individuals to act with integrity and to ignore the temptation to share what has been disclosed in trust with people outside of the group.

Be discerning. We can usually tell who might use our disclosure for tale-telling by waiting a while when talking with them. It won't be long before they tell us a story about someone else, giving us a warning sign about the level of vulnerability we want to take with them. Most of us are familiar with the person who tries to draw out personal information and stores it away for future use in conversations with others.

Begin by disclosing to like-minded people. At the outset, we need to feel that the person with whom we would like to share has our values, and can understand our experience. Also, that they interested in personal growth. We need to feel them out. We have to judge whether they will respect our story. If we feel that, due to circumstances, it is not the right time to practice disclosure, we should trust our instincts. It can take time to develop enough rapport and safety with someone or a group to offer our secret self.

This is a tricky rule, however. We need to be careful we are not using this rule to avoid practicing vulnerability altogether.

Be authentic. Own the disclosure. Sometimes when we share important information we tend to separate ourselves from others by using the third person and talking around our own experience. We say things like, "I have seen that when people feel sad about this they tend to close up," or "one can become upset when this happens," when it is ourselves about whom we are talking. There are many variations of this. Using awareness we can watch for this evasion. In my experience, many of the most powerful teachers are willing to be vulnerable, to use disclosure, to touch others by offering that which is true for them. The power of vulnerability lies in being real. Our truth is much more real when we own it, not when we talk about it in the third person. Thus "I" statements are important. In some groups only "I" statements are allowed. This is a powerful way to communicate and not slide into philosophy and general opinion.

Let it be real. Our disclosure has to be real because we are all very sensitive to the slightest whiff of phony empathy. With a kind of sixth sense we can detect when others are protecting the real story, when all the pieces are not there. It helps if our disclosure is not simply the understanding we gained, but is the actual experience that led us to that understanding. We need to disclose the true story. Deep and true disclosure often rewards us with a reduction in our own pride and shame.

Be patient. Being vulnerable and accepting another person's vulnerability is a real skill. It takes practice to share the truth of our inner world clearly and without fear, and it takes practice to be a good listener, to offer yourself without distraction. It takes time to develop discernment as well.

"Disclose each other," the shaman says. Part of our work is being a safe container for someone else's stories. This means we make a sacred contract with ourselves not to reveal that which is obviously private and sensitive information when someone shares with us regardless of how tempting this is. We practice being good listeners (see *Deep Listening*).

Expect nothing. This is an important spiritual component of any offering we make. Because disclosure can have such a powerful effect on our relationships, we can be tempted to expect that this is what happens every time. We think, "I'll go for the reward." This kind of expectation often creates disappointment and disillusionment. We disclose ourselves as an offering with no expectation, no strings attached. Sometimes nothing will happen. That something must happen is not the point. We lose our compassionate focus when we exchange an offering for reward. Regardless of what happens as we disclose, when we are vulnerable, we can honor ourselves for speaking the truth and coming from good intention. The response or reaction of others is not as important as our personal integrity.

Disclosure is one of the best mediums for deep communication and teaching, and it is also a powerful way to deliver relief and comfort to others. Most of us keep our troubling issues locked inside. We don't want others to think us weak, or crazy, or susceptible to emotional pain. Sometimes the pain gets so bad that we feel compelled to share our story with someone. We might pick a counselor we respect, a friend, a relative, or some other guide. When instead of simply offering you advice and sympathy, they share their very similar story, we realize, that we are not the only person who suffers or has suffered in a particular way. We understand that they are speaking and sharing their truth. They are being real. At that moment something happens inside us that can only be described as relief. Our feeling of isolation dissolves. One moment we were alone in the world with our seemingly private and individual problems and the next we have an ally, someone who has been there, who deeply understands and can actually express what we are feeling. They might share how they responded to the same situation. I have seen this happen many times at workshops and retreats as the group, feeling safe, begins to share experiences. At retreats, after spending a few days together in a safe atmosphere and having shared their stories, participants often show relief plainly in their faces and bodies. The departing people are often very different than those that arrived. When, without foreknowledge, people find themselves together in a group of folks with exactly the same issues they are rewarded with what Rumi called a "glimpse of the mirror" shinning beneath everything. They come to see the universality of their condition. This synchronicity can also be seen as a part of the "elegant patterning" and the mystery.

Disclosure is a pathway to the realization of similarity. Dr. Brene Brown says, "If we are going to find out way back to each other, vulnerability is going to be that path." By sharing our personal experiences and the lessons we are all learning, without expectation for change in others, without judgment and in trust, we come to realize how we are all alike. As we disclose, and our lives are affirmed by each other and our offerings, we expand the collective mesa. Vulnerability breaks down the walls of separation. We grow into and with the group; we acknowledge our basic intimacy; our likeness becomes our focus rather than our differences. Unity replaces separation. We affirm life. We experience our connection to each other. We care for each other, and we grow old together in joy and peace.

Hanging Out in the Don't Know
Becoming comfortable with uncertainty

*"But he never reflects. He has never known a single moment of awe
for the beauty of creation. He hates silence so he knows nothing."*

Ian McEwan

Practicing awareness can bring about major shifts in our
understanding of the world and the part we play in the grand
unfolding. As we have discovered, new perspectives often reveal the
need for change. Using awareness, personal responsibility, inner
work and action we can shape and define those changes, and
incorporate new ways of being into our lives. The adjustments we
make are not necessarily easy. Sometimes an awakening awareness
can engender aversions so strong that we suddenly quit one well-
established pattern without knowing what is next. For instance, we
might become aware that we have been accepting someone's
emotional abuse in the workplace or in our personal life. Our desire
to end the relationship overcomes our usually cautious, planning
nature. We free ourselves from the situation without considering
how we are going to fill our physical or emotional needs in the
future. Thus, as we grow stronger, experience personal power, and
learn to have mercy for ourselves, we find ourselves ending things
sometimes before we have considered how we will replace them.
This can be a very healthy development. In our progress, we have
overcome the old "safety pattern", the belief that we have to be sure
of the future before we let go of the present, even if what is occurring
in the present is painful, harmful or simply not serving us any

longer. The safety pattern is a big "hold back", one of those oh-so-logical ways we circumvent change (and stay miserable). Sometimes, it can be more important and healthy to simply end one thing before making sure the next thing is in place.

Things ending without a replacement is not just limited to change we create through awareness. Outer conditions or events in our immediate environment can be of equal cause. We might finish a big project on which we have been working for a long time and suddenly find ourselves with no work and nothing to do. Someone close to us may die, or a long-standing relationship might end and suddenly there is a big hole and we find it hard to move forward. We don't know what to do. The organization that employed us for many years might cease to exist, and unexpectedly we find ourselves without work, without income. We might be spending a little too long between jobs. We may get sick and be forced to slow down or make changes to our life that we never expected.

This ending of a large and accepted piece of our lives often lands us in a place we can call "the don't know." We become aware that we *don't know* how to proceed. We *don't know* what is going to happen next. We *don't know* how we are going to fill the gap, replace the job, deal with the loss, spend our days, live our future. We feel disoriented. We suddenly realize that we are in some form of transition and, almost simultaneously, realize that we *don't know* where or to what we are transitioning. This phenomenon is amazingly common, and it seems that we usually respond to it in classical ways. We try as hard as we can to come up with answers; we try to force the next step; we try to know the unknowable. As in that old Tibetan saying about trying to know the future, we find ourselves "casting our nets in dry riverbeds."

Here's an old riddle. It is as close to us as breathing, and, although it tires us, we never tire of it. What is it? The answer is "thinking." To see the galloping nature of mind, all we have to do is meditate for a few minutes. Similarly, when we find ourselves in the "don't know," we will think and think and think in a hopeless attempt to extricate ourselves from the discomfort of not knowing where we are going or what is going to happen next. Our thinking will start looping back on itself, becoming compulsive as we review the same ideas over and over.

Another common response to the "don't know" is urgently trying to find something to do or to compulsively start doing something or anything. We say, "I have to find something to do" as if we will find the answer to pour worry simply in "doing." Since we usually arrive in the "don't know" because some great piece of "doing-ness" has ceased, we tend to believe that, by simply doing something, we can fill the void it has left. For instance, we might rush out and quickly take the wrong job or rush into a relationship we know in our heart is not quite right. Often the imperative "do something" response ends in unhappiness and failure because it did not come from the heart, it came from fear in the mind. If simply doing something (taking immediate action) is not the solution, what is?

We interpret the "don't know" as a threatening and dangerous situation. Our mind fears the very idea of not knowing what is next. But the "don't know" is an important part of our life cycle. Our lives move from yin to yang, from rest to activity and from certainty to uncertainty. The big gaps in the "doing" part of our lives represented by the "don't know" are an opportunity to learn how to deal with uncertainty, to improve our trust in things, to discover how we create our reality and perhaps deepen our understanding of the source of all our ideas. In the "don't know" we come face to face with the mystery of life. Doing isn't the answer because the "don't know" is the time for being. Because we don't have much practice at being, we do not recognize its importance, its necessity, or its function.

When we find ourselves in the "don't know" there are outer difficulties and inner difficulties. The outer difficulties usually have to do with describing our place in the world so that others will be comfortable and won't judge us. We like to do this in a way that satisfies their need to place us. "What do you do?" people ask, or "What are you going to do now?" Since we are more defined in our culture by *what we do*, rather than by *who we are*, the answer to these questions is considered very important, and we feel uncomfortable when we are unable to give a good response. It helps when we are in the "don't know" to develop plausible and easy responses that do not provoke further inquisition and discomfort.

A while ago Babbie and I travelled, going back and forth to Panama every year. We never knew what our schedule was going to be. Everyone wanted to know exactly when we were leaving and exactly when we were coming back, but we like to respond to events and opportunities, as much as possible, as they are occurring. We like to stay flexible and open to change. As a consultant, if I get some good work, then I may change my plans. Changing plans, once you have made them, seems to bother people. When friends used to ask the "what are you doing and when exactly" question we answered honestly, "we don't know," but this answer caused all sorts of consternation. Like being in the "don't know" most of us are also not comfortable with flexible schedules or changing occupations. When we can't fit someone into a precise time and occupation slot, we sometimes feel uncomfortable because our personal fear of uncertainty is activated.

Babbie developed a good answer to "what and when" questions, which is "we don't have enough information at this time to make a precise decision." This is a true statement and it is interesting that it should be more successful in calming others than "we don't know" although it means exactly the same thing. The difference is that it demonstrates that we are considering possibilities and are not simply operating at the whim of the winds (although sometimes we might be doing just that). Handling the outer world in this or some other manner, creating an acceptable phrase or response, improves the outer difficulties with the "don't know", but we still have to deal with the more ominous inner confusion and fear.

The common view is that, to be safe in the world, we need always know exactly what's next. The "don't know" challenges this belief. Hanging out in the "don't know" offers us a unique opportunity to learn a big lesson: that our safety has less to do with outer conditions and our future, than it does with the condition of our inner world right now.

The first step in dealing with the "don't know" is to understand that it is a completely normal part of our path through life. It happens to everyone; if it didn't, or when it doesn't, life can be pretty dull or extremely stressful. Taking the view that the "don't know" is a normal condition can release us from the anxiety that occurs when we feel like we are in a unique and threatening situation.

The next step is learning how to respond to the "don't know", rather than reacting to it blindly. When we understand that simply doing something is not the most effective response, we might want to try the opposite approach. We can make this a time for gathering and strengthening ourselves. Instead of "doing" we can choose "being." Our focus can turn to strategies for "being" that, when we are constantly "doing," get less time in our lives. These are parts of our inner work: meditation, spiritual journeys, self-improvement strategies and disciplines, quiet time, and withdrawal from the world, perhaps with a personal retreat. This is the exact opposite of what the mind would have us do. As we enter the "don't know," the voice of fear begins to rise demanding we do something immediately. By choosing "being" before "doing" we choose to ignore this voice and put our trust in a deeper and more profound source of creativity. Moving into "being" in the face of fear shouting, "do something!" is a supreme act of faith. Like Mojud, we are trusting that our heart rather than our mind will show us the way. We are trusting that what is necessary will appear in its own time and when we are ready.

This type of action is hard for the mind to understand. It is wonderfully illogical and mysterious. It is a spiritual gesture, giving up control and trusting the dance. There is never any guarantee we will make discovery, but it is certain that we cannot reap the rewards of our faith in the greater plan without the perilous leap. We cannot equivocate with the heart. It is through "being" that we come into contact with the elegant patterning of life. "Being" is taking the action of non-action.

The rewards of responding to the "don't know" by focusing on "being" are multiple. In "being," possibilities that the mind declared dead are reborn and new and unexpected vistas are miraculously revealed. In "being," we open to our full creative nature, and our vision expands. Away from the voice of fear and the anguished need to know, we come into contact with possibilities we could never have discovered with our endless and often myopic thinking. "Being" is the foundation, the actual ground of creativity. The more still we are; the more present we become; the more we

337

tune in to the natural plan and more of that plan is revealed. Through "being," we open ourselves to possibility. We jump out of the ruts our minds create.

In the "being" response to the "don't know," we learn that there is another path in this world that can bring equal or greater rewards than the cautious plans we so carefully construct. By taking the leap of faith, by responding to fear with stillness rather than activity, we discover new and greater possibilities, and more powerful pathways. When we add this incredibly rich action of non-action to our life, we learn how to listen to the heart and let it guide us. We strengthen our intuition. Ironically, it is in "being" we may also discover, not just something to do to replace what we were doing, but that which we are meant to be doin; that which satisfies our heart. We learn to listen to and be guided by the heart. Rather than a fearful time, the "don't know" is transformed into a time of great opportunity.

To hang out in the "don't know" and be comfortable with this place, we first have to do the difficult work of creating stillness in the midst of confusion and emotional discomfort. We have the tools. Usually when we are in the "don't know" there is some extra time in our day that is the byproduct of less "doing." We can create quiet space for meditation and slowing down. We can take long walks. We can dance and sing or work out to free up energy and feel our aliveness. We can listen to powerful music. Inspirational reading helps us to remember the bigger vision, reinforcing the idea of a life path while reminding us about what is truly important. What is our ultimate goal as a human being? Usually it is more than a new job or relationship. Inspiration removes us from fearful urgency and gives us the necessary spiritual sustenance to accept change. This is also an ideal time to go on a personal retreat.

By focusing on receiving and creating vision rather than on fear and urgency, we give power and depth to our time in the "don't know." Times of uncertainty provide an opportunity to reassess our current vision or create new vision about our lives and our work. We reassess our current vision by asking ourselves some important questions about the fundamental path of our life or work. These questions are different from the ones we usually ask ourselves when we feel ungrounded, disconnected or suddenly without purpose.

Our usual questions are functional and practical, "What am I going to do now? How will I make this work? How will I survive without this person or thing? These are questions that often provide unsatisfactory or no answers at all, and deepen our distress. They are all about what we are going to do. Slowing down, and focusing on being still and receptive, we can ask deeper questions such as: "What is my work supposed to be? What is the work I love? What do I really want to do with my life? What is my purpose? What kind of relationship do I really want? What makes me feel content? What do I want to change in my life as a result of the condition in which I now find myself?" These are fundamental questions about our inner world, and the beliefs we hold that shape our outer world. From these inquiries we can create a new vision for ourselves.

Because our focus is on "being," on what is sometimes called "calm abiding," or staying grounded and quiet, we create a fertile field in which vision can emerge. This process is intuitive and different from our normal worry "looping." In this process we let go and trust that answers will come. They can come at any time, in the form of words or images. Because our intention is to make discovery, we will. We can relax, knowing that we will receive what we need when we are ready. If we become aware that we are growing anxious and are asking ourselves the usual anxious questions, it is time to come back to simply "being."

Responding to the "don't know" with "beingness" also permits our creative side to be an ally in any vision of a new reality. Creativity cannot function well in the myopic atmosphere created by a fearful response to outer conditions. When we calm ourselves and let possibilities arise rather than trying to force answers into existence, our creative nature is free to work with the clues and insights we are having. It can shape events and possibilities into a living vision. Our creative energy is not absorbed in or distracted by endless mind loops.

By "being" we are not blinding ourselves or closing the world out, as some may think. Being quiet and reflective does not mean we are numb and objective. We have not shut down our ability to act and feel. Rather, by focusing on "being" we are working to be more present and therefore more sensitive to what is happening "now." We are increasing our awareness, while simultaneously decreasing our anxiety (which is so future oriented). In this state, we broaden our ability to receive valuable hints and clues that may be doorways into our future. These clues will often lead us one by one, like bread crumbs, right toward what we truly want in our lives. The clues can be synchronicities, coincidences, something we read or people we meet. They are identifiable by their similarity or connection to that which we are envisioning. They may be a small part of our vision, something that winks out at us and then quickly recedes. Because we are not desperately responding to the "don't know" with busyness, doing, and trying to find the next thing; because we have calmed ourselves and created a vision about our life and our path, these important keys to our evolution and growth are not lost to us.

Unfortunately, until we have really tried this approach and have experienced the extraordinary clarity of its results, there will be a part of us that doubts and tries to bring us back to mind oriented problem solving. But, once we have experienced the wisdom gained through being comfortable with the "don't know," we will come to appreciate this action as a reliable and deep ally.

The "being" response to the "don't know" is a wisdom response. It works well in any stressful situation. It asks that we replace fear with vision when we experience doubt about the future; that we replace unconscious reaction and worry with measured response and intuition. To do this, we ground ourselves and stay present. We learn to trust that the answers we need are always available, but that we can't "push the river" to make them appear. The extent to which we can respond to the "don't know" portion of our life's cycles with "beingness" is a measure of our maturity, growth and trust in the elegant perfection of life. Hanging out in the "don't know" is an important, reoccurring, spiritual opportunity.

Hanging Out With Yama

The Action of Dying

*"When the wise knows that it is through
the great and omnipresent spirit in us
that we are conscious in waking or in dreaming,
then he goes beyond sorrow."*

Yama to Nachiketas – *Katha Upanishad*

Even though it is helpful to take the view in our daily lives that there is plenty of time, we need to remember that our time here is relatively short. This is yet another spiritual paradox because both views, though contrary, are simultaneously viable and, more importantly, useful. It is not unusual to spend much of our life in denial of death. We do not get up every day, at least when we are generally healthy, and say "I might die today." Unlike many sages, we don't use death as an impetus for the appreciation of life or as an important teacher.

Our lack of attention to death is entirely reasonable, because death seems remote, especially when we are young. We are so busy. And who wants to dwell on the frightening prospect of non-existence? The Masters and gurus teach that we must learn to die before we die. This is necessary for reaching the still center, the clear consciousness core. Coming to a place of peace with our own mortality is an important part of creating inner peace. Fear of dying is often considered our deepest, our root fear.

We can begin our study of death at any age. Although we usually don't believe it, death can obviously occur at any moment. Although death and dying seem more real as we age, they are worthy of consideration when we are young. Don Juan frequently reminded Carlos Castenadas to keep a lookout over his left shoulder for death. The implication is that death flirts with us more often than we think.

In ancient India there was a prince, Siddhartha Gautama. He lived the kind of life millions still desperately aspire to, a life filled with riches, ease and pleasure. His royal parents worked hard to placate his every material need and shield him from any sorrow or suffering. You know the story. One day a crack appeared in his reality and through it he saw the suffering in the world and felt the desire to awaken stir in him. One of the items that woke him up from his long dream and illusion was a dead body. He had been shielded from death, but this vision shocked him into becoming a seeker after truth, a wandering monk. It was death that awoke him to his own impermanence and to the suffering that attachment to the body, and all things impermanent, causes. Eventually, he became the Buddha, the awakened one. Whether this is a literal story or not makes no difference, encountering death can awaken our own awareness of impermanence as well.

Death is referenced in many spiritual traditions to inspire us to use our lifetime wisely. How much of our precious life are we spending overcoming the obstacles to our spiritual evolution? In order to encourage practitioners, the Buddhists say we have about as much chance of incarnating into a human life as surfacing through the hole in a life ring in the middle of the ocean. For religions that believe in reincarnation, the karma (action) we create in this lifetime affects our birth in the next life. Christianity teaches that our actions in this life will determine an afterlife in heaven or hell. Again, which it will be depends on our current choices.

In the ancient Katha Upanishad, a young boy, Nachiketas, seeks out Yama, the Lord of Death, and Yama, impressed with his humility and his persistent curiosity, shares with him the secrets of spiritual life. Becoming acquainted with death, as Nachiketas did, is a way in which we can embrace a deeper spirituality and deepen our compassion. It is interesting that Nachiketas is such a young person. While we may be afraid of death, we don't have to be afraid of exploring death. We won't die from the exploration, and such an exploration does not need to be morbid.

The ancient Egyptians paid close attention to death throughout their lives and prepared themselves for death in an elaborate way. For literally thousands of years their civilization endured. The reverence for death and the afterlife was an important part of their culture, a spiritual center. It created a simultaneous reverence for life which is demonstrated in the exquisite funerary poems inscribed into the inner tops of sarcophagi, poems meant to be recited as the dead "came forth by day," into the next dimension.

According to Ernst Becker, in his Pulitzer prize-winning work *Denial of Death*, much of the suffering and war in the world finds its source in the denial of death. Those who deny death can actually tempt it through foolish acts or the belief that they are invincible. He postulates that without the denial of death there might not be any war. By necessity or choice, every warrior believes he will be the one to live through the battles. Only others will be killed. As young boys, it is usual to deny death, to play at games that simulate heroic death scenes. We are young, open and vulnerable; death is mysterious and troubling. We assuage our fear by overcoming death in our playacting. Toy companies and video game companies rely on this form of denial; this "toying" with death. They sell "virtual" murder, mayhem and death. However, dwelling on destruction and virtual death is not really helpful to our spiritual progress. Stoking our subconscious fear of death with recreational games and sports doesn't move us any closer to actually dealing with the reality of our own death. This kind of playing at death simply reminds us of our fear. Virtual war on a computer and real, deadly war rely on excitement, the rush of adrenalin, and escapism. They are not an acknowledgement of the the deep reality of death. We can choose to honor death in a way that serves us spiritually, or we can deny its inevitability until we are in the midst of our own dying.

If we are prepared to enter this investigation, one of the best ways is to hang out with Yama like Nachitketas did. Often this occurs without warning, as when someone close to us is dying. We are thrust into an upsetting encounter with death. We are challenged by the unfamiliar and sometimes we encounter a deep and unacknowledged fear. With awareness, we notice what we are feeling. What will happen if we move into these emotions instead of avoiding them? How do thoughts about our own death and dying then change? What happens when we let go of our preconceived conditions for being with a dying person and stay in the experience? We then learn things that we can only learn at someone's deathbed, and we grow. Our compassion expands. We are rewarded.

The grief we experience when someone close to us dies is another way that death creates an opportunity for learning. Our grief is not just for the person who dies. Their death often highlights our own impermanence, our own eventual non-existence. It can be used to reveal and explore other loses we have failed to acknowledge, especially when the grieving period is overly long and our grief does not seem to diminish.

We can use our grieving time for reflection and for a personal investigation of our own relationship to death. In our grief, we may experience anger or deep sorrow or both. Our feelings and emotions are often volatile, raw and near the surface. In this state there is less obscuration by the filters we often use to shield ourselves from the knowledge of death and of ourselves. This is a good time to investigate and come to grips with our own life process. Once acknowledged grief is healed by time but, in the early stages, when grief is strongest, we are given the opportunity to see our feelings and fears about our own mortality very clearly.

As mentioned earlier, joining a hospice as a volunteer is another way to hang out with Yama, a conscious choice that can put us in the presence of death more often. While each experience is unique, there is a fundamental understanding that comes with the privilege of being present when the spirit leaves the body. We see the undeniable truth that the life spirit and the body are separate; we learn how different people suffer and approach death, and we become a participant in another person's last passage. I have made some great friendships with people who are dying. There is little pretense at this stage of life, so we begin with who we are. Many people are very open near the end of their lives, when they can still communicate.

It is said that if we come to peace with death during our lifetime, our own death will be eased. Death itself is not usually the difficult part of dying; it is the pain and suffering that precedes it that can be difficult. In this age, palliative care and pain management have become a medical art, greatly easing the suffering of dying. However, the mental and emotional anguish is something we need to attend to by exploring death and working to accept our own death. Ironically, when we do this, life becomes more precious and more vital. With the absolute knowledge of death before us, we enter the present moment with more joy and deeper reverence. We experience more aliveness.

Born in 1016 Gampopa, Milarepa's most famous student had this to say about the stages of our relationship with death:

"At first you should be driven by a fear of birth and death like a stag escaping from a trap. In the middle, you should have nothing to regret even if you die, like a farmer who has carefully worked his fields. In the end you should feel relieved and happy, like a person who has just completed a formidable task."

Notice how, in this statement, we evolve. This evolution takes conscious work. We must explore that which we fear. There are many wonderful books and teachers who explore death and dying.

We will all take the action of dying. It is good to respect this and to use our awareness of this truth to bring more consciousness and compassion into our living. We will each do this work in a different way, but, regardless, we can be sure that hanging out with Yama will bring change in our relationship to life and in our own final days and moments; in our final action. By learning what our life is trying to teach us we learn who we really are. This is our purpose. We cannot do this without working with all parts of our life, including the parts we fear, deny and do not understand, especially death. In answer to Nachiketas's clear yearning and intent, Yama, finally teaches Nachiketas the way to live life and become immortal.

"And Nachiketas learnt the supreme wisdom taught by the god of after life, and he learnt the whole teaching of inner union of Yoga*. Then he reached Brahman, the Spirit Supreme, and became immortal and pure. So in truth will anyone who knows his Atman, his higher self."

The great teachers of the east often say, "Learn to die so that you may live." Like Nachiketas, by doing this we may also come in contact with the higher self. This is a worthy goal.

*Yoga refers to physical, mental and spiritual disciplines.

Conclusion

Wake Up!

"There is no rest. The act is now. In your lives you will make children, make peace, make errors, you will make trouble, you will dance under the sun and moon. As long as you live you will create life. You will rise and fall many times. It is like the making of a good loaf of bread. You will be nourished."

Becoming the Craftsman
Awakening Osiris

By now we understand that the happiness and equanimity we seek in life is to be found in compassionate action and the opened heart. In order to keep our heart opened we need to arrive at and maintain the realization that all beings are alike, that we all seek the same inner peace, whether we are aware of this or not. We all suffer in the same ways. We are all part of the whole. Waking up is realizing this truth. It is saying "no" when the ego wants control and listening instead to a higher voice. As we wake up we are naturally compelled to be more loving, helpful and kind. We are waking up to the reality of who and what we really are.

The world reflects our beliefs and our inner reality. When we ignite our awareness, we discover what is *really* happening in the world, and in our life, beneath the familiar stories. We begin to see more clearly the areas that contain our personal lessons, the areas that are our teachers. When we take personal responsibility for our lives we truly empower ourselves. Then we can investigate our conditioning and resulting beliefs, and do the inner work to change

347

what isn't skillful or working; the places where we are not whole. When we take action from this inner work, we create that change, we make it so. With consecrated action, our life takes on more depth, and we find ourselves in a more profound dimension.

Opening the heart, especially when it wants to close, is a simple but profound path. It is real. It is not out in the future somewhere. It is a choice we can make every moment. The heart is either opened or closed because love is unequivocal. Opening the heart becomes each day's mission. It is a supremely holy gesture. Every time we do this, we receive a rich reward, and we feel what Joseph Campbell called "the rapture of being alive." We discover the precious nature of life, and we feel a continuing gratitude.

Remember, the four strategies are circular. Indigenous people see life as a circle, a hoop. How wise and true. Jump in the river anywhere but do it. Jump off the cliff. You know what that means!

May this book inspire and empower you to make the changes that you discover are necessary for your personal growth and wholeness. May it aid you in bringing more joy and love into the world around you and help you be more merciful with yourself and others. May it inspire you to practice love as a subversive activity every day and to sweeten the world with your own particular heart song. As an Egyptian wrote some 4000 years ago, may you "set up a light in the darkness."

Start right now and, using your discernment, find your own, unique way. The work is not always easy, but it is real and always rewarding. As Rumi said, "There are hundreds of ways to kneel and kiss the earth." Find as many as you can or find the one that is just right for you.

Acknowledgments

I am grateful to Babbie, the greatest gift in my life, for her patience during the years of the book project. Life companion, best friend, wife, and mother of the five wonderful ones, kind grandmother, editor, teacher, gardener, beautiful singer, actress, director, great helmsperson and travel companion, fierce standard bearer of consciousness, wise woman and excellent cook. Thank you for finally doing the important content edits. Blessings be upon you, my beauty.

I would like to acknowledge the generosity of Don and Martha Rosenthal for sharing their accumulated understanding of the spiritual life with me, without reservation, over twenty years ago. They generously opened a door into another world.

I would like to acknowledge all the teachers who freely shared their work for this book, especially those who provided encouragement in their permissions: Jack Kornfield, Eckhart Tolle, Daniel Goleman, and Stephen Buhner.

I especially want to thank Coleman Barks. First, for his translations of Rumi without which the English speaking world would be a spiritually drier and less inspiring place, and, second, for his kind permission to use any material I needed.

I want to thank my kids for all their support and patience over the years and for all the lessons they have taught me. I am particularly grateful to John and Tate, who were the first readers of the early text. Thank you two for the support and the encouragement you have given. I want to thank Elliot for the help he gave me in getting the website up, a necessary component of the modern book.

I want to acknowledge Jamie Clem for her editing and steady enthusiasm and encouragement.

I want to thank the people at Dragons Flight Studio for their guidance and professionalism is setting up the website and for their help with all the details of putting the book up on the internet. Special thanks to Fene Cartlidge for her crisp responses to my numerous questions and for her design acumen.

Stay Connected With **WAKING UP**
Visit the website at www.wakinguponline.com

Learning What Your Life is Trying to Teach You

Share ideas and ask questions. As you take new action in the world, share your results with others. Form an online sangha and get ideas from the group.

You will find dialogue, links, as well articles and responses to questions by John Earle.

CPSIA information can be obtained at www.ICGtesting.com
Printed in the USA
LVOW131614261212

313292LV00001B/171/P